Johnny,

Good luck and

Best wishes.

Don Langevin

How-to-Grow
World Class
GIANT PUMPKINS
III

By Don Langevin

World Record Pumpkin
1,337.6 Pounds
Can you believe it?

Annedawn Publishing
P.O. Box 247, Norton, MA 02766
508-222-9069

Copyright © 2003 by Donald G. Langevin
First Printing 2003
Printed in the United States of America
Library of Congress Cataloging in Publication Data
Langevin, Donald G.
How-to-Grow World Class Giant Pumpkins III / Don Langevin
1st edition.
Library of Congress Catalog Card Number:
ISBN 0-9632793-1-9

1 2 3 4 5 6 7 8 9 10

shows Jim Kilbert's
in the patch. This
r front page feature
*nal Home
Club* magazine,
How-To in
1998.

eding page,
2001, 893.5,
oungster trying to
scale's digital
weight.

"You're not growin' salad,
you're growin' fruit."

•

"If you're not blowin' 'em,
you're not growin' 'em."

•

"If you're blowin' 'em,
you're not showin' 'em."

•

"The bullshit stops,
when the tailgate drops,
at the weigh off."

Left: Ray Barenchi's 2000, 954 on the fork lift heading for the scale at the Santa Rosa, CA Harvest Fair weigh off.

Dedication

The Tuesday Night Supper Club

*John Castellucci,
Dick and Ron Wallace,
and Dave Hampton
To friends,
all made as a result of
growing giant pumpkins,
I cannot imagine
a better life without you.*

The Tuesday Night Supper Club meets every Tuesday night in a revolving format at a different home where the hosts: John Castellucci of Smithfield, RI; Dick and Ron Wallace of Coventry, RI; Dave Hampton of Waquoit, MA; or myself; takes a turn at serving up the best he can offer. Giant pumpkins are the center of conversation, but food finishes a very close second.

To the right : from the left, the Tuesday Night Supper Club: Dick Wallace, Dave Hampton, Don Langevin, on Wallace, and hn Castellucci.

The Tuesday Night Supper Club

The essence of the sport of giant pumpkin growing is not in the dreaming and planning, or in the acquired knowledge of growing the unique, and always surprising, *Atlantic Giant* pumpkin variety. It is not in the competing, although it may start there, and it cannot be found in isolation, because in growing alone, we limit the rewards of growing giant pumpkins.

The essence, pure and simple, is in the friendships we make, pursuing with others our mutual interests in bettering our own, individual, personal achievements. Friendship thrives within a group setting where competition exists, but respect wins out over personal gratification. The essence of the sport of giant pumpkin growing lies in the friends we make as a result of being mutually attracted by the same dream.

It is in this friendship and sharing that the greatest joy is found.

If you've seriously grown giant pumpkins, look around you at your friends. Can anyone, honestly, say that these friends could have been made in any other way, but through the pursuit of growing giant pumpkins?

The *Tuesday Night Supper Club* is a place and time for sharing food, laughter, and loving ridicule of one another, where offense is never intended, and the butt of the joke never feels shame or disappointment. Outside of this circle of friends, remarks made in similar fashion to others would ignite feelings of hurt, jealousy, anger, and revenge. But, within the *Tuesday Night Supper Club,* friendship ultimately wins over disappointment, and the common bonds of charity and love flourish.

Table of Contents

NEW RECORD
1,337.6 lbs.
Charles Houghton
NEW BOSTON, NH.

Preface

As I sit here pondering the reasons why another book on growing giant pumpkins should be published, my mind harks back to Saturday, October 5, 2002, when I witnessed the weighing of Charlie Houghton's new world record, 1,337.6 pound pumpkin, and brought my own personal best of 953 pounds to the scale. Pictured here, many who saw the 953 consider it the finest looking giant pumpkin ever grown over 700 pounds. As the grower, I could not agree more. When asked by an onlooker how I did it, I could only murmur, "Luck." A grower standing nearby said, "Looks like you've finally read your own books."

It dawned on me that, indeed, people read my books. With 35,000 copies in the hands of backyard gardeners all over the world, it is likely that many people got their start in this sport by way of my books. I cannot claim an ounce of recognition for what those people have achieved, but I can feel some pride in the fact that because of the information that I have made universally available though my books, many have experienced success, and that success has helped keep

them in the sport. Perhaps the grower was right when he said, "Looks like you've finally read your own books." Maybe there is something there that even the writer has not yet discovered, but the reader has.

I wrote this third book because new information had to be made available to everyone. That has always been my reason for writing on this subject. Everyone deserves the chance to compete fairly, and up-to-date information is the great equalizer in any competitive endeavor. Virtually nothing in this book is the product of my own creation or imagination, but rather it is the careful observation of those who year after year succeed where others fail. It is an observation of the methods of success, which have changed and evolved since my first book in 1993 and second book in 1998, and likely, are not yet through in gravitating to irrefutable answers. Perhaps this evolution in methods will never end – I certainly hope so, because the challenge of growing bigger pumpkins is ultimately what attracts and keeps people in the sport.

I had to write this book because what I had written earlier came from the theories of their day, and some of those theories have been either modified or entirely refuted. New ideas about plant size and pruning strategies throws a whole new light on the grower with only a small area to devote to giant pumpkins. New discoveries involving the use of considerably more calcium in feeding programs, the role of manure, a steadily growing consensus on the use of nitrogen, the beginnings of a real effort at applying genetic theory in pollination strategies, and the controversial subject of genetic manipulation, all required an airing here. Also, the explosion in the number of growers gathering information via the internet, either through websites, or through open forums with other growers via message boards, has become a major accelerator in the learning curve of all growers.

Left: Don & An... Langevin pose behind the 2002, 953.

Seed auctions, message boards, and a site devoted entirely to maintaining a database of pumpkin parentage, all contribute to a shortening of the time it takes to succeed in this sport. I would be remiss if I did not spend the time to write about these valuable resources, and convey any new discoveries to you.

Acknowledgements

The giant pumpkin growing community functions like a living organism of individuals – all working towards a common goal of increasing average weights of *Atlantic Giant* pumpkins, and raising the standard by which we judge a pumpkin to be world class.

A universal attitude of cooperation exists that makes it quite easy for anyone to readily acquire the information and seed that will make him immediately competitive in this sport. For me, any information I have ever sought has been always quickly given, so I acknowledge all giant pumpkin growers, as a whole, for their generosity, enthusiasm, sincerity, kindness, intelligence, and friendship.

Don Langevin

Ron Wallace and friends position his 2002, 860 on a lifting tarp, just prior to weighing on a digital scale. This pumpkin was harvested early because of a hole caused by a "Dill ring."

Introduction

A lot has happened in the sport of giant pumpkin growing in the last 100 years. In fact, 2003 marks the centennial year of William Warnock's historic display of a 403 pound pumpkin at the 1903, St. Louis World's Fair. He was immediately crowned the undisputed *Pumpkin King* of the world, a title he would not relinquish, even unto death. In 1979, the bell sounded for the beginning of a new era of giant pumpkin growing when Howard Dill of Windsor, Nova Scotia, Canada broke the 1903 record with a 438.5 pound pumpkin. The significance of this feat was not so much in the weight of the pumpkin, but rather in the fruit of his arduous 30 year experiment with giant pumpkin varieties. Out of this experiment came the *Atlantic Giant* pumpkin variety, and to the present day, this variety, by selective planting and pollination, has increased the world record three-fold, and elevated an average weight by an ordinary backyard gardener to well over 400 pounds.

Left: When not growing them, Dave Morgan of Santa Rosa, CA goes fishing.

...ht: Proud growers ...ob and Jo Liggett ...e while onlookers ...look in awe at the Circleville, OH Pumpkin Show. ...ront pumpkin set ...l-time Circleville ... off record at 935.

2003 marks the tenth anniversary of my first book on growing giant pumpkins, *How-to-Grow World Class Giant Pumpkins*. In that book, still in print and still considered "bible" reading for any serious giant pumpkin grower, a lot was made of the meteoric rise in world record weights since the introduction of the *Atlantic Giant* pumpkin variety. When the book was published on October 1, 1993, the world record belonged to Joel Holland of Puyallup, WA with his 1992 achievement of 827 pounds. However, within days of the book's publication, the record was broken by Donald Black of Winthrop, NY with an 884 pound pumpkin. In the thirteen years, from Dill's 1979 record to Holland's 1992 world record, the record weight had gone from 438.5 pounds to 827 pounds – an increase of 388.5 pounds, or an average increase in the world record weight of almost 30 pounds per year. In 1993, we were all stunned by what was happening. Seemingly, every year, the world record was being broken, and as the world record went up, so also did the average weights of all *Atlantic Giant* pumpkins. But, no one could have foreseen what was about to happen.

In 1994, with the world record at 884 pounds (still below the 900 pound mark), four growers across the United States and Canada stunned everyone who grows giant pumpkins competitively. Early in the day on the east coast, in a small town that boasts one of the largest agricultural fairs in the U.S., Topsfield, MA, Craig Weir from Salisbury, MA brought a 914 pound pumpkin to challenge the world record. I was there when it was weighed; in fact, eleven other men and I dragged it to the scale. We all thought that no pumpkin would ever beat this ever (never mind this year). As the day unfolded from east to west, the Canadians from Ottawa, Ontario reported results that showed two pumpkins over 900 pounds – Brockville, Ontario resident, Barry DeJong's, 945 pounder, and a stone's throw from Brockville, Lyn, Ontario native, Herman Bax's, 990 pounder. Then, an hour later, the news from Bethel, MN that Glen Brown had weighed a 923 pounder. On one day in October of 1994, four different people broke the world record and surpassed the 900 pound mark. After that, everyone thought that 1000 pounds was within sight, and many thought they would be the first to do it. The bell sounded in 1994 for a new era of optimism.

2003 also marks the fifth anniversary of my second book on growing giant pumpkins, *How-to-Grow World Class Giant Pumpkins II*. This was a book which I never intended to write, but wrote because of the many changes in cultural methods and record weights that had occurred since my first book, a stream of new names into the sport, and an incessant cry for more information. In it I explore the evolution of the best planting methods that were just beginning to solidify, and I marvelled at how the world record had gone from Holland's 827 pound record in 1992, to mythical achievement by Paula and Nathan Zehr of Lowville, NY with their 1,061 pound pumpkin in 1996 (a feat that earned them $53,000 in prize money). Four years, an increase of 234 pounds, or an average increase in the world record weight of 58.5 pounds per year. In 1996, the bell sounded for 1000 pounds.

The focus of this book covers the years from 1998 through the 2002 growing season. From Gary Burke's, 1,092 pound pumpkin to Charlie Houghton's, 1,337.6 pounder – an increase of 276.6 pounds, or an average increase in the world record of more than 61.4 pounds per year. Rather than slowing down, the average yearly increase in the world record is increasing, and the average weight of a competitive giant pumpkin has increased just as much. In 1998, there were fewer than 50 growers who could boast that they had grown a pumpkin exceeding 700 pounds. In 2002 alone, thirty-six growers officially weighed pumpkins exceeding 1000 pounds at sanctioned giant pumpkin growing association weigh offs, and another ten were unofficially recognized, making the significance of growing a 700 pound pumpkin barely mediocre. In 2001, five people broke the world record, and in 2002 the bar was raised for all who compete. Nine hundred pounds has become common place, and the goal of growing a 1000 pound pumpkin by any individual grower is only a stepping stone to the dream of growing a world record. In 2002, the bell sounded again.

If you are really serious about growing the biggest pumpkin you can, this book will be a source of priceless information for you. It is not

intended to replace either of my previous books on the subject, and anyone serious enough about giant pumpkin growing should explore those books for tips, and view the new book from the perspective of the first two. Learning to grow giant pumpkins is a work-in-progress.

The only thing you will have to ask yourself after reading these books is, "Am I ready to compete?" If you have your sights set on 1000 pounds, you're not. The next bell sounds at 1,500 pounds!

*Left:
ellie Cramer and
Mike Brock at
Moon Bay, CA.*

*t: A six-segment
female flower.*

*w: Drew Papez's
02, 1012.5 at a
local school.*

Contributors

The following have contributed photos, slides, digital images, data, or information for this book: Tim Bailey, Tom Beachy, Jim Beauchemin, Bill Bobier, Gary Burke, Fred Calai, John Castellucci, Gerry Checkon, Steve Daletas, John Deary, Ken Desrosiers, Scott Dixon, Al Eaton, Alan Gibson, J. Glover, Debbie Haeggens, Paul Handy, Stephen Handy, Ben Hebb, Brett Hester, Marv Hicks, Joel and Mari Lou Holland, Charlie Houghton, Paul Huffer, Art Kaczenski II, Jim Kilbert, Clarence Koch, Mark Korney, James Kuhn, Greg Kurkowski, Fred Macari, Kathie Morgan, Mike Nepereny, Drew Papez, Tim Parks, Dan Parson, Joe Pukos, Martin Reiss, Alan Reynolds, Rock Rivard, Jerry Rose, Ned Sandercock, Dave Stelts, Kim Thomas, Bob Troy, Cliff Warren, Nic Welty, and Quinn Werner.

How-to-Use this Book

There is some new and exciting information in this book that will raise the accomplishments of anyone who takes the time to read and understand it. As in my two previous books, I proceed from the beginning of the growing season to the end, covering as little as possible on subjects that were covered more thoroughly in either *How-to-Grow World Class Giant Pumpkins I or II.* Rudimentary gardening techniques, explicit feeding programs, discussions on sunlight, how to control pesky critters, and soil preparation, are not covered here, can be found in my first two books.

What will be covered will, however, help even a beginner to succeed, and an experienced grower will find information that will elevate his performance and make him/her considerably more consistent from year to year. Every giant pumpkin grower will find something here that will help him to grow bigger pumpkins.

I would ask you to read from chapter to chapter starting here. Then, after you've read the entire book, go back to places of interest, or places you had trouble understanding on your initial read. This book can be read by jumping from one chapter to another, but the best understanding of my intent will come from a reading that starts with me at the beginning of the season, and ends with me at the weigh off.

I will introduce you to a whole new group of *Heavy Hitters,* and refresh your memories about those who have already earned this distinction and continue to have outstanding performances every year. You will also see pictures of many growers as members of associations all over North America. If you're a member of a giant pumpkin grower association, you may very well be already a part of *How-to-Grow World Class Giant Pumpkins III.* See the chapter on *Groups & Associations* later in this book.

You will be introduced to new strategies on selecting a seed to plant, and a pollination strategy that will help you develop your own "hot" seed stock. We will cover the subject of the minor element, Calcium, in a major way, dabble in genetic engineering with descriptions of the novel properties of gibberellins, auxins, cytochinins, and colchicine, and finally give credence to the notion of growing giants on small plants.

Are you ready to break your personal best – break your state record – or the unthinkable, break the world record? Are you ready to meet the people that are setting the records in your area, and make friends that will last a lifetime? If you are, the next chapter will show you what you have to beat and who you should meet.

Good luck!

Records

World Champions and World Records

To the right are the official results for the years 1979 through 2002 showing the largest pumpkin grown in each year. An asterisk (*) denotes a world record. It took 76 years to break the world record 403 pound pumpkin grown in 1903, but in the 24 years since 1979, the world record has been broken 15 times. In eighteen years since 1984, the world record has been broken twelve times, and it has been broken in each of the last five years, 1998-2002.

If you are from the USA, the weight to beat is 1337.6 pounds, and if you are from Canada, the weight to beat is 1215 pounds. Consider this for a moment. If the average pumpkin grows, from pollination to harvest, between 60-80 days, to beat 1337.6 pounds, your pumpkin must gain an average of between 16.7 to 22.3 pounds per day. I will cover this observation of daily gain in more detail in the chapter, *Estimating Weight - Estimating Growth,* where you will discover how to tell early if you have a world class giant pumpkin or not, and how to estimate an end of season weight.

The world championship has been claimed by Canada 11 times during this 25 year time-span, and 14 times by growers from the United States. In the last 10 years, the US has had a decided advantage with championships in 8 of the 10 years. This is a trend worth noting and observing over the next 10 years. With better techniques being employed to cool plants during the summer, more and more southern US growers are becoming competitive, whereas, northern growers have little they can do in lengthening the growing season or increasing their frost free days. But, I've been wrong before, so we'll see.

Year	Grower	Place	Wgt
*1903	William Warnock	Goderich ON	403.0
*1979	Howard Dill	Windsor NS	438.5
*1980	Howard Dill	Windsor NS	459.0
*1981	Howard Dill	Windsor NS	493.5
1982	Howard Dill	Windsor NS	445.0
1983	Owen Woodman	Falmouth NS	481.0
*1984	Norm Gallagher	Chelan WA	612.0
1985	Michael Hodgson	River Philip NS	531.0
*1986	Bob Gancarz	Wrightstown NJ	671.0
1987	Don Fleming	Morrisville VT	604.5
1988	Keith Chappell	Upper Granville NS	633.0
*1989	Gordon Thomson	Hemmingford PQ	755.0
*1990	Ed Gancarz	Wrightstown NJ	816.5
1991	Waterman/Ogunbuyi	Collins NY	780.5
*1992	Joel Holland	Puyallup WA	827.0
*1993	Donald Black	Winthrop NY	884.0
*1994	Herman Bax	Brockville ON	990.0
1995	Paula Zehr	Lowville NY	968.0
*1996	Paula Zehr	Lowville NY	1061.0
1997	Chris Andersen	Moraga CA	977.0
*1998	Gary Burke	Simcoe ON	1092.0
*1999	Gerry Checkon	Spangler PA	1131.0
*2000	Dave Stelts	Leetonia OH	1140.0
*2001	Geneva Emmons	Sammamish WA	1262.0
*2002	Charlie Houghton	New Boston NH	1337.6

*Denotes World Record

*The NH boys rea...
Charlie Houghto...
world record 200...
1337.6 for loadi...*

The All-Time Top 1000
(through 2002 Growing Season)

Although this list has been compiled by Vince Zunino with the very best intentions, it does not represent the true number of pumpkins grown over the weight of the 1000th entry in this list (717 pounds). Growers only bring one or two pumpkins to a weigh off each year, leaving behind some that would easily surpass 717 pounds. In addition, the data here represents only pumpkins that were officially sanctioned. But, this list will easily show you who you have to compete against, and what you have to grow to gain any measure of respectability among the very best in the sport of giant pumpkin growing.

In reviewing this list, note that in the top-50 pumpkins, only 4 were grown before 2000, and in the top-100 only 17 were grown before 2000. 15 of the pumpkins in the top-100 were grown in 2000, and 68 of the top-100 on this list were grown in either 2001 or 2002 (68%), and 44 were grown in 2002 alone. With the list of all-time-top pumpkins changing at such an alarming rate (44% of them joined the list this year), it is easy to predict that this list will probably be drastically different in 3-5 years.

The average of the top-100 is 1055 pounds. If we extrapolate for four years to 2006 using the largest pumpkin grown in the most recent four years, we get an increase in weight of 245.6 pounds (1337.6 - 1092 = 245.6) or an average weight of a top-100 pumpkin of 1301 pounds (1055 + 246). If the difference in weight from the average to the lowest pumpkin on the list remains the same, 87 pounds (1055 - 968), then in order to be on this list in 2006, you will have to grow a pumpkin exceeding 1214 pounds (1301 - 87). That would knock off all but the top 5 on the present list. If you don't grow a 1300 pound pumpkin soon, serious growers are going to leave you in the dust. So, that's what this book aims to do – get you over 1300 pounds!

The Top 1,000 Pumpkins All-Time

Rank	Weight	Grower	City	State	Year
1	1,337.0	Charles Houghton	New Boston	NH	2002
2	1,262.0	Geneva Emmons	Sammamish	WA	2001
3	1,260.4	Craig Weir	Salisbury	MA	2001
4	1,230.0	Steve Daletas	Pleasant Hill	OR	2001
5	1,215.0	Ben Hebb	Bridgewater	NS	2002
6	1,186.4	Bruce Whittier	Henniker	NH	2002
7	1,178.0	Rock Rivard	Ville-de-Becancour	QC	2002
8	1,177.8	Jim Kuhn	Goffstown	NH	2002
9	1,173.0	Kirk Mombert	Harrisburg	OR	2002
10	1,172.0	Bill Greer	Picton	ON	2002
11	1,167.0	Paul Handy	Vancouver	WA	2001
12	1,156.0	Dave Larsen	Longview	WA	2002
13	1,153.0	Al Eaton	Richmond	ON	2001
14	1,144.0	Geneva Emmons	Sammamish	WA	2001
15	1,140.0	Dave Stelts	Leetonia	OH	2000
16	1,131.0	Gerry Checkon	Spangler	PA	1999
17	1,112.5	Steve Handy	Vancouver	WA	2002
18	1,111.0	Geneva Emmons	Sammamish	WA	2001
19	1,109.0	Todd Skinner	Barnesville	OH	2000
20	1,105.0	Greg Stucker	Napa	CA	2002
21	1,101.0	Jake Van Kooten	Port Alberni	BC	2002
22	1,097.8	Tony Ciliberto	Wilkes-Barre	PA	2002
23	1,097.5	Tom Beachy	Woodburn	IN	2002

OHIO VALLEY GIANT
PUMPKIN GROWERS
WORLD RECORD PUMPKIN
1140 lbs.
GROWN BY DAVE STELTS
LEETONIA, OHIO

Dave Stelts with his 2000 1140 pound world record

24	1,097.0	Kirk Mombert	Harrisburg	OR	2001
25	1,096.8	Joe Pukos	Leicester	NY	2000
26	1,096.0	Pete Glasier	Napa	CA	2002
27	1,092.0	Gary Burke	Simcoe	ON	1998
28	1,092.0	Dennis Daigle	Moncton	NB	2002
29	1,090.0	Mike Fisher	Springfield	OR	2002
30	1,083.5	Jerold Johnson	Clearbrook	MN	2002
31	1,076.5	Quinn Werner	Saegartown	PA	2002
32	1,075.0	Scott Daletas	Pleasant Hill	OR	2001
33	1,074.0	Fred Calai	Canfield	OH	2002
34	1,066.0	Jack Vezzollo	Salinas	CA	2002
35	1,064.0	Jack LaRue	Tenino	WA	2002
36	1,062.0	Rock Rivard	St Etienne-des-Gres	QC	2001
37	1,061.5	Tony Ciliberto	Wilkes-Barre	PA	2001
38	1,061.0	Nathan & Paula Zehr	Lowville	NY	1996
39	1,061.0	Joe Pukos	Leicester	NY	2001
40	1,058.0	Charles Houghton	New Boston	NH	2002
41	1,058.0	Craig Sandvik	Chemainus	BC	2002
42	1,056.5	Leonard Stellpflug	Rush	NY	1998
43	1,056.5	Bob Ruff	Garnavillo	IA	2002
44	1,053.5	Dave Stelts	Leetonia	OH	2001
45	1,049.5	Mary Calai	Canfield	OH	2002
46	1,049.0	Joel Holland	Sumner	WA	2001
47	1,049.0	Clarence Koch	Wisconsin Rapids	WI	2002
48	1,048.0	Neil Cox	Waterford	ON	2000
49	1,047.0	Bill Bobier	Windsor	NY	2002
50	1,038.0	Geneva Emmons	Sammamish	WA	2002
51	1,037.5	Bill Bobier	Windsor	NY	2002
52	1,036.5	Todd Kline	Shawville	QC	1999
53	1,035.0	Paul Handy	Vancouver	WA	2002
54	1,028.0	Brett Hester	Canby	OR	2001
55	1,027.0	Lisa Hester	Canby	OR	2002
56	1,026.5	Joel Holland	Puyallup	WA	2000
57	1,024.0	Joe Pukos	Leicester	NY	2002
58	1,023.0	Arnold Vader	Cherry Valley	ON	2002
59	1,023.0	Brett Hester	Canby	OR	2002
60	1,020.2	James Kuhn	Goffstown	NH	2001
61	1,020.0	Andrew Papez	St. Catherine's	ON	2001

*Papez,
2001, 1020.*

62	1,016.0	Steve Deletas	Pleasant Hill	OR	2001		85	982.8	Geoffery Peirce		NH	2002
63	1,013.6	Dave Hampton	Waquoit	MA	2002		86	981.5	Adrien Gervais	Barrie	ON	1999
64	1,012.5	Andrew Papez	St. Catherine's	ON	2002		87	981.5	Clyde Wilson	Chehalis	WA	2002
65	1,010.0	Bob & Elaine MacKenzie	Tiverton	ON	1998		88	979.5	Craig Lembke	Forestville	NY	2002
66	1,010.0	Jack LaRue	Tenino	WA	2000		89	977.0	Chris Andersen	Moraga	CA	1997
67	1,009.6	Steve Connolly	Sharon	MA	2000		90	977.0	Ray Barenchi	Santa Rosa	CA	2000
68	1,009.5	Al Eaton	Richmond	ON	1999		91	976.0	Todd Kline	Shawville	QC	2002
69	1,009.2	Joe Scherber	Wheat Ridge	CO	2000		92	975.6	Adrian Gervais	Barrie	ON	1999
70	1,007.0	Kevin Brown	Milan	PA	2000		93	974.5	Al Eaton	Richmond	ON	2000
71	1,006.0	Bill Greer	Wellington Forest	ON	1996		94	974.0	Lincoln Mettler	Eatonville	WA	1998
72	1,005.0	Kirk Mombert	Harrisburg	OR	2002		95	973.0	Claude Girard	Grand St-Esprit	QC	2001
73	1,002.0	Wes Dwelly	Oakham	MA	2001		96	972.0	Ron LeGras	St. Claude	MB	1998
74	996.5	Geneva Emmons	Sammamish	WA	2000		97	972.0	Bill Bobier	Windsor	NY	2000
75	996.5	Paul Handy	Vancouver	WA	2002		98	969.6	Steve Krug	Amana	IA	2001
76	995.8	Peter Carter	Goffstown	NH	2001		99	968.0	Harley Sproule	Ormstown	QC	1998
77	991.0	J. Hunt / C. Armstrong	Elk Grove	CA	1999		100	968.0	Brett Hester	Canby	OR	2000
78	990.0	Herman Bax	Brockville	ON	1994		101	966.0	Adrian Gervais	Barrie	ON	1998
79	989.5	Brett Hester	Canby	OR	2002		102	966.0	Joel Holland	Sumner	WA	2001
80	989.5	Dave Stelts	Leetonia	OH	2002		103	963.0	Nathan & Paula Zehr	Lowville	NY	1995
81	987.0	Bill Bobier	Windsor	NY	1999		104	963.0	Greg Stucker	Napa	CA	2002
82	986.0	Larry Checkon	Cambria	PA	2002		105	962.0	Harry Willemse	Wellington Forest	ON	2000
83	984.0	Gary Miller	Napa	CA	2001		106	961.0	Steve Daletas	Pleasant Hill	OR	2001
84	983.6	Tony Ciliberto	Wilkes-Barre	PA	2000		107	960.0	Jerry Rose	Huntsburg	OH	2001

108	960.0	Mary Vader	Cherry Valley	ON	2001
109	959.0	Reggie Noonan	Lower Freetown	PE	2002
110	955.0	Dave Stelts	Leetonia	OH	2001
111	955.0	Jack LaRue	Tenino	WA	2002
112	954.0	Ray Barenchi	Napa	CA	2000
113	953.0	Don Langevin	Norton	MA	2002
114	951.4	John Castellucci	Smithfield	RI	2002
115	948.5	Alan Nesbitt	Conesus	NY	2002
116	948.0	Ben Hebb	Bridgewater	NS	2001
117	947.2	Mark Patrick	Kylertown	PA	1999
118	947.0	Bert Dornwaard	Winchester	ON	2001
119	946.5	Pete Geerts	Arkona	ON	1996
120	946.5	Debbie Haegens	St. Williams	ON	1999
121	946.5	Lincoln Mettler	Eatonville	WA	2000
122	945.5	Barry DeJong	Brockville	ON	1994
123	945.0	Bill Vanderstine	Victoria Cross	PEI	2001
124	944.0	Arnold Vader	Cherry Valley	ON	2001
125	943.0	Mike Brock	Booneville	CA	2001
126	942.5	Alan Cox	Waterford	ON	1998
127	942.0	Jake VanKooten	Port Alberini	BC	2000
128	941.0	Al Eaton	Richmond	ON	1996
129	940.0	Kirk Mombert	Harrisburg	OR	1998
130	940.0	Kirk Mombert	Harrisburg	OR	2000
131	940.0	Joe Kurilich	Litchfield	OH	2001
132	939.0	Geneva Emmons	Issaquah	WA	1995
133	937.0	Kirk Mombert	Harrisburg	OR	1998
134	937.0	Lincoln Mettler	Eatonville	WA	1998
135	936.5	Paul Handy	Vancouver	WA	1998
136	936.0	Kirk Mombert	Harrisburg	OR	2001
137	935.0	George Lloyd	Simcoe	ON	1997
138	935.0	Glenn Needham	Braeside	ON	2002
139	935.0	Robert Liggett	Circleville	OH	2002
140	934.0	Kirk Mombert	Harrisburg	OR	2000

*Below:
Dave Hampton of
Waquoit, MA
with his 2002,
1013.6.*

*Pages 24 & 25:
...n "Kil'r" Kilbert
with his 2002,
800.5.*

State	Grower	Weight	Year	Hometown
CA	Greg Stuckier	1105	2002	Napa, CA
CA	Pete Glasier	1096	2002	Napa, CA
CA	Jack Vezzollo	1066	2002	Salinas, CA
CA	Jon Hunt	991	1999	Elk Grove, CA
CA	Gary Miller	984	2001	Napa, CA
CA	Chris Andersen	977	1997	Moraga, CA
CA	Ray Barenchi	977	2000	Santa Rosa, CA
CA	Greg Stucker	963	2002	Napa, CA
CA	Ray Barenchi	954	2000	Santa Rosa, CA
CA	Mike Brock	943	2001	Boonville, CA
CO	Joe Scherber	1009.2	2000	Wheat Ridge, CO
CO	Marc Sawtelle	852.4	2002	Colorado Springs, CO
CO	Joe Scherber	838.6	2001	Wheat Ridge, CO
CO	Kevin Holman	827.6	2000	Denver, CO
CO	Marc Sawtelle	785.6	2002	Colorado Springs
CO	Joe Scherber	760.5	2002	Wheat Ridge, Co
CO	Joe Scherber	746.8	1997	Wheat Ridge, CO
CO	Joe Scherber	730.5	1998	Wheat Ridge, CO
CO	Marc Sawtelle	713.6	2002	Colorado Springs, CO
CO	Marc Sawtelle	711.8	2001	Colorado Springs, CO
CT	Ken Desrosiers	840	2002	Broad Brook, CT
CT	David Garrell	821	2002	Fairfield, CT
CT	Bob & Sue McNamee	776.5	1998	Tolland, CT
CT	Bob & Sue McNamee	774.6	1999	Tolland, Ct
CT	Wayne Hackney	737.8	1999	New Milford, CT
CT	Wayne Hackney	729.4	1996	New Milford, CT
CT	Bart Toftness	707	2001	Wallingford, CT
CT	David Garrell	704	2001	Fairfield, CT
CT	John Deary	695	2002	Oakville, CT
CT	Cindy Chaponis	691.8	1995	Manchester, CT
GA	Mike Nepereny	615	2002	Cleveland, GA
GA	Mike Nepereny	592	1999	Cleveland, GA
GA	Mike Nepereny	584.5	2002	Cleveland, GA
GA	Mike Nepereny	565	1999	Cleveland, GA
GA	Mike Nepereny	554	1999	Cleveland, GA
GA	Brian Hildebrand	537	2002	
GA	Mike Nepereny	520	2002	Cleveland, GA
GA	Mike Nepereny	514	2002	Cleveland, GA
GA	Mike Nepereny	495.5	2000	Cleveland, GA
GA	Mike Nepereny	492.5	2000	Cleveland, GA
IA	Jake VanKooten	1101	2002	Port Alberni, B.C.
IA	Craig Sandvik	1058	2002	Chemainus, B.C
IA	Jake VanKooten	942	2000	Port Alberni, B.C.
IA	Art Carefoot	907	2001	Nanaimo, B.C.
IA	Archie Lingl	903	2001	Kelowna, B.C
IA	Craig Sandvik	803	2002	Chemainus, B.C.
IA	Eric Hanna	772	2002	Fort St. John
IA	Jake VanKooten	764	1998	Port Alberni, B.C.
IA	Jake VanKooten	757	2001	Port Alberni, B.C.
IA	Arne Eggen	747	2000	Chemainus, B.C.
ID	Gary Wilson	353	2001	Twin Falls
ID	Brian Christensen	847.5	2001	Rexburg, Idaho
ID	Brian Christensen	545	2001	Rexburg, Idaho
ID	Brian Christensen	487	2000	Rexburg, Idaho
ID	Brian Christensen	472	2002	Rexburg, Idaho
ID	Robyn Henrie	367.5	2002	Ribgy, Idaho
ID	Harold Jorgensen	340	2002	Blackfoot, Idaho
ID	Steve Sorensen	335.5	2002	Rexburg, Idaho
ID	Cliff Warren	325	2000	Pocatello, Idaho
IL	George Kopsell	679	1997	Hebron, Il
IL	George Kopsell	648	1999	Hebron, Il
IL	George Kopsell	645	1999	Hebron, Il
IL	Donna Kopsell	629	1998	Hebron, Il
IL	Donna Kopsell	621	2001	Hebron, Il
IL	George Kopsell	620	1999	Hebron, Il
IL	Dave Kopsell	578.5	2001	Hebron, Il
IL	George Kopsell	574	1997	Hebron, Il
IL	Gene McMullen	572	2002	Streator, IL
IL	Donna Kopsell	568	1997	Hebron, Il
IN	John Barenie	896	2000	Griffith, IN
IN	Brad Walters	826.5	2001	Greenwood, IN
IN	Josh Mappes	815	1999	Morgantown, IN
IN	Dave Beachy	807	2002	Woodburn, IN
IN	Tom Beachy	801	2002	Woodburn, IN
IN	Richard Luzzi	769	1999	Valparaiso, IN
IN	Jim Gatewood	743	2001	Fulton, IN
IN	Kelly Klinker	740	2002	Woodburn, IN
IN	Jim Gatewood	728.5	2001	Fulton, IN
IN	Bill Hughes	697	2001	Versailles, IN
MA	Craig Weir	1260.4	2001	Salisbury, MA
MA	David Hampton	1013.6	2002	Waquoit, MA
MA	Steve Connolly	1009.6	2000	Sharon, MA
MA	Wes Dwelly	1002	2001	Oakham, MA
MA	Don Langevin	953	2002	Norton, MA
MA	Joe Goetze	917.2	1998	Pittsfield, MA
MA	Craig weir	914	1994	Salisbury, MA
MA	Fran Dalton	859.4	1998	Newburyport, MA
MA	Rick Skrypczak	845.8	1998	Barre, MA
MA	Jim Maxymillian	835	1999	Pittsfield, MA
MI	Bob Schlutt	884	1996	Bridgeman, MI
MI	Mark Clemantz	848.5	2002	Holly, MI
MI	Bill Edwards	841	1996	Marshall, MI
MI	Jerry Eason	812	2001	
MI	Don VanHoutte	796.5	1994	Armada, MI
MI	Michael VanHoutte	791	1996	Ray, MI
MI	Bill Hall	791	2000	Fenton, MI
MI	Mark Clementz	789	2001	Holly, MI
MI	Don VanHoutte	785	1998	Armada, MI
MI	Bob Schlutt	781.5	1996	Bridgeman, MI
MN	Jerold Johnson	1085.5	2002	Clearbrook, MN
MN	Margie Johnson	926	2002	Clearbrook, MN
MN	Glen Brown	923	1994	Bethel, MN
MN	Glen Brown	867	1994	Bethel, MN
MN	Steve Thorson	837	1999	Bemidji, MN
MN	Glen Brown	790	1994	Bethel, MN
MN	Wayne Peters	768	2000	Rochester, MN
MN	Steve Thorson	757	2000	Bemidji, MN
MN	David Bhaskaran	728	2001	Rochester, MN
MN	Wayne Peters	722.5	1996	Rochester, MN
MT	Kim Thomas	296	2002	Hamilton, MT
MT	Kim Thomas	212	2002	Hamilton, MT
MT	Kim Thomas	199	2002	Hamilton, Mt
MT	Clarence Fogel	180	2002	Hamilton, MT
MT	Larry Peterman	149	2002	Missoula, MT
MT	Andrea Morgan	93	2002	St. Ignatius, MT
MT	Andrea Morgan	87	2002	St. Ignatius
MT	Cindy King	45	2002	Corvallis, MT
MT	Ben Schmidt	33	2002	Missoula, MT
MT	Andrea Schmidt	4	2002	Unknown
NH	Charlie Houghton	1337.6	2002	New Boston, NH
NH	Bruce Whittier	1186.4	2002	Henniker, NH
NH	Jim Kuhn	1177.8	2002	Goffstown, NH
NH	Charlie Houghton	1058	2002	
NH	Jim Kuhn	1020.2	2001	Goffstown, NH
NH	Peter Carter	995.8	2001	Goffstown, NH
NH	Jeffrey Peirce	983	2002	New Boston, NH
NH	Jim Kuhn	929.2	1997	Goffstown, NH
NH	Jim Kuhn	929	2002	Goffstown, NH
NH	Joseph Letourneau	914.6	2002	Goffstown, NH
NY	Joe Pukos	1096.8	2000	Leicester, NY
NY	Nathan and Paula Zehr	1061	1996	Lowville, NY
NY	Joe Pukos	1061	2001	Leicester, NY
NY	Len Stellpflug	1056.5	1998	Rush, NY
NY	Bill Bobier	1047	2002	Windsor, NY
NY	Bill Bobier	1037.5	2002	Windsor, NY
NY	Joe Pukos	1024	2002	Leicester, NY
NY	Bill Bobier	987	1999	Windsor, NY
NY	Craig Lembke	979.5	2002	Forestville, NY
NY	Bill Bobier	972	2000	Rush, NY
OH	Dave Stelts	1140	2000	Leetonia OH
OH	Todd Skinner	1109	2000	Barnesville, OH
OH	Fred Calai	1074	2002	Canfield, OH
OH	Dave Stelts	1053.5	2001	Leetonia, OH
OH	Mary Calai	1049.5	2002	canfield, OH
OH	Dave Stelts	989.5	2002	Leetonia, OH
OH	Jerry Rose	960	2001	Huntsburg, OH

OH	Nathan Stelts	955.5	2001	Leetonia, OH
OH	Joe Kurlich	940	2001	Litchfield, OH
OH	Bob Liggett	935	2002	Circleville, OH
OR	Steve Daletas	1230	2001	Pleasant Hill, OR
OR	Kirk Mombert	1173	2002	Harrisburg, OR
OR	Steve Handy	1112.5	2002	Vancouver, WA
OR	Kirk Mombert	1097	2001	Harrisburg, OR
OR	Mike Fisher	1090	2002	Springfield, OR
OR	Scotty Daletas	1075	2001	Pleasant Hill, OR
OR	Brett Hester	1028	2001	Canby, OR
OR	Lisa Hester	1027	2002	Canby, OR
OR	Brett Hester	1023	2002	Canby, OR
OR	Steve Daletas	1016	2001	Pleasant Hill, OR
OR	Kirk Mombert	1005	2002	Harrisburg, OR
PA	Gerry Checkon	1131	1999	Spangler, PA
PA	Tony Ciliberto Jr.	1097.8	2002	Wilkes-Barre, PA
PA	Quinn Werner	1076.5	2002	Saegertown, PA
PA	Tony Ciliberto	1061.5	2001	Wilkes-Barre, PA
PA	Kevin Brown	1007	2000	Milan, PA
PA	Larry Checkon	986	2002	N. Cambria, PA
PA	Tony Ciliberto	983.6	2000	Wilkes-Barre, PA
PA	Mark Patrick	947.2	1999	Kylertown, PA
PA	Anthony Ciliberto	923	2001	Wilkes-Barre, PA
PA	Len Knauss	898	2001	Rome, PA
RI	John Castellucci	951.4	2002	Smithfield, RI
RI	Warren Cole	920	1998	Warwick, RI
RI	Ron Wallace	885	2000	Coventry, RI
RI	Tim Adams	845.2	2001	Wood River Junction, RI
RI	Dick Wallace	832.2	2001	Coventry, RI
RI	Tim Adams	828	1998	Wood River Junction, RI
RI	Ethan Jervis	818	1998	Wood River Junction, RI
RI	Ron Wallace	779.8	2001	Coventry, RI
RI	John Castellucci	743	1997	Smithfield, RI
RI	Warren Cole	729	1998	Warwick, RI
RI	John Castellucci	724	1997	Smithfield, RI
TN	Bryan Saylor	683	2002	Herndon, TN
VA	John Robinette	823	1999	Duffield, VA
VA	Brent Richey	637	2002	South Hill, VA
VA	Tim Herring	586	2001	Crew, VA
VA	Tim Herring	568	2000	Crew, VA
VA	Tim Herring	457	2002	Crew, VA
VA	Dixie Turner	447	2001	Crew, VA
VA	Bert Turner	421	2001	Crew, VA
VA	Patricia Herring	411	2002	Crew, VA
VA	Patricia Herring	356	2001	Crew, VA
WA	Geneva Emmons	1262	2001	Sammamish, WA
WA	Paul Handy	1167	2001	Vancouver, WA
WA	David Larsen	1156	2002	Longview, WA
WA	Geneva Emmons	1144	2001	Sammamish, WA
WA	Genevy Emmons	1111	2001	Sammamish, WA
WA	Jack LaRue	1064	2002	Tenino, WA
WA	Joel Holland	1049	2001	Sumner, Wa
WA	Geneva Emmons	1038	2002	Sammamish, Wa
WA	Paul Handy	1035	2002	Vancouver, WA
WI	Clarence Koch	1049	2002	Wisconsin Rapids
WI	John Barlow	930.5	2002	Gays Mills, Wi
WI	Dave Creuziger	908.5	2001	Sturtevant, WI
WI	Mike Fritz	835	2002	Knapp, WI
WI	John Barlow	829	2000	Gay Mills, WI
WI	Dave Creuziger	826.5	2000	Sturtevant, WI
WI	Mark Shymanski	825.5	1996	Montello, WI
WI	Scott Freeman	809	1998	Krakow, WI
WI	Joe Ailts	798.5	2001	Deer Park, WI
WI	Dave Creuziger	784	2000	Sturtevant, WI
WV	John Robinette	823	1999	Duffield, VA
WV	Bryan Saylor	683	2002	Herndon, TN
WV	Brent Richey	637	2002	South Hill, VA
WV	Tim Herring	586	2001	Crew, VA
WV	Tim Herring	568	2000	Crew, VA
WV	Tim Herring	457	2002	Crew, VA
WV	Dixie Turner	447	2001	Crew, VA
WV	Bert Turner	421	2001	Crew, VA
WV	Patricia Herring	411	2002	Crew, VA
WV	Patricia Herring	356	2001	Crew, VA
WY	Ron Hoffman	648	2002	Riverton, WY
WY	Roy Birt	601	2001	Wheatland, WY
WY	Ron Hoffman	549	2001	Riverton, WY
WY	Connie Hoffman	481	2002	Riverton, WY
BC	Jake VanKooten	1101	2002	Port Alberni, B.C.
BC	Craig Sandvik	1058	2002	Chemainus, B.C.
BC	Jake VanKooten	942	2000	Port Alberni, B.C.
BC	Art Carefoot	907	2001	Nanaimo, B.C.
BC	Archie Lingl	903	2001	Kelowna, B.C.
BC	Craig Sandvik	803	2002	Chemainus, B.C.
BC	Eric Hanna	772	2002	Fort St. John
BC	Jake VanKooten	764	1998	Port Alberni, B.C.
BC	Jake VanKooten	757	2001	Port Alberni, B.C.
BC	Arne Eggen	747	2000	Chemainus, B.C.
MAN	Ron Le Gras	972	1998	St Claude, MB
MAN	Ron Le Gras	819	2001	St Claude, MB
MAN	John Goertzen	779.5	2000	Winkler, MB
MAN	Duane Jonsson	707	2000	Oakbank, MB
MAN	Ron Le Gras	705.2	1997	St Claude, MB
MAN	Ted Storey	689.7	1999	Miami, MB
MAN	Alvina Goertzen	668	2000	Winkler, MB
MAN	Ryan Goertzen	664.5	2000	Winkler, MB
MAN	Lorne Nuefeld	648	2001	Roland, MB
MAN	Dennis Friesen	647	1998	Wawanesa, MB
NB	Dennis Daigle	1092	2002	Moncton, N.B.
NB	Iroi LeBlanc	852	2000	Cocagne, N.B.
NB	Luc LeBlanc	808	2001	Cocagne, N.B.
NB	Dennis Daigle	786	2001	Moncton, N.B.
NB	Ken Reinsborough	741	1999	Dalhousie, N.B.
NB	Dennis Daigle	719	2002	Moncton, N.B.
NB	Ken Reinsborough	711	1997	Dalhousie, N.B.
NB	Iroi LeBlanc	690	2001	Cocagne, N.B.
NB	Herman Dixon	688	1998	Riverside-Albert, N.B.
NB	Shelden Stubbert	678	1999	Lower Cloverdale, N.B.
NS	Ben Hebb	1215	2002	Bridgewater, NS
NS	Ben Hebb	948	2001	Bridgewater, NS
NS	David Hebb	934	2002	Bridgewater, NS
NS	Roger Wentzell	914	1998	Bridgewater, NS
NS	Donna Hebb	901	2002	Bridgewater, NS
NS	Lisa Wentzell	900	2002	Bridgewater, NS
NS	Howard Dill	881	1998	Windsor, NS
NS	Howard Dill	875	1999	Windsor, NS
NS	Lisa Wentzell	871	2001	Bridgewater, NS
NS	Mathew Corkum	857	2001	Bridgewater, NS
ON	Bill Greer	1172	2002	Picton, ON
ON	Alan Eaton	1153	2001	Richmond, ON
ON	Gary Burke	1092	1998	Jericho, ON
ON	Neil Cox	1048	2000	Waterford, ON
ON	Arnold Vader	1023	2002	Cherry Valley, ON
ON	Andrew Papez	1020	2001	St. Catharines, ON
ON	Andrew Papez	1012.5	2002	St. Catharines, ON
ON	Bob Mackenzie	1010	1998	Tiverton, ON
ON	Alan Eaton	1009.5	1999	Richmond, ON
ON	Bill Greer	1006	1996	Picton, ON
PEI	R. Noonan	959	2002	Freetown, PEI
PEI	B. Vanderstine	945	2001	Victoria Cross, PEI
PEI	B. Vanderstine	862	1999	Victoria cross, PEI
PEI	C. Picketts	818	2002	French River, PEI
PEI	R. Noonan	805	1999	Freetown, PEI
PEI	L. Shaw	786	2002	Charlottetown, PEI
PEI	E. Shaw	786	2002	Charlottetown, PEI
PEI	B. Vanderstine	770	2002	Victoria Cross, PEI
PEI	P. Paynter	753	2000	French River, PEI
PEI	E. Vanderstine	751	1999	Victoria Cross, PEI
QB	Rock Rivard	1178	2002	St-Etienne-des-Gres, QB
QB	Rock Rivard	1062	2001	St-Etienne-des-Gres, QB
QB	Todd Kline	1036.5	1999	Shawville, QB
QB	Todd Kline	976	2002	Shawville, QB
QB	Claude Girard	973	2001	Grand St-Esprit, QB
QB	Harley Sproule	968	1998	Ormstown, QB
QB	Lorraine Orr	887	1995	Howick, QB
QB	Mike MacDonald	887	1999	North Hatley, QB
QB	Todd Kline	877	2002	Shawville, QB
QB	Todd Kline	864	2002	Shawville, QB

Data courtesy of Jim Gatewood

25

141	934.0	David Hebb	Bridgewater	NS	2002
142	934.0	Wayne Kennedy	Orono	ON	2002
143	931.0	Pete Glasier	Napa	CA	2002
144	930.5	John Barlow	Gay Mills	WI	2002
145	929.2	James Kuhn	Goffstown	NH	1997
146	929.0	Jim Kuhn	Goffstown	NH	2002
147	927.0	Bruce Kaye	Stittsville	ON	2002
148	926.0	Margie Johnson	Clearbrook	MN	2002
149	924.5	Jerry Rose	Huntsburg	OH	2001
150	923.0	Glen Brown	Bethel	MN	1994
151	923.0	Anthony Ciliberto	Wilkes-Barre	PA	2001
152	923.0	Bob Marcellus	Spencerville	ON	2002
153	923.0	Dave Hampton	Waquoit	MA	2002
154	922.5	Geneva Emmons	Sammamish	WA	2001
155	922.0	Joel Holland	Puyallup	WA	2002
156	920.0	Warren Cole	Warwick	RI	1998
157	920.0	Geoffery Peirce		NH	2002
158	918.0	Paul Handy	Vancouver	WA	1998
159	917.4	Andy Wolf	Allegany	NY	2002
160	917.2	Joe Goetze	Pittsfield	MA	1998
161	917.0	Nathan & Paula Zehr	Lowville	NY	1996
162	916.0	Jack LaRue	Tenino	WA	1997
163	916.0	Steve Krug	Amana	IA	2002
164	915.0	Jack LaRue	Tenino	WA	1998
165	914.6	Joseph Letourneau	Goffstown	NH	2002
166	914.0	Craig Weir	Salisbury	MA	1994
167	914.0	Roger Wentzell	Bridgewater	NS	1998
168	911.0	Harold Waterbury	Selkirk	ON	1997
169	911.0	Dave Stelts	Leetonia	OH	2001
170	910.0	Ron Nelson	Bremerton	WA	1994
171	910.0	Len Stellpflug	Rush	NY	2000
172	910.0	Brant Timm	Pembroke	ON	2002
173	910.0	Jack LaRue	Tenino	WA	2002
174	910.0	Vince Zunino	Los Altos Hills	CA	2002
175	909.5	George Lloyd	Simcoe	ON	1996
176	908.5	Sharon Eaton	Richmond	ON	1999
177	908.5	Dave Creuziger	Sturtevant	WI	2001
178	908.0	Bruce Whittier	Henniker	NH	2002
179	907.5	Alan Gibson	Winona	OH	2002
180	907.0	Art Carefoot	Naniamo	BC	2001
181	907.0	Kirk Mombert	Harrisburg	OR	2002
182	906.5	George Lloyd	Simcoe	ON	1998
183	906.0	Paul Handy	Vancouver	WA	1997
184	906.0	Brett Hester	Canby	OR	2002
185	906.0	Jim Kuhn	Goffstown	NH	2002
186	905.5	Robert Aller	Washougal	WA	2002

187	903.5	Archie Lingi	Kelowna	BC	2001
188	903.5	Jack Vezzollo	Salinas	CA	2001
189	901.5	Joe Kurilich	Litchfield	OH	2002
190	901.0	Glenn Needham	Braeside	ON	2000
191	901.0	Donna Hebb	Bridgewater	NS	2002
192	900.0	Lisa Wentzell	Windsor	NS	2002
193	899.0	Don Emmons	Sammamish	WA	2000
194	898.0	Len Knauss	Rome	PA	2001
195	897.5	Jack LaRue	Tenino	WA	1996
196	897.0	Paul McIntyre	Oxford Mills	ON	1996
197	897.0	Buddy Conley	Circleville	OH	2001
198	896.0	John Barenie	Griffith	IN	2000
199	894.4	Arnold Vader	Cherry Valley	ON	2001
200	894.0	Pete Geerts	Arkona	ON	1996
201	894.0	Geneva Emmons	Sammamish	WA	2000
202	894.0	John Lyons	Baltimore	ON	2002
203	893.5	Joe Pukos	Leicester	NY	2001
204	893.0	Jack LaRue	Tenino	WA	2002
205	892.5	Adrian Gervais	Barrie	ON	2002
206	891.0	Joel Holland	Puyallup	WA	2000
207	890.2	Charles Houghton	New Boston	NH	2001
208	890.0	Bruce Whittier	Henniker	NH	2002
209	889.0	Vince Zunino	Los Altos Hills	CA	2002

210	889.0	Geneva Emmons	Issaquah	WA	1998
211	888.0	Kirk Mombert	Harrisburg	OR	1998
212	888.0	Ben Hebb	Bridgewater	NS	2002
213	887.0	Lorraine Orr	Howick	QC	1995
214	887.0	Tony Ciliberto	Wilkes-Barre	PA	1996
215	887.0	Mike MacDonald	North Hatley	QC	1999
216	887.0	Jack LaRue	Tenino	WA	2000
217	885.0	Harry Willemse	Wellington Forest	ON	2000
218	885.0	Ron Wallace	Coventry	RI	2000
219	884.0	Don Black	Winthrop	NY	1993
220	884.0	Bob Schlutt	Bridgeman	MI	1996
221	884.0	Chris Geerts	Arkona	ON	1996
222	884.0	Jeff Patrey			2002
223	883.5	Utoni Ruff	Garnavillo	IA	2002
224	882.0	Jack LaRue	Tenino	WA	2000
225	881.0	Howard Dill	Windsor	NS	1998
226	880.2	Bill Greer	Picton	ON	2002
227	880.0	Deanna Lloyd	Simcoe	ON	1997
228	880.0	Richard Smith	Brampton	ON	2002
229	879.5	Adam Timpf	Walsingham	ON	2002
230	879.0	Joel Holland	Puyallup	WA	1997
231	879.0	Bill Greer	Picton	ON	2001
232	878.5	Bill Greer	Picton	ON	1998
233	878.5	Jim Beauchemin	Goffstown	NH	2002
234	878.0	Clyde Wilson	Chehalis	WA	1998
235	877.0	James Martin			2002
236	877.0	Todd Kline	Shawville	QC	2002
237	876.5	George Lloyd	Simcoe	ON	1996
238	876.0	Pat Papez	Brantford	ON	2000
239	876.0	Chin Ly	Dover	NH	2001
240	875.4	Larry Checkon	Spangler	PA	2000
241	875.0	Jack LaRue	Tenino	WA	1995
242	875.0	Howard Dill	Windsor	NS	1999
243	874.5	Jim Beauchemin	Goffstown	NH	2002
244	874.4	Deanna Lloyd	Simcoe	ON	2001
245	874.0	Buddy Conley	Circleville	OH	2001
246	874.0	Stan Pugh	Puyallup	WA	2001
247	873.5	Bill Moss	Salem	OH	2001
248	872.0	Ian Gervais	Barrie	ON	2002
249	871.6	Morgan Inglis	Walkerton	ON	2000
250	871.0	Ken Armstrong	Vittoria	ON	1997
251	871.0	Lyle Richert	Vancouver	WA	1997
252	871.0	Al Berard	Sanford	ME	2001
253	871.0	Lisa Wentzell	Windsor	NS	2001
254	869.6	Fred Calai	Canfield	OH	2000
255	869.5	Ed Reynolds	Wyebridge	ON	2002

256	868.3	Ron Nesbitt	Conesus	NY	2001
257	868.0	Sherry LaRue	Tenino	WA	1997
258	867.0	Glen Brown	Bethel	MN	1994
259	867.0	Kirk Mombert	Harrisburg	OR	2000
260	866.5	Don Emmons	Sammamish	WA	2000
261	866.0	Kirk Mombert	Harrisburg	OR	1996
262	866.0	Ben Hebb	Bridgewater	NS	2002
263	865.6	Peter Carter	Goffstown	NH	2002
264	865.5	Alan Nesbitt	Conesus	NY	2001
265	865.0	Lincoln Mettler	Eatonville	WA	1998
266	865.0	Gary Miller	Napa	CA	2001
267	864.0	Todd Kline	Shawville	QC	2002
268	863.8	Jess Smith	Weere	NH	2001
269	862.0	Bill Vanderstine	Victoria Cross	PEI	1999
270	862.0	Geneva Emmons	Sammamish	WA	2002
271	861.0	Clyde Wilson	Chehalis	WA	1998
272	860.0	Kirk Mombert	Harrisburg	OR	2001
273	859.5	Debbie Haegens	St. Williams	ON	2002
274	859.0	Frances Dalton	Newburyport	MA	1998
275	859.0	Kirk Mombert	Harrisburg	OR	1999
276	859.0	Takao Hoshijima	Kurashiki	Japan	1999
277	858.0	Harold Baird	Kinburn	ON	1997
278	857.0	Matt Corkum	Windsor	NS	2001
279	856.0	Wallace Simmons		NC	2000
280	856.0	Joe Kurilich	LitchField	OH	2001
281	855.0	Ralph Giffen	Arrie	ON	2000
282	855.0	Nick Oxner	Antigonish	NS	2001
283	855.0	Joel Holland	Sumner	WA	2001
284	854.6	Al Berard	Sanford	ME	2002
285	854.1	Joel Holland	Puyallup	WA	1998
286	854.1	Jim Kuhn	Goffstown	NH	2001
287	854.0	Geneva Emmons	Issaguah	WA	1997
288	854.0	Joel Holland	Puyallup	WA	1998
289	854.0	Pete Glasier	Napa	CA	2001
290	854.0	Jim Kuhn	Goffstown	NH	2001
291	854.0	Ken Reinsborough	Dalhousie	NB	2002
292	854.0	Rock Rivard	Ville-de-Becancour	QC	2002
293	854.0	Roger Wentzell	Windsor	NS	2002
294	853.0	Al Eaton	Richmond	ON	1997
295	853.0	Chris Hebb	Bridgewater	NS	1999
296	853.0	Adrien Gervais	Barrie	ON	2000
297	853.0	Pat Papez	Brantford	ON	2001
298	852.4	Marc Sawtelle	Colorado Springs	CO	2002
299	852.0	Iroi LeBlanc	Windsor	NS	2000
300	851.0	Peter Carter	Goffstown	NH	2001
301	851.0	Shellie Cramer	Rochester	WA	2002
302	850.5	Jack LaRue	Tenino	WA	1995
303	850.5	Brett Hesterby		OR	1999
304	850.5	Sharon Eaton	Richmond	ON	2001
305	850.0	Mark Fortinasewaga		NY	2000
306	847.5	Brian Christensen	Rexburg	ID	2001
307	847.5	Deanna Lloyd	Green Corners	ON	2002
308	847.0	Steve Daletas	Pleasant Hill	OR	1998
309	846.5	Lyle Richart	Vancouver	WA	1995
310	846.0	Nathan & Paula Zehr	Lowville	NY	1996
311	846.0	Fred Calai	Canfield	OH	1999
312	846.0	George Lloyd	Simcoe	ON	2000
313	845.5	Rick Skrzypczak	Barre	MA	1998
314	845.2	Tim Adams	Wood River Junction	RI	2001
315	845.0	Tony Ciliberto	Wilkes-Barre	PA	1995
316	845.0	Bill Bobier	Windsor	NY	1999
317	845.0	Alan Nesbitt	Conesus	NY	2001
318	845.0	Frank Lanterman	Youngstown	OH	2002
319	844.0	Kirk Mombert	Harrisburg	OR	1998
320	844.0	Winston Wykcoff	Burbank	OH	2001
321	843.0	Eileen Kennedy	Orono	ON	2002
322	842.5	Ken Mitchell	Elk Grove	CA	2001
323	842.0	Larry Squires	Port Rowan	ON	2000
324	842.0	Al Eaton	Richmond	ON	2002
325	842.0	Seth			2002
326	841.5	Ken Armstrong	Vittoria	ON	2002
327	841.0	Bill Edwards	Marshall	MI	1996
328	841.0	David Hebb	Bridgewater	NS	1999
329	841.0	Linda Lanterman	Canfield	OH	2001
330	841.0	Greg Stucker	Napa	CA	2002
331	840.5	Dale Lanterman	Canfield	OH	1998
332	840.0	Kathy Joynson	Enniskillen	ON	2002
333	840.0	Ken Desrosiers	Topsfield	MA	2002
334	839.5	Adrien Gervais	Barrie	ON	2000
335	839.0	Pat Ruelle	Redway	CA	1995
336	839.0	Mike Brock	Booneville	CA	2001
337	838.7	Joe Scherber	Wheat Ridge	CO	2001
338	838.0	George Lloyd	Simcoe	ON	2001
339	838.0	Bill Bobier	Windsor	NY	2002
340	837.5	Frank Catapano	Woodbridge	ON	2000
341	837.2	Greg Waller	Nineveh	NS	1999
342	837.0	Steve Thorson	Bemidji	MN	1999
343	837.0	Dave Harrod Jr.	Angus	ON	2000
344	837.0	Jack LaRue	Tenino	WA	2000
345	836.0	Norm Craven	Stouffville	ON	1993
346	835.0	Paul McIntyre	Oxford Mills	ON	1998
347	835.0	James Maxymillian	Pittsfield	MA	1999

348	835.0	Mike Fritz	Knapp	WI	2002	394	821.4	Nancy Wellington	Forest	ON	2000
349	833.8	Bob Ruff	Garnavillo	IA	2000	395	821.0	Leo Swinimer	Windsor	NS	1999
350	833.5	Kirk Mombert	Harrisburg	OR	1995	396	821.0	John-Michael Werking	Ashville	PA	2001
351	833.5	Loren Vanderschoot		CA	2002	397	821.0	David Garrell	Fairfield	CT	2002
352	833.0	Paul Handy	Vancouver	WA	1997	398	820.5	Dave McCallum	Hanover	ON	2000
353	832.2	Ron Wallace	Coventry	RI	2001	399	820.5	Quinn Warner	Sagertown	OH	2001
354	832.0	Angus Bruce	Inverary	ON	1998	400	819.0	Paul Brown	New Berlin	NY	1995
355	832.0	Kirk Mombert	Harrisburg	OR	2000	401	819.0	Jack LaRue	Tenino	WA	1997
356	831.0	Vince Zunino	Los Altos Hills	CA	2001	402	819.0	Lincoln Mettler	Eatonville	WA	2000
357	831.0	Gary Miller	Napa	CA	2002	403	819.0	Ron LeGras	St. Claude	MB	2001
358	830.0	Mark Fortinasewaga		NY	2002	404	819.0	Clyde Wilson	Chehalis	WA	2001
359	829.5	Chris Gregory	La Crescenta	CA	2002	405	818.8	Dan Carlson	Clinton	IA	2001
360	829.0	John Barlow	Gray Mills	WI	2000	406	818.0	Ben Hebb	Bridgewater	NS	1999
361	829.0	George Lloyd	Green Corners	ON	2002	407	818.0	Ron Covert	Picton	ON	1999
362	828.8	Mark Bresnick	Pittsford	VT	2000	408	818.0	Clifford Picketts	Kensington	PE	2002
363	828.6	Chin Ly	Dover	NH	2000	409	818.0	Geoff Gould	Mill Creek	WA	2002
364	828.4	Timothy Adams	Richmond	RI	1998	410	817.0	Sherry LaRue	Tenino	WA	1997
365	828.0	Kirk Mombert	Harrisburg	OR	1998	411	817.0	Kirk Mombert	Harrisburg	OR	2000
366	828.0	Steve Daletas	Pleasant Hill	OR	1999	412	816.5	Ed Gancarz	Wrightstown	NJ	1990
367	828.0	Winston Wyckoff	Burbank	OH	2000	413	816.0	Jerry Rose	Huntsburg	OH	1995
368	827.6	Kevin Holman	Denver	CO	2000	414	816.0	Christa Parks	Salem	OH	1998
369	827.0	Joel Holland	Puyallup	WA	1992	415	816.0	John Handbury	Derbyshire	ENG	1999
370	827.0	Howard Dill	Windsor	NS	1995	416	815.6	Dan Hajdas	Cheshire	MA	2002
371	827.0	Bob Mackenzie	Tiverton	ON	2000	417	815.5	Lorraine Orr	Howick	QC	1994
372	826.5	Rick Veens	Forest	ON	1996	418	815.5	Luke Van Aert	Watford	ON	1996
373	826.5	Brett Hester	Canby	OR	2000	419	815.5	Richard Baird	Canfield	OH	1998
374	826.5	Ashley Creuziger	Sturtevant	WI	2000	420	815.5	Bill McIver	Staffa	ON	2000
375	826.5	Brad Walters	Greenwood	IN	2001	421	815.4	Jim Ford	Hillsboro	NH	2002
376	826.5	Harry Willemse	Wellington Forest	ON	2001	422	815.0	Larry Checkon	Spangler	PA	1998
377	826.2	David Hilstolsky	Wyoming	PA	2002	423	815.0	Josh Mappes	Morgantown	IN	1999
378	826.0	Vince Zunino	Los Altos Hills	CA	2002	424	815.0	Joel Holland	Puyallup	WA	2000
379	825.5	Mark Shymanski	Poynette	WI	1996	425	814.0	Gretchen Schwarz	Shawville	QC	1997
380	825.0	Lisa Hester	Canby	OR	2002	426	814.0	Scott Armstrong	Valley Stream	NY	2001
381	824.5	Wendy Veens	Forest	ON	1995	427	814.0	Jim Sherwood	Mulino	OR	2001
382	824.5	Jerry Rose	Huntsburg	OH	2002	428	814.0	Art Franek	Munson	PA	2002
383	824.0	Shellie Cramer	Rochester	WA	2000	429	813.5	Ron Sass	Barrie	ON	1999
384	823.8	Heide Edwards	S. Beloit	WI	2000	430	813.5	Winston Wykcoff	Burbank	OH	2000
385	823.0	Pete Glasier	Napa	CA	1998	431	813.2	Robert Demers		NH	2002
386	823.0	Danny Dill	Windsor	NS	1999	432	813.0	Bill Grant	Warkworth	ON	1997
387	823.0	John Robinette	Duffield	VA	1999	433	813.0	Jenna Hebb		NS	2002
388	823.0	Howard Dill	Windsor	NS	2000	434	812.5	Eric Carlson	Portola Valley	CA	2002
389	823.0	Eric Carlson	Portola Valley	CA	2001	435	812.0	Jack LaRue	Tenino	WA	1997
390	822.5	Carson Willemse	Forrest	ON	2001	436	812.0	Eric Sundin	Stoney Creek	ON	2000
391	822.4	Brian Staring	Waterville	NY	2002	437	812.0	Gerald Eason	Fowlerville	MI	2001
392	822.0	Arnold Vader	Cherry Valley	ON	2002	438	811.5	Deanna Lloyd	Simcoe	ON	2001
393	821.5	Bill Sturman	Port Colbourne	ON	2000	439	811.5	Mike Brock	Booneville	CA	2002

440	810.5	Randy Warren	Auburn	CA	2002
441	810.0	Fenton McInnis	Hubbards	NS	1996
442	810.0	Lionel Boutet	Mississauga	ON	1996
443	810.0	Howard Dill	Windsor	NS	1999
444	810.0	Paul Handy	Vancouver	WA	1999
445	810.0	David Snow	Vittoria	ON	2001
446	809.0	Scott Freeman	Krakow	WI	1998
447	809.0	John Elliott	New Berlin	NY	2000
448	809.0	Phil Joynson	Enniskillen	ON	2002
449	808.5	Stan MacDonald	Kateville	QC	2001
450	808.5	Joan Gibson	Winona	OH	2002
451	808.0	Kirk Mombert	Harrisburg	OR	1996
452	808.0	Mark Woodward	Leominster	MA	1997
453	808.0	Steve Daletas	Pleasant Hill	OR	2000
454	808.0	Joel Holland	Puyallup	WA	2000
455	808.0	Jack LaRue	Tenino	WA	2000
456	808.0	Luc LeBlanc		NB	2001
457	808.0	Jerry Rose	Huntsburg	OH	2002
458	807.5	Nancy Wellington	Forest	ON	2000
459	807.5	Lisa Hester	Canby	OR	2000
460	807.0	Joel Holland	Puyallup	WA	1996
461	807.0	Sherry LaRue	Tenino	WA	1998
462	807.0	Dave Beachy	Woodburn	IN	2002
463	806.5	Dick Baird	Canfield	OH	1998
464	806.0	Ken Rose	New Waterford	NS	1999
465	806.0	Daniel Kruszyna	Cheshire	MA	2002
466	805.5	Al Eaton	Richmond	ON	1996
467	805.0	Reggie Noonan	Freetown	PEI	1999
468	805.0	Joe Pukos	Leicester	NY	2000
469	804.0	Nathan Zehr	Lowville	NY	1994
470	804.0	Pete Glasier	Napa	CA	2000
471	804.0	Steve Daletas	Pleasant Hill	OR	2000
472	804.0	Gary Miller	Napa	CA	2001
473	804.0	Dan Carlson	Clinton	IA	2002
474	803.5	Al Eaton	Richmond	ON	1999
475	803.5	Gretchen Schwarz	Shawville	QC	1999
476	803.4	Steven Davies	Dennisport	MA	2002
477	803.0	Bob Ruff	Garnavillo	IA	1993
478	803.0	David Martin	Little Brittan	NY	2000
479	803.0	Craig Sandvik	Chemainus	BC	2002
480	802.0	Wendy Veens	Forest	ON	1997
481	802.0	Lisa Wentzell	Windsor	NS	1998
482	802.0	Tim Gieger	Canfield	OH	2001
483	802.0	Howard Dill	Windsor	NS	2002
484	801.5	Dave Stelts	Leetonia	OH	1997
485	801.0	David Hampton	Waquoit	MA	1998
486	801.0	Don Black	Winthrop	NY	1999
487	801.0	Eric Carlson	Portola Valley	CA	2002
488	801.0	Tom Beachy	Woodburn	IN	2002
489	800.5	Kirk Mombert	Harrisburg	OR	1994
490	800.5	Dale Lanterman	Canfield	OH	2002
491	798.5	Mary Calai	Canfield	OH	2000
492	798.5	Gary Miller	Napa	CA	2001
493	798.5	Joe Ailts	New Richmond	WI	2001
494	798.5	Chris Lyons	Scarborough	ON	2002
495	797.9	Nancy Atkinson	Hamilton	ON	2000
496	797.5	Winston Wykcoff	Burbank	OH	2002
497	797.0	Bob Troy	Torrance	CA	2001
498	797.0	Ned Sandercock	Honesdale	PA	2001
499	796.5	Don VanHoutte	Armada	MI	1994
500	796.0	Kirk Mombert	Harrisburg	OR	1997
501	796.0	Clyde Wilson	Chehalis	WA	1997
502	796.0	Dick Burke	Canby	WA	1999
503	796.0	Bill Greer & Arnold Vader	Picton	ON	2000
504	795.5	Bill Bobier	Windsor	NY	1996
505	795.5	Deanna Lloyd	Simcoe	ON	1998
506	795.0	Herman Bax	Lyn	ON	1996
507	795.0	Jose Ceja	Napa	CA	2002
508	794.5	Ron Covert	Picton	ON	1999
509	794.0	Jerry Rose	Huntsburg	OH	2002
510	794.0	Robert Liggett	Circleville	OH	2002
511	793.5	Arnold Vader	Cherry Valley	ON	1999
512	793.5	Art Milburn	Brockville	ON	2000
513	793.5	Ellis			2002
514	793.0	Nathan Zehr	Lowville	NY	1995
515	793.0	Brett Hester	Canby	OR	1999
516	793.0	Lisa Wentzell	Windsor	NS	2000
517	793.0	Amy Dopp	Turbotville	PA	2001
518	792.0	Joel Holland	Puyallup	WA	1993
519	792.0	Pete Geerts	Arkona	ON	1998
520	792.0	Hilly Armstrong	Port Elgin	ON	1999
521	792.0	Warren Buscho	Applegate	WI	2002
522	791.6	Cone/Wiberg	Andover	MA	2001
523	791.0	Mike MacDonald	Sherbrooke	QC	1994
524	791.0	Michael VanHoutte	Ray	MI	1996
525	791.0	Pete Glasier	Napa	CA	1998
526	791.0	Mark Woodward	Leominster	MA	1998
527	791.0	John Lyons	Baltimore	ON	1998
528	791.0	Bill Hall	Fenton	MI	2000
529	790.2	Debbie Haegens	St. Williams	ON	1997
530	790.0	Glen Brown	Bethel	MN	1994
531	790.0	Steve Daletas	Pleasant Hill	OR	2000

532	790.0	Quinn Werner	Saegartown	PA	2002	578	782.5	Greg Stucker	Napa	CA	2002
533	789.2	Bill Greer	Picton	ON	2001	579	782.0	Joel Holland	Puyallup	WA	1993
534	789.0	Norm Craven	Stouffville	ON	1995	580	782.0	Roger Wentzell	Bridgewater	NS	1997
535	789.0	Brett Hester	Canby	OR	1998	581	782.0	George Cook	Florence	ON	1998
536	789.0	Vince Zunino	Los Altos Hills	CA	2000	582	782.0	Doug Timpf	Walsingham	ON	2002
537	789.0	Mark Clememtz	Holly	MI	2001	583	781.5	Barb McCallum	Hanover	ON	2000
538	788.6	Amy Dopp	Turbotville	PA	2000	584	781.4	Anne Braun	Dundas	ON	1996
539	788.6	Kevin Companion	Huntington	VT	2002	585	781.0	Ben Hebb	Bridgewater	NS	1993
540	788.5	Bob Webber & Sons	Loretto	ON	1996	586	781.0	Bob Schlutt	Bridgeman	MI	1996
541	788.5	Eric Carlson	Portola Valley	CA	2000	587	781.0	Stan MacDonald	Katevale	QC	1996
542	788.0	Steve Radich	Bow	WA	1998	588	781.0	Don Emmons	Issaquah	WA	1998
543	788.0	Jim Martin	Hayward	CA	2001	589	781.0	Phil Daignault	Hinsdale	MA	1999
544	787.5	Bill Greer & Arnold Vader	Picton	ON	2000	590	781.0	Joe Lazzaro	Cannastota	NY	2000
545	787.5	Ron Wray	Simcoe	ON	2000	591	781.0	Dave McCallum	Hanover	ON	2000
546	787.0	Todd Kline	Shawville	QC	1997	592	780.5	Ray Waterman	Collins	NY	1991
547	787.0	Paul Handy	Vancover	WA	2000	593	780.0	Al Eaton	Richmond	ON	1998
548	787.0	Eric Carlson	Portola Valley	CA	2002	594	780.0	Kirk Mombert	Harrisburg	OR	1998
549	787.0	Todd Skinner	Barnesville	OH	2002	595	780.0	Mike MacDonald	Sherbrooke	QC	1998
550	786.8	Matt Mongeon	Newmarket	NH	2001	596	780.0	John Elliott	New Berlin	NY	2002
551	786.5	Mary Calai	Canfield	OH	2001	597	780.0	Ray Fancy	Bridgewater	NS	2002
552	786.1	Eddie Shaw	Charlottetown	PE	2002	598	779.8	Ron Wallace	Coventry	RI	2001
553	786.0	Len Stellpflug	Rush	NY	1994	599	779.5	Bill Bobier	Windsor	NY	1997
554	786.0	David Wray	Vanessa	ON	1996	600	779.5	John Goertzen	Winkler	MB	2000
555	786.0	Owen Woodman	Falmouth	NS	1997	601	779.5	Frank Valenza	Balston Spa	NY	2001
556	786.0	Don Emmons	Issaquah	WA	1997	602	779.5	Wayne Kennedy	Orono	ON	2001
557	786.0	Jack LaRue	Tenino	WA	2000	603	779.5	Lloyd Rose	Erie	PA	2001
558	786.0	Dennis Daigle		NB	2001	604	779.5	Paula McGeary	Oxford	MA	2002
559	786.0	Laurie Shaw	Charlottetown	PE	2002	605	779.0	Don VanHoutte	Armada	MI	2001
560	785.5	Grant McGregor	Hensall	ON	1997	606	779.0	Bruce Whittier	Henniker	NH	2001
561	785.5	Marc Sawtelle	Colorado Springs	CO	2002	607	778.6	Arnold Vader	Cherry Valley	ON	2002
562	785.0	Jenna Hebb	Bridgewater	NS	1997	608	778.0	Bob Ruff	Garnavillo	IA	1995
563	785.0	Don VanHoutte	Armada	MI	1998	609	778.0	Frank Woodman	Falmouth	NS	1997
564	785.0	Andy Wolf	Allegany	NY	2001	610	778.0	Mark Carter	Orion	MI	1998
565	785.0	Frank Catapano	Woodbridge	ON	2001	611	778.0	Wayne Swinimer	Windsor	NS	1998
566	785.0	Kirk Mombert	Harrisburg	OR	2002	612	778.0	Peter Robinson	Simcoe	ON	2000
567	784.0	Pete Glasier	Napa	CA	1996	613	777.5	Bruce Orchard	Bountiful	UT	2001
568	784.0	Bill Trautwein	Goleta	CA	2000	614	777.0	Rod Harvey	Newport	NS	1995
569	784.0	Dave Creuziger	Sturtevant	WI	2000	615	777.0	Jeremy Veens	Forest	ON	1996
570	783.6	Ellie George	West Charlton	NY	2001	616	776.5	Bob & Sue McNamee	Tolland	CT	1998
571	783.4	Herbert Smith	West Charlton	NY	2001	617	775.5	Rick Veens	Forest	ON	1998
572	783.4	Mary Vadar	Cherry Valley	ON	2001	618	775.5	Bob MacKenzie	Tiverton	ON	2002
573	783.0	Scott Solomon	San Jose	CA	1996	619	775.0	Larry Werth	Lanesboro	MA	1998
574	783.0	Harold Baird	Kinburn	ON	1999	620	775.0	Joyce Armstrong	Vittoria	ON	2002
575	783.0	Neil Lanterman	Salem	OH	2000	621	774.6	Bob & Sue McNamee	Tolland	CT	1999
576	783.0	Steve Daletas	Pleasant Hill	OR	2000	622	774.5	J. Perkins	Devizes	ENG	1994
577	783.0	Richard Teals & Dennis Parr	Moses Lake	WA	2001	623	774.0	Harold Baird	Kinburn	ON	1996

624	774.0	Kirk Mombert	Harrisburg	OR	2000
625	774.0	Gretchen Schwarz	Shawville	QC	2002
626	773.8	Dan Kruszyna	Cheshire	MA	1999
627	773.5	Rob Lanterman	Canfield	OH	1999
628	773.0	Jack LaRue	Tenino	WA	1998
629	773.0	John Girgus	Derry	NH	2002
630	772.5	Matt Klaver	Kippen	ON	1997
631	772.5	Eric Hanna	Fort St. John	BC	2002
632	772.5	Ron Wilson	Canby	OR	2002
633	772.0	Bob Ruff	Garnavillo	IA	1994
634	772.0	Ashley Creuziger	Sturtevant	WI	1999
635	772.0	Ken Rose	New Waterford	NS	2000
636	771.6	Rocky Rockwell	Sayre	PA	2000
637	771.5	Steve Krug	Amana	IA	2001
638	771.0	Mark Fortin	Canasewaga	NY	1998
639	771.0	Mark Shymanski	Poynette	WI	1998
640	771.0	Jack Vezzolo	Salinas	CA	1999
641	771.0	Steve Daletas	Pleasant Hill	OR	2000
642	771.0	Joel Holland	Sumner	WA	2001
643	771.0	Amy Krug	Amana	IA	2002
644	770.5	Todd Kline	Shawville	QC	2001
645	770.0	R. McKenzie	Tiverton	ON	1995
646	770.0	Bill Van Iderstine	Victoria Cross	PE	2002
647	769.5	Mark & Kyle VanHoutte	Armada	MI	1995
648	769.5	B. Colley	Paisley	ON	1995
649	769.5	Jean-Paul Mercier	Gentilly	ON	1998
650	769.5	Bruce Kaye	Stittsville	ON	2001
651	769.0	Eric Brown	Milan	PA	1996
652	769.0	Lincoln Mettler	Eatonville	WA	1998
653	769.0	Richard Luzzi	Valparaiso	IN	1999
654	769.0	Dave Creuziger	Sturtevant	WI	2002
655	768.0	Bill Greer	Picton	ON	1997
656	768.0	Steve Radich	Bow	WA	1998
657	768.0	Wayne Peters	Rochester	MN	2000
658	768.0	Lincoln Mettler	Eatonville	WA	2000
659	768.0	Ron Vahlerberghe	Chesterfield	MI	2001
660	768.0	Robert Buggerhagen	Hamburg	NY	2001
661	768.0	Joseph Lew Yohe	Pittsburgh	PA	2002
662	768.0	Mark Bresnick	Pittsford	VT	2002
663	767.0	Chris Lyons	Scarborough	ON	1994
664	767.0	Douglas Wyman	Dundas	ON	1996
665	767.0	Craig Robinson	Windsor	NS	1998
666	767.0	Debbie Geerts	Arkona	ON	1998
667	767.0	Steve Krug	Amana	IA	2001
668	767.0	Clyde Truax		OH	2001
669	767.0	Frank Catapano	Woodbridge	ON	2002
670	767.0	Renald Provencher	Ville de Becancour	QC	2002
671	766.2	Lorraine Willemse	Forest	ON	2000
672	766.0	Sandy MacPherson	Sydney	NS	1999
673	766.0	Kirk Mombert	Harrisburg	OR	2001
674	765.5	R. Gancarz	Wrightstown	NJ	1990
675	765.5	Angus Bruce	Inverary	ON	1998
676	765.0	David Baird	Kinburn	ON	1996
677	765.0	Kirk Mombert	Harrisburg	OR	1997
678	765.0	John Weidman	Marshfield	WI	2001
679	764.0	Sherry LaRue	Tenino	WA	1995
680	764.0	Jake VanKooten	Port Alberini	BC	1998
681	764.0	Kirk Mombert	Harrisburg	OR	2000
682	764.0	Charles Houghton	New Boston	NH	2001
683	763.6	Dave Hilstolsky	Wyoming	PA	2002
684	763.2	Gary Soutier	Pittsfield	MA	1999
685	763.0	Joyce Schlutt	Bridgeman	MI	1996
686	762.5	Mike Eyre	Dorchester	ON	1999
687	762.0	Pat Ruelle	West Charlton	NY	1998
688	762.0	Herbert Smith	West Charlton	NY	1998
689	762.0	Casey Neuville	Amherst	WI	2000
690	761.0	George Lloyd	Simcoe	ON	1997
691	761.0	Kirk Mombert	Harrisburg	OR	2001
692	761.0	Matthew Corkum	Windsor	NS	2002
693	760.5	Len Stellpflug	Rush	NY	1996
694	760.5	Jason Jongeneel	Port Elgin	ON	1998
695	760.5	Joe Scherber	Wheat Ridge	CO	2002
696	760.0	Fenton McInnis	Hubbards	NS	1998
697	760.0	Mark Patrick	Kylertown	PA	1999
698	760.0	Mark Patrick	Kylertown	PA	2001
699	759.5	Pam Vanderschoot		CA	2002
700	759.0	Don Black	Winthrop	NY	2000
701	759.0	Mike Brock	Booneville	CA	2002
702	758.5	Eric Brown	Milan	PA	1997
703	758.5	Margo Baird	Canfield	OH	1998
704	758.5	Cindy Kolb	Chico	CA	2002
705	758.0	Mike MacDonald	Sherbrooke	QC	1996
706	758.0	Robert Ferry	Martinsburg	PA	1998
707	758.0	Art Franek	Munson	PA	1998
708	757.5	Kevin Companion	Huntington	VT	2002
709	757.4	Joe & Todd Hedrich	Presque Isle	ME	1999
710	757.0	Steve Thorson	Bemidji	MN	2000
711	757.0	Kirk Mombert	Harrisburg	OR	2000
712	757.0	Jake VanKooten	Port Alberini	BC	2001
713	757.0	Stan Pugh	Puyallup	WA	2001
714	757.0	Kurt Herrmann	Genesee Depot	WI	2002
715	756.6	Bruce Whittier	Henniker	NH	2001

#	Score	Name	City	State	Year
716	756.5	Ken Myers	Spanish	ON	2002
717	756.0	Don VanHoutte	Armada	MI	1995
718	756.0	David Hebb	Bridgewater	NS	1996
719	756.0	Takao Hoshijima	Kurashiki	Japan	1996
720	756.0	Pete Geerts	Arkona	ON	1997
721	756.0	John Barenie	Griffth	IN	1999
722	756.0	Bill Trautwein	Goleta	CA	2001
723	756.0	Bill Greer	Picton	ON	2002
724	756.0	Jim Ford	Hillsboro	NH	2002
725	755.8	Mark Woodward	Leominster	MA	2000
726	755.5	Cliff Webb	Seeley's Bay	ON	1998
727	755.5	Kevin Brown	Milan	PA	1998
728	755.0	Gordon Thompson	Hemmingford	QC	1989
729	755.0	Norm Craven	Stouffville	ON	1993
730	755.0	Zach & Ryan Gunderman	Lowman	NY	1999
731	755.0	Wallace Simmon	Canston	NC	2000
732	755.0	Cliff Webb	Seeleys Bay	ON	2001
733	755.0	Frank Catapano	Woodbridge	ON	2001
734	755.0	Glenn Needham	Braeside	ON	2002
735	754.0	Bert Veens	Forest	ON	1996
736	754.0	Pete Glasier	Napa	CA	2001
737	754.0	Quinn Werner	Saegertown	PA	2002
738	753.5	Geneva Emmons	Issaquah	WA	2000
739	753.0	Peter Paynter	French River	PEI	2000
740	753.0	Ellie George	West Charlton	NY	2001
741	753.0	Adam Sampson	Tenino	WA	2001
742	753.0	Doug Keel	Boutliers Point	NS	2002
743	752.8	Norm Craven	Stouffville	ON	1994
744	752.6	Tom Accardo	Derry	NH	1997
745	752.5	Len Stellpflug	Rush	NY	1993
746	752.5	Carrie Papez	St-Catherines	ON	2002
747	752.0	Shinichi Sugenga		Japan	1996
748	752.0	Ashley Creuziger	Sturtevant	WI	1998
749	752.0	Bill Trautwein	Goleta	CA	2000
750	752.0	Dick Wallace	Coventry	RI	2002
751	752.0	Doug Fisher	Goderich	ON	2002
752	751.0	Scott Solomon	San Jose	CA	1996
753	751.0	John Lobay	Smokey Lake	AB	1999
754	751.0	Elayne Vanderstine	Victoria Cross	PEI	1999
755	751.0	Lincoln Mettler	Eatonville	WA	2000
756	750.5	Pete Glasier	Napa	CA	2001
757	750.5	Mike Angelucci		OH	2001
758	750.2	Mary Vader	Cherry Valley	ON	2002
759	750.0	Jess Smith	Weere	NH	1997
760	750.0	Joel Holland	Puyallup	WA	1998
761	750.0	Sherry LaRue	Tenino	WA	1998
762	749.5	Jack LaRue	Tenino	WA	2002
763	749.0	Verne Lawrence	Bellevue	WA	1997
764	749.0	Kirk Mombert	Harrisburg	OR	1999
765	749.0	Geneva Emmons	Issaquah	WA	1999
766	749.0	Steve Daletas	Pleasant Hill	OR	2000
767	749.0	Lincoln Mettler	Eatonville	WA	2000
768	748.8	Bob Ruff	Garnavillo	IA	2001
769	748.5	Paul McCallum	Shallow Lake	ON	1997
770	748.0	Tim Parks	Salem	OH	1995
771	748.0	Clifford Picketts	French River	PEI	1998
772	748.0	Ken Mitchell	Elk Grove	CA	2001
773	748.0	Ken Mitchell	Elk Grove	CA	2002
774	748.0	Mike Olivio			2002
775	747.6	Al Berard	Sanford	ME	1999
776	747.5	Gary Burke	Simcoe	ON	1999
777	747.0	Ben Hebb	Bridgewater	NS	1997
778	747.0	Winston Wykcoff	Burbank	OH	1998
779	747.0	Deanna Lloyd	Simcoe	ON	1999
780	747.0	Arne Eggen	Chemainus	BC	2000
781	747.0	Jack LaRue	Tenino	WA	2000
782	746.8	Joan Daignault	Hinsdale	MA	1996
783	746.8	Joe Scherber	Wheat Ridge	CO	1997
784	746.7	Joe Lazzolo	Cannastota	NY	2001
785	746.5	Pete Glasier	Napa	CA	1999
786	746.0	Joe Hendrick	Presque Isle	ME	1994
787	746.0	Don Black	Winthrop	NY	1997
788	746.0	Geneva Emmons	Issaquah	WA	1997
789	746.0	Len Stellpflug	Rush	NY	1999
790	746.0	Jack Heffernan	Ariss	ON	1999
791	746.0	Jack LaRue	Tenino	WA	2000
792	746.0	Al Berard	Sanford	ME	2001
793	746.0	Art Franek	Munson	PA	2001
794	746.0	Jack & Sherry LaRue	Tenino	WA	2001
795	745.0	Bill Grant	Warkworth	ON	1996
796	745.0	Joe Lazzaro	Cannastota	NY	1998
797	745.0	Marvin Hicks	Williamsburg	PA	1998
798	745.0	Lincoln Mettler	Eatonville	WA	2000
799	745.0	Steve Krug	Amana	IA	2002
800	744.0	Mike Brock	Booneville	CA	1998
801	744.0	John Yandoh	Winthrop	NY	1999
802	744.0	Jack LaRue	Tenino	WA	2002
803	743.5	Sharon Eaton	Richmond	ON	2000
804	743.2	John Castellucci	Smithfield	RI	1997
805	743.0	Robert Grohs	Simcoe	ON	1996
806	743.0	Alun Jones	Liverpool	ENG	1997
807	743.0	Brett Hester	Canby	OR	1999

808	743.0	Jim Gatewood	Fulton	IN	2001		854	737.0	Joe Vesperman	Madison	WI	1996
809	743.0	Bruce Normand	Goffstown	NH	2001		855	737.0	Raymond Getson	LaHave	NS	1997
810	742.5	Joanne Donkers	Sarnia	ON	1995		856	737.0	Michael Prysby	Bath	MI	2000
811	742.2	Bob Ruff	Garnavillo	IA	1996		857	737.0	David Hebb	Bridgewater	NS	2001
812	742.0	Karen Waterman-Fisher	Collins	NY	1991		858	737.0	Kevin Companion	Huntington	VT	2002
813	742.0	Ray Waterman	Collins	NY	1993		859	736.5	Nic Welty	Smithville	OH	2000
814	742.0	Pete Glasier	Napa	CA	1996		860	736.5	Dempsey Lanterman	Canfield	OH	2001
815	742.0	Stephen Pachucki	Wilkes-Barre	PA	1999		861	736.0	Clarence Normand			1998
816	742.0	Ray Barenchi	Santa Rosa	CA	2001		862	736.0	Mark Woodward	Leominster	MA	2001
817	741.5	Debbie Geerts	Arkona	ON	1997		863	736.0	Bill Sturman	Port Colborne	ON	2002
818	741.5	Fred Calai	Canfield	OH	2000		864	736.0	John Weidman		WI	2002
819	741.2	Bob Ruff	Garnavillo	IA	1997		865	735.8	Mark Woodward	Leominster	MA	1996
820	741.0	Ken Reinsborough	Dalhousie	NB	1999		866	735.5	Paul McIntyre	Oxford Mills	ON	2001
821	741.0	Peter Carter	Goffstown	NH	2001		867	735.5	John Papez	Brantford	ON	2002
822	740.8	Matthew Mongeon	Newmarket	NH	1999		868	735.0	Howard Dill	Windsor	NS	2001
823	740.5	D. VanHoutte	Ray	MI	1994		869	735.0	Joe Pukos	Leicester	NY	2001
824	740.5	Cynthia Dillon	Brockville	ON	1998		870	735.0	Roger Drake	Niagara Falls	NY	2002
825	740.5	Gene Butzer		MO	2000		871	734.5	Glenn Needham	Braeside	ON	2000
826	740.5	Kathy Andolina	Gowanda	NY	2000		872	734.5	Neil Cox	Waterford	ON	2000
827	740.0	Joel Holland	Puyallup	WA	1993		873	734.2	Bruce Gray	Olin	IA	1993
828	740.0	J Collver	Wellandport	ON	1996		874	734.0	Tony Ciliberto	Wilkes-Barre	PA	1993
829	740.0	Kirk Mombert	Harrisburg	OR	1996		875	734.0	Fred Hain	London	ON	1997
830	740.0	Jayson Pahlmeyer	Napa	CA	1998		876	734.0	Bob Marcellus	Spencerville	ON	1998
831	740.0	Doris Wray	Simcoe	ON	1998		877	734.0	Glenn Cheam	Stittsville	ON	2002
832	740.0	Jose Ceja	Napa	CA	1999		878	733.5	Gary Gow	Barrie	ON	1997
833	740.0	Mark Fortin	Canasewaga	NY	2000		879	733.0	John Castellucci	Smithfield	RI	1997
834	740.0	Kelly Klinker			2002		880	733.0	Don Black	Winthrop	NY	1998
835	739.5	Waterman/Fisher	Collins	NY	1995		881	733.0	Joel Holland	Puyallap	WA	1999
836	739.5	Dale Lanterman	Canfield	OH	1999		882	733.0	Stan Pugh	Puyallup	WA	2001
837	739.4	Utoni Ruff	Garnavillo	IA	2000		883	732.5	Don Crews	Lloydminster	AB	2002
838	739.0	Sharon Eaton	Richmond	ON	1996		884	732.4	Kurt Herrmann	Genesee Depot	WI	1996
839	739.0	Joel Holland	Puyallup	WA	1996		885	732.4	Wayne Kennedy	Orono	ON	2002
840	739.0	Mark Clement	Port Elgin	ON	1998		886	732.0	Tony Lezzi	Tillsonburg	ON	1999
841	739.0	Bill Moss	Salem	OH	1999		887	732.0	Joe Kurilich	Litchfield	OH	2002
842	739.0	Clyde Wilson	Chehalis	WA	2001		888	732.0	Joel Holland	Puyallup	WA	2002
843	739.0	Jerry Kohlstaedt	Turnwater	WA	2002		889	731.5	Richard Goodhue	Lennoxville	QC	1998
844	739.0	Ron Wallace	Coventry	RI	2002		890	731.0	Gregg Bindel	Bancroft	WI	1998
845	738.5	Eric Brown	Milan	PA	1998		891	731.0	Fred Carter	Orion	MI	1999
846	738.0	Ron Wray	Simcoe	ON	1997		892	731.0	Greg Stucker	Napa	CA	2000
847	738.0	Ann Baird	Kinburn	ON	1999		893	731.0	Rita Veens	Forrest	ON	2001
848	738.0	Ken Mitchell	Elk Grove	CA	2001		894	730.5	Milton Barber	Delanson	NY	1991
849	738.0	Jane Herrmann	Waukesha	WI	2001		895	730.5	Joe Scherber	Wheat Ridge	CO	1998
850	738.0	Kyersti Olson	Bancroft	WI	2002		896	730.5	Ron Lewis	Naughton	ON	2002
851	737.8	Wayne Hackney	New Milford	CT	1999		897	730.0	David Hebb	Bridgewater	NS	2000
852	737.8	Craig Liembike	Fontsville	NY	2001		898	730.0	Jim Sherwood	Mulino	OR	2000
853	737.8	Bob Duffy	Topsfield	MA	2002		899	730.0	Chris Gregory	La Crescenta	CA	2002

900	729.4	Wayne Hackney	New Milford	CT	1996
901	729.2	Marvin Meisner	Holundayburg	PA	2000
902	729.0	Don VanHoutte	Armada	MI	1996
903	729.0	Joe Lazzaro	Canastota	NY	1999
904	729.0	Shellie Cramer	Rochester	WA	2000
905	729.0	Al Berard	Sanford	ME	2002
906	729.0	Glenn Needham	Braeside	ON	2002
907	728.5	Julie Eyre	Dorchester	ON	1999
908	728.5	Jim Gatewood	Fulton	IN	2001
909	728.5	Eric Geery	Lafayette	NY	2001
910	728.0	Sherry Solomon	San Jose	CA	1996
911	728.0	Jeremy Veens	Forest	ON	1998
912	728.0	Dave Creuziger	Sturtevant	WI	1998
913	728.0	Bill Blair		OH	2001
914	728.0	Kevin Brown	Milan	PA	2001
915	728.0	Darrel Roulst	Mossyrock	WA	2002
916	728.0	Ron Wallace	Coventry	RI	2002
917	727.5	Craig Lembke	Forestville	NY	1995
918	727.0	Kirk Mombert	Harrisburg	OR	1993
919	727.0	Don Black	Winthrop	NY	1996
920	727.0	John Baehr	Medford	OR	1997
921	727.0	Chris Hebb	Bridgewater	NS	1998
922	727.0	Steve Radich	Bow	WA	1999
923	726.6	Don Eisenhaur	Derry	NH	2001
924	726.5	Stan MacDonald	Katevale	QC	1995
925	726.5	Jim Lanterman	Canfield	OH	2001
926	726.5	Yvon Guay	Bromont	QC	2001
927	726.0	Bill Grant	Warkworth	ON	1993
928	726.0	Rick Dickow	Menlo Park	CA	1997
929	726.0	Jeremy Veens	Forest	ON	1998
930	726.0	John Butler	St. Thomas	ON	2001
931	726.0	R. Teals & D. Parr	Moses Lake	WA	2001
932	725.6	Rick Bartlet	Richmond	MA	1995
933	725.5	Ray Waterman	Collins	NY	1994
934	725.5	Steve Macnay	Kincardine	ON	1996
935	725.5	Glenn Needham	Braeside	ON	2001
936	725.0	B. Hartman	Honeoye Falls	NY	1993
937	725.0	Lyle Richart	Vancouver	WA	1996
938	725.0	Norm Milligan	Nanaimo	BC	2001
939	724.5	Bert Veens	Forest	ON	1998
940	724.5	Jack Lanterman	Salem	OH	2000
941	724.0	Harry Willemse	Wellington Forest	ON	1993
942	724.0	Don VanHoutte	Armada	MI	1996
943	724.0	John Castellucci	Smithfield	RI	1997
944	724.0	Paul Handy	Vancouver	WA	1999
945	724.0	Bill Van Waaden	San Jose	CA	2001
946	724.0	Beth Carlson	Clinton	IA	2002
947	723.8	Chris Moul	New Boston	NH	2001
948	723.0	Ken Armstrong	Vittoria	ON	1996
949	723.0	Kirk Mombert	Harrisburg	OR	1997
950	723.0	Dave Bhaskaran	Rochester	MN	2001
951	723.0	Steve Radich	Bow	WA	2001
952	723.0	John Castellucci	Smithfield	RI	2002
953	723.0	Scott Solomon	San Jose	CA	2002
954	722.5	Wayne Peters	Rochester	MN	1996
955	722.0	Joel Holland	Puyallup	WA	1992
956	722.0	Cliff Picketts	French River	PEI	1999
957	722.0	Don Emmons	Sammamish	WA	2002
958	721.5	Al Eaton	Richmond	ON	1993
959	721.5	Chris Lyons	Scarborough	ON	1997
960	721.5	Clarence Koch	Wisconsin Rapids	WI	2000
961	721.2	Roy Lendt	Chicago City	MN	1996
962	721.0	Mitchell Brewster	Windsor	NS	1999
963	721.0	Peter Carter	Goffstown	NH	2001
964	721.0	Joel Holland	Puyallup	WA	2002
965	720.6	Wallace Simmons	Canton	NC	2001
966	720.5	Jim Lee	Salem	OH	1996
967	720.5	Nic Welty	Smithville	OH	1999
968	720.5	Fred Muermann	Chetek	WI	2002
969	720.0	Bill McIver	Staffa	ON	1996
970	720.0	Brett Hester	Canby	OR	1998
971	720.0	Bill Thorpe	Windsor	NS	1999
972	720.0	Renald Provencher	Gentilly	QC	1999
973	720.0	Pam Wile	Windsor	NS	2000
974	720.0	Tim Parks	Salem	OH	2000
975	720.0	Brian Toyzan	Pinconning	MI	2001
976	720.0	Charles Pelletier	St. Alexandre	QC	2001
977	719.5	Michael VanHoutte	Ray	MI	1994
978	719.5	Al Gibson	Winona	OH	1998
979	719.5	George Spence	Mildmay	ON	2001
980	719.0	Jerry Rose	Canfield	OH	1994
981	719.0	Mark & Kyle VanHoutte	Ray	MI	1996
982	719.0	Don VanHoutte	Armada	MI	1997
983	719.0	Mike MacDonald	Sherbrooke	QC	1997
984	719.0	Dave Gowan	Philo	CA	1998
985	719.0	Lincoln Mettler	Eatonville	WA	1998
986	719.0	Chris Lyons	Scarborough	ON	2001
987	719.0	Peter Carter	Goffstown	NH	2002
988	718.5	John Robinette	Duffield	VA	1998
989	718.0	Mark Woodward	Leominster	MA	1992
990	718.0	Marvin Mitchell	Fenton	MI	1999
991	718.0	Jerry Rose	Huntsburg	OH	2002

992	717.5	Mike MacDonald	North Hatley	QC	1991
993	717.5	Pat Ruelle	Redway	CA	1995
994	717.5	Herbert Smith	West Charlton	NY	2001
995	717.4	Ken Armstrong	Vittoria	ON	2000
996	717.0	Norm Craven	Stouffville	ON	1993
997	717.0	Richard Goodhue	Lennoxville	QC	1994
998	717.0	Rod Harvey	Newport	NS	1995
999	717.0	Howard Shelly	Napa	CA	1996
1000	717.0	Hoshiko Hoshijima		JAP	1996
1001	717.0	Pete Geerts	Arkona	ON	1998
1002	717.0	Sheila Parks	Salem	OH	2000
1003	717.0	Ken Mitchell	Elk Grove	CA	2001

Data compliments of Vince Zunino

Country, & Regional Records

Starting with the United States and Canada, and their respective states and provinces, this list includes, in alphabetical order, other countries that compete in this sport.

If there is no entry in a row, no record has been officially recognized. If there is no entry in a column, information is incomplete for this record.

Far Left: Vince Zu and his 2000, 789 waiting to be weig at the Half Moon CA weigh off.

Left: Mike MacD with his 1991, 71 a pumpkin of con able merit which endured 11 years top-1000.

Page 37: Kevin S of Torrance, CA w his 2001, 594 at Elk Grove, CA Fa Festival and Weig

Below: Bob Troy his legendary 20 654 – one of the beautiful giant pumpkins ever gr

			lbs.	Year
United States	Charles Houghton	New Hampshire	1337.6	02
State	Grower	City/Town		
Alabama	Massey Goree	Quinton	401.5	96
Alaska	David Schroer	Homer	347.1	99
Arizona	Sam Kelscell	Gilbert	51.5	96
Arkansas				
California	Greg Stucker	Elk Grove	1105.0	02
Colorado	Joe Scherber	Wheat Ridge	1009.2	00
Connecticut	Ken Desrosiers	Broad Brook	840.0	02
Delaware				
Wash. DC	Joe Mills	Washington DC	470.0	98
Florida	Tim Canniff	Cortez	610.0	01
Georgia	Mike Nepereny	Monroe	615.0	02
Hawaii				
Idaho	Brian Christensen	Rexburg	847.5	01
Illinois	George Kopsell	Hebron	679.0	98
Indiana	John Barenie	Griffith	896.0	00
Iowa	Bob Ruff	Garnavillo	1056.0	02
Kansas	Doug Bush	Wichita	402.0	94
Kentucky	Belle Davis	Dawson Springs	204.0	94
Louisiana	Frank Milli	Zachary	578.0	99
Maine	Al Berard	Sanford	871.0	01
Maryland	Greg Carrico	McHenry	379.6	00
Massachusetts	Craig Weir	Salisbury	1260.4	01
Michigan	Bob Schlutt	Bridgeman	884.0	96
Minnesota	Jerald Johnson	Clearbrook	1083.0	02
Mississippi				
Missouri	Dan Westfall	Springfield	647.5	99
Montana	Clarence Fogel		180.0	02
Nebraska	Blase Biga	Omaha	320.0	02
Nevada	Scott Goodpasture	Fallon	715.0	00
New Hampshire	Charles Houghton	New Boston	1337.6	02
New Jersey	Ed Gancarz	Wrightstown	816.5	90
New Mexico				
New York	Joe Pukos	Leicester	1096.8	00
North Carolina	Wallace Simons	Waynesville	856.0	00
North Dakota	Gaylen Marzolf	Martin	410.0	97
Ohio	Dave Stelts	Canfield	1140.0	00
Oklahoma	Tiffany Hathorn	Apache	317.6	02
Oregon	Steve Daletas	Pleasant Hill	1230.0	01
Pennsylvania	Gerry Checkon	Spangler	1131.0	99
Rhode Island	John Castellucci	Smithfield	951.4	02
South Carolina				
South Dakota	Greg Kurkowski	Watertown	713.0	01
Tennessee	Jim Asberry	Allardt	716.0	91

State	Grower	City/Town		
Texas	Audie Starkey	Mount Pleasant	620.0	01
Utah	Bruce Orchard	Bountiful	777.5	01
Vermont	Mark Breznick	Pittsford	828.8	00
Virginia	John Robinette	Duffield	823.0	99
Washington	G. Emmons	Sammamish	1262.0	01
West Virginia	Steve Cline	Princeton	790.0	02
Wisconsin	Clarence Koch	Nekoosa	1049.0	02
Wyoming	Ron Hoffman	Riverton	648.0	02

Canada	Ben Hebb	Nova Scotia	1215.0	02
Province	Grower	City/Town		
Alberta	John Lobay	Smoky Lake	751.0	99
BC	Jake VanKooten	Port Alberni	1101.0	02
Manitoba	Ron Legaras	St. Claude	972.0	98
New Brunswick	Dennis Daigle	Moncton	1092.0	02
Newfoundland	Bill Williton	Torbay	380.0	00
Northwest Ter.	Horace Karnes	Fort Smith	168.0	98
Nova Scotia	Ben Hebb	Bridgewater	1215.0	02
Ontario	Bill Greer	Richmond	1172.0	02
PEI	Reg Noonan	Freetown	959.0	02
Quebec	Rock Rivard	St. Etieneces	1178.0	02
Saskatchewan	Dustin Coupal	Saskatoon	693.5	01
Yukon Territory				

Country	Grower	lbs.	kilos	
Australia	Ken & Rosemary Holden	970.2	440.0	02
A.C.T.	John Paul	495.0	224.5	
N. Territory				
NSW	Ben Boynton	950.6	431.1	02
Queensland	Geoff Frohloff	662.6	300.5	02
S.Australia	Ken & Rosemary Holden	970.2	440.0	02
Tasmania	Noel Button	319.7	145.0	
Victoria	T Knight	604.2	274.0	02
W.Australia	Ron Wilson	511.1	231.8	00
Austria	Penny Lichtenecker	381.5	173.0	99
Belgium	Paul Boonen	932.7	423.0	01
Denmark	Erik Lund	375.0		01
England	John Handbury Chesterfield	816.0		99
Germany	Martin Reiss	658.0		02
Italy	Alessandro Menzio	760.7	345.0	
Japan	Takao Hoshijima	861.3	390.6	99
Mexico	Lupita Caro	389.0		00
Netherlands	Hendrik Orde nijhuis	314.0		98
New Zealand	Graham Smith	519.7	235.7	98
Sweden	Börje Gustavsson	756.3	343.0	01
Switzerland	Giovanni Betti	591.0	268.0	98
Wales	Bernard Lavery	710.0		89
Yugoslavia	Instit'ue of F & V Crops	244.8	111.0	96
Zimbabwe	Lance Kennedy	137.2	62.2	97

Martin Reiss with the German record 2002, 658.

irk Mombert reacts to
in at Half Moon Bay,
A in 2000 with a 940
pound pumpkin.
ed from this pumpkin
ced Geneva Emmon's
I, world record, 1262.

w: Clarence Koch, on
right, with his 2002,
1049 Wisconsin state
d, and the "Father" of
nt pumpkin growing,
Gary Keyzer.

Joe Pukos in the patch in early September with his 2000, 1096.8

The Heavy Hitters

Since my first book, *How-to-Grow World Class Giant Pumpkins,* 34 growers have earned the distinction of being called *Heavy Hitters* in this sport, and 5 of the 34 were honored again in my second book, *How-to-Grow World Class Giant Pumpkins, II.*

In this book, I decided that there would be no repeats of former *Heavy Hitters* but instead decided to honor previous honorees by including them in a special section of this chapter. There are now so many good growers in the United States and Canada, that picking any list of the most outstanding is bound to ignite heated discussion among growers – especially those loyal to their region.

As in my past books, designation of *Heavy Hitter* status has not been granted exclusively on weight of pumpkins grown, but rather on a subjective mix of variables which may include: contributions to the sport either in the management of competitions or the leadership of an association, contributions that have led to a better understanding of the growing of giant pumpkins, and those growers who have been particularly innovative or generous.

There are at least 100 growers in North America that have a legitimate claim to the distinction of being called a *Heavy Hitter.* If I tried to include them all here, this book would be little more than a *Who's Who* of the sport. Since the major emphasis of this book is to introduce new information on growing giant pumpkins and teach, not only experienced growers but inexperienced growers, it was necessary to limit the number of entries for this publication. As with my first two books, the goal has been to write a book that could stand on its own. Therefore, everything from seed starting to competing has to be touched-on so that someone new to my books can fully grasp the fundamentals of growing giant pumpkins without any previous required reading. As a result, I have whittled down a list of 100 or more growers to a list that includes just 23.

Someday, perhaps I will publish a *Who's Who in Giant Pumpkin Growing,* but for now, these 23 growers have earned the right to be recognized by all as *Heavy Hitters.*

Left and right: Charlie Houghto world record, 20 1337.6: sculptu in the patch, and the scale at the Topsfield, MA All-New Englan Championship a GPC weigh off.

Right: Kathy Houghton show enormous pride her husband's accomplishment

New Hampshire's Finest

New Hampshire giant pumpkin growers captured the first 3 places in the GPC world rankings for the year 2002. This feat boggles the mind, when you consider that all three of these pumpkins were grown within 20 miles of one another. I have seen a continuous rotation in regional superiority over the 10 years in which I have covered the sport. First it was the growers from New York, then those from Ontario, then the Pacific Northwest, with the Ohio growers nipping at their heels, and now New Hampshire and New England seem to dominate as a region. I'm smart enough, and experienced enough to know that this is a "moveable feast." Weather and good fortune can make us all look good, so before you decide to move to New Hampshire, maybe all you need to do is get to know some of its best growers.

The top growers in NH include: Charlie Houghton, Bruce Whittier, Jim Beauchemin, Jim Ford, Robert Demers, Matthew Pollack, Matt Mongeon, Chin Ly, Jess Smith, Peter Carter, Geoff Peirce, Jim Kuhn, and Joseph Letourneau.

Charlie Houghton   1337.6

I've known Charles Houghton since the very beginning of my own career of growing giants. In fact, before I wrote my first book in 1993, he was in an audience I addressed at the New England Pumpkin Growers Association annual winter dinner, where I had asked to present my ideas on writing a book on giant pumpkins. Quiet, unassuming, and always in the company of New Hampshire friends, Charlie Houghton would astound us all in 2002 by growing the largest pumpkin the world has ever seen.

1337.6 pounds is only a number here, but in the flesh, at the actual weigh off in Topsfield, MA where I witnessed the event, that vision belies the number assigned to it. Measuring an incredible 174 inches in circumference (that's 14 1/2 feet for those of you trying to visualize a pumpkin that weighed more than 3 times the weight of the world record up to the year 1979), the 1337.6 was a veritable mountain to behold. Standing, side to side, at over 5 feet wide, Houghton's world record 1337.6 left little doubt in anyone's mind present that something very special had just happened.

Remembering when 1000 pounds was thought to be impossible, yet seeing the digital scale slowly settle at 1337.6 pounds, I pondered the future of this record, and how Charlie Houghton had just elevated the minds, hearts, and expectations of every competitive giant pumpkin grower alive.

Joe Pukos

Joe began growing giant pumpkins in 1996, but still has a rare claim to fame. He has not only grown a 1000-pound pumpkin (something no one had ever done before 1996), he has grown them three years running: 1096.8 in 2000, 1061 in 2001, and 1024 in 2002.

This graduate in forestry, and map maker for the County of Livingston, NY, has a beautiful family that includes his bride of 22 years, Terri, and 4 children including three sons: Randy, Scott, and Eric, and daughter, Emily.

His accomplishments include: finishing in first place at the WPC weigh off in Clarence, NY in 2000 where he set a new, New York state record of 1096.8 and took home a check for $25,000, a first place finish at the GPC weigh off in Oswego, NY in 2001 with a 1061, and a second place finish in Oswego in 2002 with a 1024.

Joe watched his dad grow giant pumpkins for many years before he actually began planting them himself. He first became interested in

giant pumpkins as a result of searching for better seed for his father to plant. Joe's father passed away in 2002. The experience of seeking-out superior seed has helped this relatively young grower to leap in front of most of the world's best – proving that years of trial and error can be avoided with proper seed selection.

Joe has contributed some hot seeds to the world's gene pool. His 2000, 652 and 805; and 2001, 735 have all produced 1000 pound pumpkins.

Above: Joe with family and the 1096.8, Claren NY, 1st place, $25,000 prizew

Left: Joe's 200 893.5 in patch.

There are many reasons why Joe Pukos stands out as a *Heavy Hitter* but none is more evident than his insistence on growing small, carefully pruned plants. Joe is one of a new breed of giant pumpkin growers that has chosen to reduce plant size to encourage fruit growth. Disregarding advice from my previous books, Joe and many other new young growers, either for reasons of lack of space, or the intuition that we are growing pumpkins not leaves, has opened the eyes of most of the competitive giant pumpkin community, including myself, the past 4-5 years.

As my good friend, Alan Reynolds, once told me, "We're not growin' salad, we're growin' fruit," and Joe Pukos can certainly grow fruit! He has to. He has two *Heavy Hitters* in his backyard. Both Len Stellpflug and Alan Nesbitt, *Heavy Hitters* in *WCGP I,* live less than 10 miles away. With neighbors like that, you have to grow big just to be respectable.

ve: 2002, 1024
2001, 735 with
and Joe's dad.
t: 2001, 1061
at weigh off.

Steve Daletas

Steve Daletas balances a busy life between family, piloting commercial aircraft, and gardening. And not surprising, when that balance was tipped in 2002, he chose to suspend pumpkin growing — even though he had one of the best giant pumpkin performances of all time in 2001.

Living in the southern end of the Willamette Valley in Pleasant Hill, Oregon, where springs are cool and wet, and summers are mild, hovering between 75 and 85 degrees with a week or so in the mid 90's, Steve shines in some of the best growing conditions imaginable for crops requiring long seasons with temperate climate. Fall cools to the mid to upper 70's with first-frost holding out until late September — providing for substantial, late, weight gains — something we all crave everywhere else in North America.

Steve began growing giant pumpkins in the mid 1980's, but didn't really get a passion for it until he moved to the country, and a larger growing area, in 1998. He worked the soil that first year, and planted his first *Atlantic Giant* in 1999.

He's been married twenty years to Susie, and has two children, a 17 year old daughter Stacey and a 12 year old son Scotty, who all witnessed his growing prowess in 2001.

Actually, Scotty grows as well, and not only witnessed the season but grew his own 1075 pound pumpkin. The whole family pitches in with Steve's mom doing a lot of the pollinating and his daughter and bride doing the mandatory cheerleading. Steve says, "My daughter says she's embarrassed about her dad's obsession, but inside she really likes it." I can attest to the fact that any father that has both a teenage daughter and a love of pumpkin growing has heard that one before.

Daletas family and friends on way to the Canby, OR weigh off with the 2001, 1230

In October of 2001, Steve Daletas' name became very well known in giant pumpkin growing circles. The world record was Dave Stelts', 2000, 1140 pounder. In fact, up until the weigh offs in 2001, only three people had ever grown pumpkins over 1100 pounds, and two were world records – Dave Stelts in 2000 and Gerry Checkon in 1999 with a 1131 pounder, plus Todd Skinner's 2000, 1109. 2001 would be a monumental year for giant pumpkin growing. I can only compare it to 1994 when no one had yet grown a pumpkin over 884 pounds, and four broke 900 pounds at the weigh offs. In 2001, Geneva Emmons broke the world record by a mind boggling 122 pounds – 1262 pounds, and adding to that excitement, and at the same time demonstrating the fact that 1200 pounds was the new level of giant pumpkin respectability, Craig Weir grew a 1260.4, Steve chipped-in with a 1230, and three other people broke the world record 1140 pounds set in 2000 (Paul Handy with an 1167, Al Eaton with an 1153, and Geneva Emmons again with an 1144).

Steve's 1230 also added a new dimension to how growers would now begin to view the physical attributes of a world class giant pumpkin. Measuring 416 total inches using the over-the-top method of estimating weight, this pumpkin had a circumference of 194" (that's over 16' if you're too engrossed to do the math) and an estimated weight of 1470 pounds. No one had ever grown a pumpkin with those kinds of measurements. Even though it was 16% below the estimated weight, the mere physical size of this pumpkin fueled the imaginations of giant pumpkin growers everywhere. Someone is going to grow a 1500 pound pumpkin, and it is likely to come sooner than anyone expected. 1500 pounds is no longer a fantasy number, it is something within grasp, and the next major barrier to break. Steve sees the 1500 pound pumpkin this way, "A few years ago my answer would have been no, but we've seen several pumpkins that, if they had just weighed "on chart," would have broken this barrier. With some seed [stocks] weighing heavy, like they are now, I see the 1500 pound mark falling soon. The upper limit? It's anyone's guess."

Steve has also opted for growing smaller, more carefully pruned plants. His plants typically measure 500 - 600 square feet, and his preferred pruning method is the Christmas Tree. He also uses a double primary vine method that I've called the "wishbone" in the past.

Steve with the 2001, 1230 cut open and revealed.

His 1230 was grown on a wishbone plant along with a 1016 pounder on the other primary. Steve says, "In my opinion, one plant can support more than one pumpkin."

Even though Steve took 2002 off, he spent the season sharing the excitement of growers who had chosen to grow his seeds. Five growers grew pumpkins over 1000 pounds and a sixth grew a 900 pounder from his seeds.

When asked what he feels is important, he answered, "I feel the soil is critical! If you don't take care of it, then the seed can't do what it's capable of doing. So, I work hard to get it balanced. After that, [you have to spend a lot of] time in the patch. There is no substitute, from heated greenhouses in the spring to covers over the patch when the fall rains come."

More on what he calls "balanced"
in the chapter – *Calcium.*

Above: Scotty and
pose for photograp
with the 1230 at t
Canby, OR weigh c

Left: Stacey, Susie
Steve & Scotty Da
with the 2001, 10
the Half Moon B
CA weigh off.

*Above: Steve and the
2000, 828, and an
earlier photo of the
Daletas' family
how you've grown!.*

*Right: Susie & Steve
with the 2001, 1230;
on a float with the
1016 at the
Moon Bay parade.*

1016

Bill Bobier

Bill started growing giant pumpkins in 1994 with seeds and a WPC newsletter from Ray Waterman, and made it look easy with a first year 667 pounder. "I can't wait to see what I can do when I know something," he remarked as he followed the 667 with a very humbling 400 pounder in 1995.

Time to go fishing. Bill isn't married to growing giant pumpkins, but he is married to doing things in a big way. He has shown no hesitation in taking a year off from pumpkin growing (he's done it twice since 1994), and when he's not growing giants, he's fishing for Tuna – giant Tuna. His best is a 260 pound bluefin – so he qualifies as a world class giant tuna fisherman as well.

Bill is a "Jack of all trades," but a master of most of them. He balances his life between family (wife, Donna and three daughters), a chimney service and restoration business (yes, he is a chimney sweep, or as he would prefer, a certified chimney professional with a Masters Degree in chemical engineering), and he also finds time for civic service (where he serves as chairman of the Board of Assessors).

His best pumpkin to date is a 2002, 1047 pounder, but he also grew a 1037.5 and a 991 in 2002, and a 1025 in 2000 – he took 2001 off. This record alone would qualify him as a *Heavy Hitter,* but he is famous in competitive giant pumpkin circles for two pumpkins that did not weigh 1000 pounds. His 1999, 723 and 2000, 845 (both unofficial weights) have gone on to produce many world class offspring. The 845 produced the 2002, Houghton world record 1337.6 and the 2001, Weir 1260.4. The 723 produced the 2002, Eaton 1236, the 2001, Eaton, 1153 along with more than 50 other pumpkins over 700 pounds. Any grower with a Bobier 723 or 845 to plant has a chance to challenge the best growers in the world.

In Bill's Own Words,

"My techniques for growing giant pumpkins are not much different from that of most serious growers. I attempt to maximize every step in the development of the plant and pumpkin. When the plants are small, they are protected and kept warm in 12' x 16' greenhouses – with colored water jugs used to retain some of the sun's heat – and an extra bubble packing cover over the plants. They remain in their houses until mid June. I have temperature sensitive window openers to vent the heat during sunny days as well as water misters on an automatic timer.

"When the plants outgrow their houses, I start pruning and burying vines. I prune almost every other side vine and all tertiary vines [third stage growth]. The side vines are grown to 8'-10', terminated, then buried. I trench ahead of the vines then cover them with soil. I have reduced my plant size over the years from 1200 sq. ft. to about 500 sq. ft. I set several fruit on the main vine only, and eventually keep the best based upon shape and position.

"Over the years, my fertilizing regimen has been cut back as well. I add alot of compost and other organics, and have drastically cut-back chemical plantfood. I try to rest some of my patches periodically, and grow green cover crops instead. My patches are as weed free as possible, and I believe it is very important to have an even growth rate for the pumpkins. You can control this with watering rates and fertilizer adjustments.

"I seek to plant the best seed I can obtain, and my "killer cross" [which produced the 2000, 845] has made this possible. Crossing the Lloyd 935 with the Mettler 865 was a lucky guess. When I made this cross I didn't recognize the genetic importance of the lines, but I did know that the 935 Lloyd had a tremendous reputation, as well as the 946 Geerts and the 567 Mombert which are the parents of the 865. This cross has become my claim to fame."

All I can say about Bill's tips is, "I could not have said it better myself." Good seeds, small strategically pruned plants, and the use of organic plantfoods in moderation, combine to produce a higher probability of success.

the "killer cross"
2000, 845.

ight: 2002, 1047.

ht: 2002, 1037.5.

ill with his 2001,
lb. Bluefin Tuna.

Paul and Stephen Handy

If your pickup truck body is only 65" wide, you better not grow anything bigger than that, and that's precisely what Paul Handy did in 2001 with a pumpkin he grew at 64.5" wide – and 1167 pounds. The state of Washington is known for big things: *Big Foot,* big trees, and big pumpkins, and in 2001, both Paul, and Geneva Emmons, also from WA, brought big pumpkins to bear on the world record set in 2000 by Dave Stelts at 1140 pounds. Geneva claimed a new world record at a staggering 1262 pounds, and the 1167 remains the second largest pumpkin ever grown in WA, and the eleventh in the world all-time.

Paul has been a leading grower in the Pacific Northwest for many years, and his kind and humorous personality has made him a perennial favorite with growers in both Washington and Oregon.

His son, Stephen is no slouch either. In 2002 he reined in a 1112.5 pound pumpkin, which ranks seventeenth all time in the world. In fact, Washington growers account for 6 spots in the top-20, all-time, all-world rankings. Geneva Emmons appears three times, the Handys twice, and David Larsen, with a 1156 pound pumpkin in 2002, ranks twelfth.

The Handy seeds have also been significant producers. Their seeds, planted by others, have produced many 800, 900, and 1000+ pound pumpkins.

Left: Paul Handy loading his 2001, 1167 with a half inch to spare.

Right: Stephen winching and posing with his Dad and the 2002, 1112.5.

Brett Hester

Welcome to Brett Hester's wonderful world of giant pumpkin growing, and equally wonderful worlds of giant squash, giant kohlrabi, giant sunflowers, giant corn, beets and turnips (and anything else giant that anyone competes with). *"Unlock the door to his world with the key of imagination. Beyond it is another dimension - a dimension of sound, a dimension of sight, a dimension of mind. You're moving into a land of both shadow and substance, of things and ideas. You've just crossed over into the Twilight Zone."*

from the Twilight Zone

As Brett relates, "The reason I do this crazy thing has changed over the years. Originally it was to be the best, then it was to do better each year, and to honor my grandpa, rest his soul. Now it has gotten to where it should be: for the fun of it. It is not the money, not the newspaper stories, not the TV appearances, not the girls (don't we wish), that drives one in this sport, but rather a feeling of pride when you stand on stage next to your entry, and say to yourself, 'I grew that thing!' – what a feeling."

Brett has spent alot of time on the stage, and he's had alot of wonderful feelings: growing a 42 pound kohlrabi in 1995 which tied the world record; growing a corn stalk over 20'; growing a sunflower almost 20'. He's grown a sunflower measuring more than 24" in diameter, and a beet and turnip that weighed 22 and 17 pounds respectively. And, he's done it all with a sense of urgency to compete, to show himself, to prove he can do it.

Add to this list of "done it," a 986 pound squash and a 968 pound pumpkin in 2000, and five, 1000+ pound pumpkins and three, 900+ pound pumpkins in 2001 and 2002, and you come away with a picture of a man totally committed to competing with giants.

But his proudest moment was not one in which he competed for bragging rights.

"In 1997, my grandfather and I worked the entire summer on a project aimed at being recognized as *Champion Gardeners* at our local fair. I even did some baking and hand-stitched a pillow, just so we could qualify for the *King of the Fair* award. On the second day of the fair, before the judging was complete, my grandfather passed away. The next day, I accepted our award as King of the Fair, and as I stood on the stage I felt his presence and knew instantly his joy."

Brett got into giant pumpkin growing after a neighbor brought a 50 pound pumpkin over to his house in the fall of 1993 and said those fateful words, "Let's see you and your grandpa beat this." The next year he grew a 133.5 pound pumpkin and forever claimed the "road" record, but the "smell of bigger fish to fry," lured him to the WPC weigh off in Oregon where he would be challenged again.

He finished dead last. Far from being discouraged, his failure made him even more determined to return with larger pumpkins in 1995. In 1995 he grew a 627.5 pound pumpkin, and two over 500 pounds (respectable weights for their time). In 1996, he bettered his personal best with a 676. 1997 was an off-year, but in 1998 he cracked the 700 pound mark with two pumpkins weighing 720 and 789. In 1999, he bettered his personal best again with a 850.5, but also grew his first competition giant squash at 862.5 pounds. In 2000, he grew a personal best squash of 986 pounds and a personal best pumpkin at 968. In 2001, he grew a pair of 1000 pound pumpkins, and in 2002, a trio of 1000 pound pumpkins (a new personal best of 1063) and a trio of 900 pounders – six pumpkins over 900 pounds in one year – a phenomenal achievement.

Left: Brett "Chainsaw" Hester ...ves pumpkin and squash in Pacific ...orthwest fashion.

...ight: 2002, 1027.

Top: 2002, 1023.

In Brett' Own Words

"I believe, that to be a good grower, it takes more than just good luck; more than just the best seeds, more than the perfect soil and the perfect patch – it takes hard work. I have never been lucky, so I grow 18 plants to compensate for all the bad things that can happen.

"I work hard all winter to get good seeds from the previous growing season, so that when those seeds prove out, I already have them before their popularity puts them out of my reach. I work hard, spring and fall, to get my soil into the best condition I can. I move, and spread by hand, hundreds of yards of manure, compost, potting soil, pumice, perlite, and anything else I can find to improve the soil. In the summer, I work each plant at least a half an hour a day [that's 9 hours a day for 18 plants]. I do everything I can to increase my chances of getting lucky – and the harder I work, the luckier I have been.

"I do the basics, but I do them right. I choose about 80% of my seeds for competition based on previous performance, and the other 20% on new seeds with interesting genetics.

"I file and soak my seeds before planting, and I keep my starting chamber at a constant 85° and 85% humidity using sterilized media inoculated with michorrizal fungi. I start my seeds in late April and set them out in early may.

"My cloches are small by comparisons to most, because the weather I experience is nice and warm this time of the year.

"I use very little fertilizer with my young seedlings, but as the plant grows, I increase feeding. I do not have a fertilizing schedule, rather, I watch the plant's growth rate and color, and when it needs a push here and there, I fertilize.

"I try to set fruit 10'-14' out on the main vine. I look for 5-lobe blossoms, and also pay alot of attention to the angle of the stem to the vine. I set 5-10 fruit on a plant, including sets on side vines, but most are culled within a week's observation. I keep 2-3 for a while to insure at least one fast grower on a plant.

I prune in the Christmas tree style, but am switching to a rectangle shape this year with a 25' main vine and side vines no longer than 12.5'.

"I watch my plants closely for insect infestations – especially aphids. I keep my patch weed free and neat until September 1st, and suspend weeding after that. I've found that I do more damage to late season brittle leaves than the benefits I derive from keeping the patch free from weeds.

"For all you new growers, be ready to learn, be open minded, work your tail off, and don't expect to break the world record your first year.

"And, here's some things not to do. Do not fail to tie-down your pumpkin in the bed of your truck. If you don't, it tends to make the bed of your truck a little rounder. [The picture on page 170 shows Brett's truck.] Do not spray *Roundup* or other weed killers on a windy day – you'll kill more than you bargained for. Do not think you have figured it all out, because when you think you have, you'll find out just how little you know. Never rest and never be satisfied.

"Never try weeding with a machete [a long knife used by laborers to cut-down sugar cane, and the weapon of choice of all serial killers]. I was cutting brush when I noticed a few weeds in my pumpkin patch. Trying to save time, I marched over to a clump of crabgrass near the stem of a very fast growing 500 pound pumpkin. I reached around the fruit, put the tip of the machete under the crabgrass and lifted. In one slice, I cut through the crabgrass, main vine and stem of the pumpkin – my stomach turned inside out."   *by Brett Hester*

"Leaving Mr. Brett Hester, still shy, quiet, very happy, and apparently in complete control of the Twilight Zone."

from the Twilight Zone

Brett's home at Halloween with inset below of his 1999, 793.

OVGPG's Finest

If it has anything to do with giant pumpkins, you're bound to see Tim Parks and Alan Gibson together. One, extremely articulate, never at a loss for words, the other, soft spoken but highly skilled at organizing and motivating the people around him. They make a perfect blend in managing one of the best giant pumpkin organizations in the world, the Ohio Valley Giant Pumpkin Growers (OVGPG).

They stage a GPC weigh off every year with Tim as master of ceremonies and Alan as the official scorekeeper at Parks' Garden Center in Canfield, Ohio. They've weighed world records there, and they've cultivated an atmosphere of mutual respect for anyone who dares to plant giant pumpkins. They have one of the tightest groups of growers in the world – sharing seeds, new ideas, and seemingly limitless enthusiasm.

There are six inductees as *Heavy Hitters* from the state of Ohio in this book, all of whom owe some debt of gratitude to Tim Parks or Alan Gibson for their unwavering support of the sport of giant pumpkin growing.

My hat is always off to those willing to do the work of administering a world class weigh off of giant pumpkins. It's not an easy task organizing an event of the magnitude in which the OVGPG presents each year. They've turned Canfield into a mecca for giant pumpkin growers, where every grower knows well in advance that they'll be efficiently weighed and duly recognized. This is no accident, and Tim Parks and Alan Gibson have much to do with the success of the GPC weigh off in Canfield.

This alone is worthy of the designation of *Heavy Hitter,* but each, in his own right, has produced world class giant pumpkins as well.

Tim Parks

Tim is one of the original steering committee members of the *Great Pumpkin Commonwealth* (GPC), and in this role, has shown a cool mind and keen vision, and has done it in a spirit of friendship without alienating people or other groups. This is no easy task when you're trying to coordinate more than 20 other sites, scores of strong personalities, and weigh offs geographically dispersed all over North America.

*Parks' Garden Ce
home of the OVG
and GPC weigh o*

After family, Tim splits time between managing a highly successful garden center business, with growing giant pumpkins, and a long list of other interests.

His best pumpkin to date is an 816 pounder in 1998, and his accomplishments have been many. His enthusiasm has lit a fire under many an Ohio grower, and his dogged persistence at making the Ohio weigh off run smoothly has paid handsome dividends to anyone associated with the OVGPG. He helped design and build a crane system for weighing giant pumpkins on weigh off day – something that makes the day a lot more enjoyable for all concerned with moving the monsters. He organizes an annual picnic that brings pumpkin growers from all over North America to Canfield for a weekend of patch tours, networking, beer drinking, and eating – and he's at the epicenter of all that's going on. If you've never been to a OVGPG picnic in July, you've missed a whole lot about what giant pumpkin growing is all about, and if you have been to an Ohio picnic, you owe alot to Tim, Alan and the OVGPG members.

Above: Tim and Nick Parks with their 2001, 779 pound pumpkin. Right: Tim Parks and Alan Gibson direct the OVGPC Weigh Off at Park's Garden Center in Canfield, OH.

Alan Gibson

Alan Gibson has been writing the Ohio Valley Giant Pumpkin Growers Newsletter for several years, and as a director, secretary, and treasurer of the association, has contributed much to the success of giant pumpkin growing in the state of Ohio. It would be difficult to imagine where giant pumpkin growing in Ohio would be if not for the administrative talent, and genuinely friendly leadership role that Alan has brought to the OVGPG. Along with Tim Parks, the late and greatly admired Dick Baird, Fred Calai, Ron Moffett, Jack and Dale Lanterman, and Dave Stelts, the OVGPG has flourished, combining an intense and serious competitive nature with a friendly and charitable treatment of every grower in their membership. This is truly the sport of giant pumpkin growing at its very best.

Alan had personal bests in 2002. He grew an exhibition only 990 and an official 907.5 weighed at the GPC weigh off in Canfield.

I am indebted to Alan for the many pictures he generously submitted for this book. He is extremely proud of the OVGPG and its members, and was a staunch advocate for the induction of the other five Ohio growers that join him here as *Heavy Hitters*.

Standing from t left, the OVGP(Directors: Jack Lanterma Alan Gibson, Dale Lanterma Dick Baird, Dave Stelts, Fred Calai, Tim Parks, ana Ron Moffett.

Top: Alan Gibs patch and his 2002, 808.5.

Fred Calai and
an Gibson pose
their unofficial
ies at the 2002
field Fair – the
ai 884 and the
Gibson 990.
an see that the
ompetition was
xtremely good.

: Alan with his
wife Joan and
ughter, Jenny,
tend to grower
registrations.

Jerry Rose

Jerry has been growing since he was 12 years old, starting in 1981, and has spent all of those 22 years "putting in his dues." We met in 1998 at the Ottawa/St. Lawrence Growers' Seminar in Ottawa, Canada, where he was honored with fourteen other growers in attendance with the distinction of having grown a pumpkin over 700 pounds. That was a huge accomplishment back then, with less than 100 growers in the world capable of making that claim. His 816 in 1995 completed a string of three straight years in which he broke the Ohio state record each year. I have always been impressed with his knowledge and his consistent improvement.

However, things were not always so "rosy" for Jerry Rose. His first entry in a local fair at the age of 12 weighed just 59 pounds, but he struck-up a friendship with an old-timer who spent the next few years showing him the ropes. I've always insisted that the mentor/student relationship is one of the best ways to learn giant pumpkin growing, and Jerry proved that by battling his mentor every year until he finally surpassed him in 1989 with a 292 pounder. His mentor, Anson Rhodes, could not have been happier.

In 1989, Jerry went to the WPC weigh off in Collins, NY, (a mecca of giant pumpkin growing), met some of the top growers in the world, saw the first pumpkin ever grown over 700 pounds, Gordon Thomson's world record 755, and began many friendships that exist to this day – all of which lead to better seeds and better information. Jerry's affable way personifies the personality of giant pumpkin growers.

Left: Jerry and his 2001, 960 a his hometown festival where it all started. And above right on the scale at GPC weigh off Canfield.

Right: Jerry congratulates Dave Stelts on 2001, 1053.5

In spite of his dogged attempts at controlling disease in a patch that was devoted to giant pumpkins for many years, Jerry finally moved to a new patch, free from pythium and fusarium buildup, and grew his personal best of 960 in 2001. He says, "I'm back," and with that, take notice Ohio and world.

Dave Stelts

Every time I meet Dave Stelts, I become more impressed with him. Every time I meet him, I like him more. The first time we met, I came away with very good feelings about this fun loving, humorous man. Never would I have deduced from that first meeting that he would become one of the best growers in the world, and one of the most innovative and committed individuals I've ever encountered in this sport.

When he first gained prominence in competitive giant pumpkin circles with his 801.5 in 1997, I was very, very, surprised. I really had not considered that here was a grower with great potential. Talking with him and his friends, I slowly began to gain insight into what drives this man to succeed. He does nothing in half-measures, leaves nothing to chance, and is always ready to gamble everything on what he believes strongly in.

In 2001, Dave showed the world what he was pursuing – a new world record 1140 pound pumpkin, and only the third pumpkin ever grown over 1100 pounds. Other growers began to emulate his cultural practices, and almost every grower in the Ohio Valley Giant Pumpkin Growers association started growing pumpkins with more zeal, using many of Dave's ideas. Much of the increase in average weights of the OVGPG has been a direct result of pruning plants more heavily, and pushing the AG like it has never been pushed before – something Dave had been doing for quite a few years. The "food factory" approach to growing giant pumpkins has much of its origin in the Stelts' patch.

Dave's good nature is legendary in Ohio, and his willingness to help any grower in need is equally appreciated and respected by all that know him. He once told me that a good giant pumpkin grower has to have "balls of stone." One pumpkin per plant, set at least 10' out on the main between July 4-10 – nothing else is pollinated. "While you're pollinating 2 or 3 more, I'm already 100 pounds ahead of you!"

Catch him if you can.

HOME OF OHIO'S LARGEST PUMPKINS

TOMATO		SQUASH				
Frank Lanterman	2.86	Deb Welty	947 State Record	Allen Kisamore	557	Sheila Parks (ex) 700
Fred Calai	2.65	Larry Welty	675	Michelle Andolina	391.5	Billy L'man 626.5
Jim Kilbert	2.56	Dave Stelts	609.5	Bill Pastor	3075	Dale L'man 650.5
MUSKMELON		Dave Skripac	609	Gene Mettle	395.5	Neil L'man 89 724.5
Marc Richard	20.88	Deb Welty	580	Frank Lanterman	445	Jerry Rose 677.5
George Bell	17.87	Nic Welty	744	Bill Morshhauser	558	Tim Parks 89 720
Nic Welty	3.00	Dick Baird	506.5	Jim Kilbert	478	Larry Welty 671
WATERMELON		Trevor Leyden	296.5	Mike Angelucci	479.5	Nic Welty 736.5
Fred Calai	139.5	Gerry Korna	407.5	Christine Wyckoff	483.5	Kathy Andolina 740.5
Bill Lanterman	134.5	Jean Scott	417	Sherri Alligretto	455.5	Tim Parks #10 717
Richard Barnes	124	Sharon Howell	465	Tom Adams	587	Jack L'man #11 709.5
Mary Calai	119	Richard Calai	267.5	Ken Ruble	511.5	Neil L'man #5 783
Marc Richard	106.25			Matt Alligretto	590.5	Fred Calai (ex) 741.5
CONN. FIELD		PUMPKINS		Dempsey L'man	560.5	Mary Calai #4 798.5
Harvey Giffin	105.17 Record	Eric Leyden	281.5	Jack Ternes	437.5	Fred Calai #2 869.5
Nic Welty	89	David Bowman	321.5	Chas. L'man	518	Winston Wyckoff 813.5
b Welty	84	Becky Snyder	237.5	Josh Jackson	451.5	Dave Stelts 1140 #1
A Giffin	79.5	Terry Kilbert	400.5	Lloyd Rose	536.5	
Lanterman	625	Joseph Chastain	251	Joan Gibson wow	614	
		Richard Calai	380.5	Alan Gibson	628	

Dave¹
Fred²
Winston³

Wow

Winston Wyckoff - 813.5 #3

1140.0

Left: Dave holds the coveted "Green Jacket," and Oooh, baby! The season begins for the 2001, 1053.5.

Above: the check, the scoreboard and the pose with the new world record 2001, 1140.

Nic Welty The Mad Scientist

In 1994, Nic grew his first giant pumpkin plants, one *Atlantic Giant*, and one *Big Max*. His largest fruit was a 91 pound *Big Max*, but every year since, through the year 2000, he has increased his personal best to where it now stands at 947 pounds. In the last two years he has spent less time on competition and more time on study with an emphasis in molecular biology and genetics at Carnegie Mellon University. Over the past three seasons he has grown hundreds of AG plants, conducting experiments to learn more about the nature of the genetics involved in giant pumpkin growing. Most of the information on genetics in this book is a product of Nic's writing and collaboration.

Nic started with giant zucchini, and by 10 years old began a serious fascination with many giant vegetables. In 1994 he grew his first giant pumpkins, and in 1995 grew a 200 pound *Burpee Prizewinner* pumpkin.

Above right: Nic displays an 18.5 pound giant parsnip.

Right: Welty family 1999, squash, gourd, and pumpkin display.

Above left: Nic inside his career best 947 pound squash.

In the winter of 1996, Nic found my first book, *How-to-Grow World Class Giant Pumpkins,* in the library, made some contacts, and received seeds from Howard Dill, and myself.

He lost most of his plants that year, but still managed a 221.5 pound AG which was weighed at his first weigh off at the GPC site in Canfield, Ohio. His 221.5 AG was classified a squash and finished last, but a 72 pound *Jumpin' Jack* pumpkin gained him first place in the field pumpkin category.

In the winter of 1997, he spent much of his time sending out seed requests to top growers, doing independent research, and committing

himself to a plan for full scale operations, with 2500 sq. ft. plants with only one fruit per plant. He lost a 636 pound squash because of inexperience, only to find out that the weigh off champ would be a 636 a few weeks later. This was the year he first began growing true, green, squash, and decided to dedicate efforts to advancing the green monsters, along with experimenting with colchicine and delving into more extensive readings in plant science.

In the winter of 1998, he went, as he says, "totally nuts," getting seeds from just about every top grower, and putting together a winning plan. That season, he learned about splitting fruit. The current Ohio state record was 816 pounds, and he had pumpkins that split early in their growing cycle at: 728, 739, and 809 pounds. Still, he managed to hold a 638 pound fruit for the contest. He also planted his first giant marrow, extended his interests into many other giant fruits and vegetables, and started a small plot of 20 extra plants for genetic observation. In subsequent years, this number would rise steadily, as he carried out a variety of experiments.

In 1999, he spent some time writing instructional articles on techniques, and took a three week vacation to Europe in July after finishing pollination. He produced his first 700+ fruit, and grew a pair of world champion bushel gourds. He also began some genetic tinkering with an extra 50 plants.

In 2000, he grew 21 competition plants, (a mind boggling number), and managed his best year. He started college in the fall, but still his patch produced a 947, 744, 736.5, 670.5, 615, 580, and more. He finished 1-2-3 in the OVGPG squash category. He also grew giant radishes, giant carrots, giant watermelons, giant cantaloupes, giant sunflowers, giant marrows, and giant gourds, along with an additional 300 plants for genetic experimentation. Is it any wonder that his interest in giant vegetable varieties should lead to college study in molecular biology and genetics?

In 2001, he backed off on competitive growing to devote more of his time to schooling and genetic research, but still grew 300 plants for experiments and observations.

In 2002 he grew 500 plants, and focused more attention on gathering knowledge on the genetics of giant pumpkins. He grew an 18.5 lb. radish, 33.6 lb. cantaloupe, and took first place in the cantaloupe and tomato competitions at the GPC weigh off, as well as second place in the *Connecticut Field* pumpkin category.

I am indebted to Nic for his collaboration with me on the information contained in this book on genetics and pollination strategies. Without this help, this book would have been diminished, and the information that is so crucial to keeping weights of AG's climbing would have been lost to the general population of growers.

Top right:
...arry Welty, Nic's
Dad, looks in
...nishment at the
...ing of the 1997,
636.

...ht: 7 consecutive
... set fruit on this
...y, 1998, squash.

...ght: Squash and
...umpkin display.

...1999 patch was
...red for a 3 week
...s with trenching
...d of vine growth
...sier burying later.

Fred Calai

If Fred Calai of Canfield, Ohio had only grown giant pumpkins in 2002, and never put another seed in the ground, he would still be considered one of the finest giant pumpkin growers of all time. What a year he had in 2002!

Very few giant pumpkin growers can make the statement that they have grown more than one 1000 pounder. Geneva Emmons and Kirk Mombert have done it 4 times, and Brett Hester, Steve Daletas, Paul Handy, and Joe Pukos have all done it 3 times. Some of these growers have spread their accomplishment over more than one year, but none has ever brought three, 1000+ pound fruit to a single weigh off. On October 5, 2002, Fred Calai showed up at Parks' Garden Center in Canfield, Ohio for the GPC weigh off with a mega load. Later in the day it would be confirmed that he had grown a 1074 pound pumpkin (which finished 2nd in Ohio, 12th in the GPC, and moved him into 33rd place, all-time in the world), a 1049.5 pound pumpkin, and a 1056.5 pound squash. The squash is the second largest ever grown in the world.

He has also held the Ohio state record with his now famous 846 in 1999. The 846 produced 18 pumpkins over 700 pounds in 2002 including: five 800-pounders three 900-pounders, two 1000-pounders, and four 1100 pounders. The 846 is a 801.5 Stelts x 876.5 Lloyd cross which, incidentally, is the same cross that produced his 2002, 1074. The 846 Calai has produced 57 official pumpkins over 700 pounds, and the offspring have done incredibly well in their own right, setting standards for size, shape, and color that will remain integral characteristics of the *Atlantic Giant*.

Fred has donated thousands of his seeds to association raffles, sales, and auctions, and is described by all who have met him as kind, generous, and extremely supportive. He is the epitome of good sportsmanship in this sport.

Fred has served as director of the Ohio Valley Giant Pumpkin Growers, and has been a tireless worker since the beginning of the organization. He also helped develop the Canfield weigh off track-lifter for pumpkins – a distinction that will not be forgotten by anyone who has ever volunteered to be on a giant pumpkin lifting team.

1999, 846

Top left: Fred's adoring family and the 1999, 846.
Top right: Fred in the patch with his 2002, 1056.5 squash.
Middle: Fred with the famous 846 again.

Below: Fred stands in the patch
and then at the weigh off
with his 2002, 1074.
Extremely tall, with broad shoulders
and great color – devoid of
limiting dill rings or stem problems –
the 1074 should get quite a run in 2003!

Tom Beachy

The next time you sit down and relax and begin to be contented with how much effort you're putting into giant pumpkin growing, remember that there are young men, like Tom Beachy, who are still working. From Indiana, and obviously possessing unlimited energy and ingenuity, Tom Beachy is, with little doubt, a force to be reckoned with in giant pumpkin growing.

His pumpkin patch appears many times in this book, and for justifiable reasons. I was enormously impressed with the amount of AGs he grows, and the attention he gives to every plant. Most growers find it difficult to keep up with care for just a few giant pumpkin plants, but Tom cares in extraordinary detail for 20 or more plants – and he does it with nothing withheld that could squeeze another ounce of life out of them. If there is strength in numbers, then Tom Beachy is marching, in close ranks, towards 1500 pounds at a cadence none of us can keep.

These two pages, and pages 152 and 153, show in a montage of photos his dogged determination to plant as many *Atlantic Giants* as any person could possibly imagine – and do it with a passion and commitment to every detail... It is absolutely frightful.

All of the basic chores of growing are attended to, and many of the not-so-basic are also addressed: shade for every fruit, pathways protected from soil compaction, aggressive pruning, heated water, and on and on.

Tom's personal best is his 2002, 1097.5 pound pumpkin, officially weighed but not officially sanctioned as the all-time Indiana state record. With only four years of experience under his belt, 1999-2002, look for much from this grower – a new state record, and maybe a new world record. If it doesn't happen, it won't be for lack of effort.

Tom credits much of his success to his dad, Dave Beachy, who helps enormously with the plants, and tends a few for himself as well.

Tom reminds me of my own son, who is also fully committed to his family and work. I take great pride in my son as Dave must also take in Tom. Behind every good son, is a good father.

Main Image: Tom checks his notes in this 2002 photo, as his best for the year, an 801 and 1097.5 are to the left of the access path, and his father's 682.5 and 807 are to the right.

The photo inset to the far left shows Tom during the 2000 season with his eventual 837.

Gerry Checkon

I had never heard of Spangler, PA, Gerry Checkon, or *Ironite* until October of 1999. That summer, rumors brewed that a PA grower had a pumpkin taping (estimated weight) over 1100 pounds. Later in the summer I heard the name Larry Checkon mentioned, and still later, just two weeks before the world weigh offs, I heard the sad news that he had lost his 1190 pound pumpkin – ending his pursuit of a new world record. Little did I know then that there was another Checkon growing giant pumpkins, and that she would arrive in Altoona, PA on weigh off day with the first pumpkin ever grown over 1100 pounds – a new world record 1131.

I saw pictures of her on the internet, even had a chance to speak with her and Larry on the telephone, but did not get to meet her in person until the International Giant Pumpkin Seminar in the Spring of 2001 at Guelph University, Ottawa, Ontario, Canada. In a crowded room of men enjoying a hospitality hour the night before the seminar, stood a diminutive woman.

Although she was lost in the shadows of the people towering over her, she was immediately recognizable, but I was stunned by her tiny size. You'd expect big people to be growing giant pumpkins, but here was the furthest you could stray from any preconceived notion of what a world record giant pumpkin grower should physically resemble. At that moment it became entirely clear to me, the sport of giant pumpkin growing is for everyone. Everyone has an equal chance at succeeding. Size, sex, brawn, or physical energy have little to do with success. Here was a woman that had focused her attention on a pumpkin she called, "Mooney," and despite her husband, Larry's disappointment, finished 1999 in style with a new world record.

Ironite became a hot commodity as a result of Gerry and Larry's testimonial, and if you say that seeds don't matter, don't say that around Gerry. The 1997, 935 Lloyd had been no accidental choice as seed in 1998. The previous year, Gary Burke of Simcoe, Ontario, Canada

Left and right: Gerry's 1999,
Right inset: Larry's 1999,

had broken the world record with it, wresting the record from Paula Zehr, who grew the first 1000 pound pumpkin in 1996 with a 1061. In 1995, three women upset all the men by finishing 1-2-3 in the world (Zehr, Geneva Emmons, and Lorraine Orr). Emmons would go on to better the world mark in 2001 with an astounding 1262 pound pumpkin. Gerry's 1131 filled in the gap in 1999. Since 1996 – six years – women have held three world records, and despite their lower profile and fewer numbers in the sport, have set extraordinary examples as growers of giant pumpkins. Neither size nor sex has anything to do with how good a pumpkin grower you can become.

Ask Gerry Checkon!

Ben Hebb – Canada's Finest

Ben is a dairy farmer from Bridgewater, Nova Scotia, Canada, not far from the birthplace of the *Atlantic Giant* pumpkin variety and the home of Howard Dill in Windsor. He's been growing AGs for eleven years and has always thought that his competitive nature, and his love of growing things, met a perfect match with growing giant pumpkins.

He has two young children, and his wife, Donna, is a nurse. The farming is hard, the weather sometimes brutal, but the joy of living family life on a farm surpasses all the sacrifices. And with that kind of love devoted to family and farming, he brings an awesome arsenal of personal virtues to bear on the growing of giant pumpkins and squash.

He broke the world record in the squash category in 2000 with a 990 pounder, and went over the 1000 pound mark with a pumpkin in 2001 with an unofficial weight of 1069. In 2002, eleven years of growing finally paid off with an all-time Canadian record 1215. One can only imagine what this young grower will produce over the next eleven years.

NEW
WORLD RECORD
990 lbs.
Ben Hebb Bridgewater, NS

*...eft: Ben with his
...02, 1215 at the
...indsor weigh off,
...nd left, with his
...ily and the new
...anadian record.*

*... right: Ben with
...is world record,
...0, 990 squash,*

*... right: Ben and
...02, 1215 pose
...he top growers at
...sor, NS, Canada
...weigh off:
...Dennis Daigle
...with 1092 left,
...nd Reg Noonan
...with 957 right.*

Drew Papez

"I try to pollinate from 15'-20' out, because I feel the plant beyond the pumpkin contributes little to the size of the fruit. I water everyday to keep consistent moisture in the soil. This helps to thwart the ill effects of heavy rain and the possibility of a huge spike in growth. I fertilize once a week with water soluble fertilizer mixed with fish emulsion and seaweed extract. I also include water soluble micro nutrients along with epsom salts. I foliar spray calcium once every 5 days and I also spray this directly on the pumpkin.

"I use heating cables in the spring to warm the soil inside a 4' x 5' cold frame with ventilating lid. I am on a clay bed and once the roots hit the clay they grow horizontal. So, I have installed drainage tiles underneath the whole garden, spaced 3' apart running lengthwise, connected to a storm drain. The patch was built on top of the drainage pipes to a depth of 3' with potting soil, leaves, and manure, and I add more every fall. I built a retaining wall around my patch to hold the soil in place, and I feel this helps warm up the soil in the spring.

"My organic level is 20 percent and my pH is 7.1, but I concentrate more on the calcium to magnesium ratio. I spread *Ironite* every spring, along with 100 pounds of agricultural gypsum, and 6 yards of manure for my 800 sq. ft. patch. I also spread granular *Merit* in the spring to control cucumber beetles and squash bugs. I will be using *Warrior T* this year to better control squash vine borers. I also add another 100 pounds of gypsum each fall.

I only pollinate on the main vine and I pinch off all females on secondaries before they open. I try to pollinate 3 on the main and then choose the best one. I cull fruit at 50 pounds, just to make sure the best fruit is in it for the long haul. Usually the second fruit is the keeper, since the first fruit pollinated has always grown slower for me. This is how I learned to pollinate only the ones that are at least 15' out. I pollinate from June 28th to July 5th.

"My pumpkins average 400 pounds by August 1st, and I have to limit fertilizer after that. I had one split on August 4th at 700 pounds, pollinated June 28th. Daily measurements are required to be able to tell you whether you need to fertilize or not. At 30-35 pounds a day, I fertilize lightly. At 40 pounds a day, I do not fertilize. My 1020 grew 45 pounds a day for 4 consecutive days in

2001. Anything that I have ever had that grew over 50 pounds a day blew-up on me, so I like to see 35 pounds a day as a peak.

"I grow in a Christmas tree style, with no vines behind the stump. I let the first couple of secondaries grow to 10'-12', and as the main grows, the secondaries get progressively smaller. At the end of the main, I let my secondaries get to about 2' before I stop all growth on July 20th. I let my main grow 25', but I only have about 50 sq. ft. of plant beyond the pumpkin.

"I feel, the plant beyond the pumpkin contributes little to fruit growth, so I keep the plant size in this area to a minimum. I plant seedlings at either end of the garden and let them grow towards each other, allowing each only 400 sq. ft. of area."

t: Drew and his 2001, 1020.

Drew works as a Pit Manager at o Niagara, and is two children, w and Danielle pear to the left. fe Carrie is the n Bee doing all he pollinating, se Drew works am to 12 noon. As Drew says, out her none of ld be possible."

ight: Drew with s 2001, 1020.

Rock Rivard – 2001... a dream season

In 2001, Rock set the Québec record with a 1062 pounder – placing hin second in Canada that year (3rd all time), and tenth in the world (15th all time).

Who could have predicted such a season? How did he get there? What's his secret?

In Rock's Own Words

"My 2001 season started in the fall of 2000. A big dumptruck of fresh manure – 15 tons worth – left me with about 6" to 8" of manure over the entire patch. On top of the manure I added about 6" of shredded leaves and tilled everything in.

"On April 28, 2001, the seeds are filed and soaked for about 6 hours, then placed in the germinator. My germinator is a simple plastic plant starter that I place on a waterbed heater. I plant in 4" peat pots, keep the soil temperature at about 85°, and keep a high level of humidity. About 24 hours later, my season started!

"I spread about 25 lbs. of gypsum, 15 lbs. of Ironite and another 15 lbs. of calcium nitrate on my patch, and then till it all in. I also prepared nutrient pits. These pits are holes dug to about 2' deep and 6' in diameter, then filled with a mixture of bagged sheep manure, shrimp compost, forestry compost, and some home-made compost. The soil removed from the hole is then mounded over the filled nutrient pit. This helps in warming up the soil in early season and with drainage later on.

"Four days after germination, I transferred the seedling into a 12" plastic pot and waited for the arrival of the first true leaf. I wait for the first true leaf so I can determine what direction the main vine will be grow – it always grows opposite the first true leaf.

"On the 6th of May, the seedling is transplanted outside. During transplant, it is very important not to disturb the root system, since it is very fragile. Each of my transplants were protected by mini greenhouses that measured about 8' x 10', and were heated with infrared light bulbs. These huts remained over the plants until the they outgrew them in early June.

May

"May is the longest month of the season (or so it seems), when nothing seems to be happening. However, during May the plant's root system is fully developing and the plant is getting ready to really take off. During this time of the season, overnight protection and watering are the most important things to take care of. The plant will not need much in the way of fertilizer as it will be feeding from the nutrient pit.

June

"The fun begins in June when the main vine starts growing at incredible rates. The end of May came with the plant having only a dozen leaves, and by mid June, the main vine has stretched to 10' with 3' secondaries. I start burying vines now. I bury vines to favor the development of a secondary root system, and to help anchor the plant against wind. For vine burial, I use a mixture of home-made compost and leaf compost from the local waste recycling program.

"By the end of June, I've been invaded by my arch-enemy, the Cucumber Beetle. These bugs have an enormous appetite and can devour young leaves and whole plants before you realize what's happening. As soon as thy arrive, I dust my plants with Sevin, which is very efficient on the bugs and relatively harmless to the plant. The first wave is neutralized, but Cucumber Beetles usually appear in waves – three or four waves during the season depending

Left and right: Rock with the 2002, 1178.

on weather conditions. You can reduce the risk of later waves by completely eliminating the first wave, which I did successfully this year.

July

"The end of June and the first two weeks of July is an important time for pollination – these weeks are the prime time for pollination. On the 6th of July, I pollinated a flower that would become a 1062 pound pumpkin a few months later. During the pollination period, I pollinate all female blossoms, taking no chance of ending a season without a fruit to weigh.

"From mid to late July, I choose the fruit I will keep on the vines for the remainder of the season. I tend to keep one fruit per plant. To make final selections, I use notes that have tracked each pumpkin's growth rate. I began removing young fruit, which were not well positioned on the vine, during the second week of July.

"By July 27th, I was down to two pumpkins on the plant when the final choice was made. This is where tracking growth rates is very important, the fruit that I decided on was not the biggest at the time, but was the fastest grower.

"When the fruit starts to really grow, watering becomes extremely important. I keep the moisture level in the soil as constant as possible. Often, fluctuations in soil moisture leads to splits in the fruit or stem. On July 31st, the estimated weight of my pumpkin was 124 pounds.

August – Wow!

"What a way to jump-start the month. During the first 10 days, the pumpkin gained over 25 lbs. per day! A minor cold wave calmed growth a bit, but once the weather improved, growth was back to 20-25 lbs. a day, with a few days in the 30's!

"At this point in the season, I stop trying to grow vines and leaves, and concentrate solely on growing the fruit. I achieve this by terminating all the vine ends. I treat the cut ends with a fungicide and then bury them. Now, the plant's energy has no where to go except to the fruit. On August 16th the estimated weight of my pumpkin is 556 lbs.

"On July 17th, I recorded the largest weight gain for a single day – 39 lbs., but horror – splits begin to appear on the stem of the pumpkin. The splits are pretty big (about 2" long and 1" deep), and I fear that they will split all the way through to the cavity of the pumpkin. I stop watering to reduce weight gains, and as I expected, growth lessens long enough to allow the splits to heal. Once healed, the fruit resumes growing again at 25+ lbs. per day. A stem split does not always mean the season is over.

"Watering, weeding, and watching are back to normal. The season goes on, but now the cold August nights have come, so I start covering the fruit with a old, thick quilt at night. A fall shelter is built measuring 45' by 24', equipped with infrared light bulbs for heat. This helped, because daily weight gains tapered off slowly. "On August 31st, the estimated weight is 896 lbs. – a 772 pound weight gain for August!

September

"September is the worst month for a grower with a big pumpkin. By this time of year, the watering, weeding, and insects are no longer major concerns. The plant has started its decline, and apart from trying to resurrect growth with additional fertilizer, all one can do is wait – hoping for the best, but expecting the worst.

"It was a happy ending, though, to an extraordinary season. A 1062 pound pumpkin."

Incidentally, Rock followed up his 2001, 1062 with a 2002, 1178, and with his insightful growing techniques, the future seems bright for this fun-loving grower from Quebec.

Gary Burke

In only his second year growing giant pumpkins, Gary Burke shocked everyone in Simcoe, Ontario, Canada, and everyone else in North America for that matter, with a new world record in 1998 of 1092 pounds. For this accomplishment, he was awarded the first ever "Orange Jacket" honoring his feat of setting new Ontario, Canada, and world records.

The awarding of this jacket is now made by the Port Elgen Pumpkinfest in conjunction with their sponsorship of the International Giant Pumpkin Growers' Seminar held in Niagara Falls, Canada annually. And, the award has expanded to include all growers – not just Canadian or those from Ontario, but anyone, internationally, who grows the largest pumpkin in the world for any given year.

This coveted award has been awarded to Ontario growers, Todd Kline, Al Eaton, and the late and beloved Bill Greer.

Above: Gary poses with his wife Elizabeth and his 1999, 747.5 pound pumpkin at the Simcoe, Ontario weigh off. Below: Gary supervises loading his world record, 1998, 1092.

John Deary

First Growing Season: 1999
Growing Area: 50' x 30' patch – 2 plants

1999: 198.2
2000: 302 & 466
2001: nothing, lost everything to borers.
2002: 695 – personal best

How I got into the giant pumpkin growing...

"One spring day in 1998, I had a conversation with a co-worker, Ken Desrosiers, about how I would like to grow some pumpkins for my son. As a result of that conversation, he gave me some extra field pumpkin seeds he had. One thing led to another, as it often does, and I never planted the seeds, but I resolved to grow a giant pumpkin the next season. This decision was reinforced later when I saw the AG that Ken had grown in his own garden that year.

"When the 1999 season began, Ken realized that I needed a nudge, so he gave me an AG seedling and a sawhorse wrapped in plastic for wind protection. Not wanting to disappoint Ken's generosity, I planted the seedling in a 6'x6' raised bed – talk about being naive. I didn't know much about gardening let alone how to grow a monster pumpkin. The plant overtook the bed in no time and began to devour the nearby lawn. Needless to say, I was hooked when I saw how fast the vines were growing. I was amazed that every night when I walked out into the garden I could see tangible growth. Although I was enamored with the progress of the vines, I almost forgot that it was really all about the pumpkin! Without knowing much at all about gardening, I was still rewarded with a beautifully shaped orange pumpkin of 198.2 lbs. and a sense of accomplishment that was unparalleled."

Ken Desrosiers

First Growing Season: 1998
Growing Area: 50' x 40' patch – 2 plants
1998: 125
1999: 302.5
2000: 604
2001: 625
2002: 840 (personal best and new CT state record)

How I got into the giant pumpkin growing...

"I started growing giant pumpkins in 1998 after getting some seeds as a gift from my mother. I put them in the corner of my vegetable garden and the plant took over the garden. I was amazed at how fast they grew! I began growing competitively in 1999, and I lost my best pumpkin with a rib split. I took the pumpkin to Alan Reynolds' house in Durham, CT., and on his scale the pumpkin weighed 457 pounds. My entry at Topsfield in 1999 weighed 305.2 pounds and finished in 87th place. Now, I was really hooked, so that fall, I sought better seeds and enlarged my garden. After losing my best pumpkin again in 2000, I finally "landed" one in 2001. It weighed 625.4 pounds and finished 28th at Topsfield, and also won the "most aesthetically challenged" [ugliest] pumpkin at the Topsfield fair. In 2002 I planted my best seeds yet, a 712 Kuhn and an 805 Pukos. Both seeds had produced pumpkins over 1000 pounds. I grew a new CT state record pumpkin of 840 pounds on the 805 Pukos plant. I named her *Wicked-Wide-Wilma* or www for short. My 840 finished 12th at Topsfield.

*Left: Screen sho
BigPumpkins.c*

*Page 85, top: Th
not Ken and Joh
it is the Deary t
as youngsters.
Bottom left: Joh
his 2002, 695 a
Durham, CT Fa
Bottom right: K
with his family
his 2002, CT, s
record, 840, "W
Wide Wilma" (*

How BigPumpkins.com was born:

"We were both working at *Software Impressions* for a little over a year and had worked together prior to that at another consulting firm. Although we were good friends and accomplished web developers, we were definitely not master gardeners. Turning to the web for advice and information about our new sport, we often came up empty handed. At about the same time, we were chronicling our current season's progress on our company's web server in the form of an online diary. We wanted to show people on the internet our current progress, and let them comment on the state of our plants.

"At the close of the 1999 season, we realized that our postings would be useful for comparison purposes next season. As web developers, we also realized that this would be a great service for other growers as well – not to mention, that if we got others to utilize this service, we would be able to learn from them too. So, that winter we set out to build an online community that was user friendly and, most importantly, accessible to newcomers. The community concept is truly the heart and soul of *BigPumpkins.com* and the key to its success. Members from all over the world contribute to the site's content. It is truly the collective work of hundreds of growers.

"*BigPumpkins.com* is in its 5th season of operation, and has over 7,500 registered users. We average 840,000 hits a month, and peak with over one million hits during weigh-off season. None of it would be possible without the generous support of *Software Impressions* who hosts our server."

BigPumpkins.com Statistics as of June, 2003

Registered users: 7,507
Average visitors per day: 1,400
Average hits per day: 28,583
Total hits for all of 2002: 10,433,099

Mike Nepereny

In the category of information dissemination, Mike Nepereny and his creations: *CucurByte, www.atlanticgiantgenetics.com,* and the *Atlantic Giant Genetics Cooperative,* stand at the epicenter of the future of giant pumpkin growing. Nowhere else in the world can someone find such a vast storehouse of information on AG pumpkins, and where anyone with intuition can utilize a number of query options to isolate from thousands of individual pumpkins a select few. Unequivocally, the AGGC website is the best tool for AG research ever created, and the great equalizer between the experienced and inexperienced giant pumpkin grower. I once had a grower tell me that my books put him on a level playing field with the best growers in the world. I can only say that Mike has not only put the average backyard gardener on a level playing field, he has actually put them right in the game.

It is rare to find someone with talent and genius in such a rare combination of diverse subject areas so as to make his work a benefit to all. Such is the case of Mike Nepereny, a self taught software developer and a state champion pumpkin grower (2002, 615, GA record).

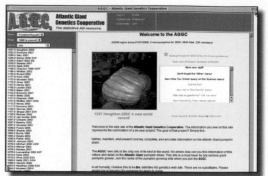

Mike went online with the AGGC website on January 1, 2000, and nothing has been the same since.

Atlantic Giant Genetics Cooperative (AGGC)

"Even though the *Atlantic Giant* Genetics Cooperative is only about 2 years old, its roots can be traced back more than 6 years. It was then that I began laying the framework for capturing and tracking the information you see on the AGGC web site today.

"I remember receiving a copy of Al Eaton's 700+ pound, pumpkin, hierarchy tree booklets. Intrigued, I began to study them intently, looking for patterns and similarities. I appreciated the work and dedication that went into creating them on paper, and admired Al for his

Above: screensh[...]
atlaticgiantgeneti[...]

Far left: Mike wit[...]
nice orange 2002[...]
Directly left: His[...]
time top Georgia[...]
2002, 615.

Page 87: Mike an[...]
bride, Debbie, wit[...]
2002, 585.

tenacity. I started developing an interest in plant genetics almost immediately. Being a software developer by trade, I knew that such information could be easily tracked and manipulated using the right software. I began to look for existing products that would do this. After failing to find such a product, I set about designing my own."   — *Mike Nepereny*

This resulted in the creation of the software application, *CucurByte,* and led to the design of a website devoted to AG genetics (www.atlanticgiantgenetics.com), and finally to an organization called the *Atlantic Giant Genetics Cooperative.* More on the AGGC and its awesome delivery of information about almost every significant giant pumpkin and grower on page 173.

A.G.G.C.

Joel Holland at the Half Moon Bay, CA weigh off in 2001 with his 966.

Marv Hicks

"One year I put some 'feed store' Dill's *Atlantic Giant* seeds in and grew my first giant weighing 118 pounds. A friend and co-worker, Dale Helsel, coached me a little in 1996. His brother, Galen, and Dr. Marvin Meisner had just started a small pumpkin weigh off in Altoona, PA which I attended that fall. That was when I really got the fever. I was amazed at Tony Ciliberto's 734. Before leaving, I approached him about getting a few of his seeds, and of course, I had them a short time later.

"In 1997, I planted Tony's 887 and made my first real attempt at growing a giant pumpkin — ending the season with a beautiful, shiny, yellow AG. I made my first trip to the Altoona weigh off — a 20-minute drive from my home in Williamsburg, PA. The pumpkin weighed 397 pounds and placed 9th.

"In 1998, I grew a 977 Andersen that had been started by Doc Meisner. Almost perfect weather and rainfall, combined with a patch that was new and not contaminated with pumpkin diseases, gave me my personal best 745.

"1999 was a mediocre year for me, but with an

interesting twist. Local growers, led by Marv Meisner, formed the PA Giant Pumpkin Growers Association, and at season's end, I was contacted by Beth Rado of VA who was organizing a pumpkin carving event in Washington D.C. at the Vice President's residence — occupied at that time by Al and Tipper Gore. She wanted my help in procuring a few big pumpkins. Beth was authorized to invite a small number of growers to attend the annual Gore Halloween party. Who would have thought that growing giant pumpkins would give an average guy like me the opportunity to take my family on an adventure such as this?

"In 2001, my younger son Julian, who was 13 at the time, became interested in growing giant pumpkins. I had a 932 McIntyre planted as a backup and was letting him do hand pollinations on it. He got one to take and his season was off, and my plan to pull the plant immediately changed. I was more worried about his pumpkin than any I've ever grown. He did 99% of the work on that plant, which was limited to about 220 sq.ft., and he took a 501 pounder to the Altoona weigh off. I planted a 946 Geerts and 801.5 Stelts in the patch. A blossom end split on the 946 ended it for that one. I kept two pumpkins on the 801 and ended the season with a 673 and 594.

I've had good years, bad years, and some in-between. I always have pre-season optimism and am full of great expectations, but am aware of the reality that this is a fairly high-risk hobby, especially when you are limited to two or three plants. For example, in 2002 I lost two of the most sought after seeds in the world — the 723 Bobier and 846 Calai — both succumbed to fusarium. Julian planted a 968 Sproule that also went down — the patch was empty by mid August.

Page 90:
Marv Hicks and his
2001, 673 at the
Altoona, PA, GPC
weigh off.

Page 91top:
Dr. Marvin Meisner
ses with his carved
1999, 622 at the
Vice Presidential
residence on
Halloween,

and bottom:
Julian Hicks peers
from within Marv's
1998, 745 during
seed removal.

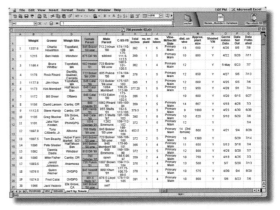

The Patch

"My patch is just over 1200 sq. ft. and I was growing two pumpkins in that space but the last two years have added a third plant that is kept at about 250 sq. ft. I like to get manure on in the fall and try to add organics but don't always get as much as I'd like. I use some water-soluble fertilizer but try not to overdo it. I'm starting to believe that many of us are getting our patches so out of balance with chemicals, that we are creating a lot of our own problems. I'm also a believer in using michorrizal fungi. I've seen good results in my patch with it in the past. Not using it last year and losing everything has me committed to not planting without it. It may not be a cure-all but I do believe it increases the plants chance to fight off disease.

The 700 Pound List

"Tony Ciliberto called me a few years ago and asked if I would be interested in taking over his 700 pound list. I had seen his list from years past and had also been involved with collecting data for Mike Nepereny's A.G.G.C. site, so I knew pretty much what I was getting into.

"I send data forms to weigh off sites and ask the coordinators to pass them out to growers of 700 pounders. In return, I send a completed copy of the list to each site coordinator and any grower who returns a form. Most of the data on my list comes directly from the growers but I also use Mike Neperene's *CucurByte* program and the AGGC website to fill in blanks. Mike, Rock Rivard, and I trade a lot of information back and forth in the months after the weigh offs. I fill in some blanks for them and they fill in some for me. It works out well and benefits everyone in the growing community.

"I hear from a lot of the top growers and many tell me they look forward to the finished list as much as anything they receive. When one gets a call or email from the likes of Paul Handy, Jack LaRue, or Jim Kuhn, it certainly is rewarding to know that the work is appreciated."

Marv Hicks' 700 pound list is one of the most valuable sources of data on giant pumpkins, and an indispensable tool in evaluating your own seed choices from year to year.

The Heavy Hitters – A pictorial tribute to those who have made past distinction, along with the book (s) they appeared in.

Heavy Hitter	Book
1 Alan Nesbitt	I
2 Donald Black	I
3 Barry DeJong	II
4 Craig Weir	II
5 Geneva Emmons	II
6 Milt Barber	I
7 Lorraine Orr	II
8 Howard Dill	I & II
9 Mark Woodward	I
(with)	
9 Hugh Wiberg	I
10 Len Stellpflug	I
11 Don Fleming	I
12 Jim Kuhn	II
13 Jack LaRue	II
14 Chris Andersen	II
15 Tom Norlin	I

	Heavy Hitter	Book
16	Bill Greer	II
17	Wayne Hackney	I
18	Bob Ruff	II
19	Pete Glasier	I
19	*(with)* Joel Holland	I & II
20	Norm Gallagher	I
21	Robert Gancarz	I
22	Edward Gancarz	I
23	Mike MacDonald	I
24	Herman Bax	II
25	George Lloyd	II
26	Jerry McGowan	I
27	Gordon Thomson	I
28	Tony Ciliberto	II
29	Glen Brown	I & II
30	Kirk Mombert	II
31	Al Eaton	I & II
32	Ray Waterman	I & II

Chapter 4 – Seed Selection

Seed selection can be said to be the single most important reason why less experienced growers have become, more and more, able to compete with seasoned veterans in recent years. First and second year growers are having tremendous success in producing world class giant pumpkins, because the strategies they use in determining what seed to plant center around the abundant amount of information available through association newsletters, the internet, and word of mouth.

Background information on almost every significant giant pumpkin grown in the last 10 years can be found somewhere. This information includes: weight, grower, seed, and pollinator, along with characteristics like: shape, color, and the amount of deviance from estimated weight to actual weight. This means that every competition seed today comes with heredity information that may go back 4-5 generations. This wealth of information has been tapped-into by every successful grower today. There are many ways to go about selecting the right seed to plant, and some of the more successful strategies are discussed here.

Following the Pack

If you look at the top pumpkins grown in any one year, you will find that 33% or more are grown from a small pool of seeds coming from fewer than 10 pumpkins. In 2002, from a list of 228 pumpkins that weighed more than 700 pounds, 47 of them (or 21%) came from just 3 different pumpkins. With information like this available to any serious giant pumpkin grower, it is not hard to predict that these same 3 seed stocks will be heavily planted again. Why? Because, they produce!

Following the pack has many advantages. You are planting high probability seed stocks that insure you much greater success than a random selection of seeds, and you are incorporating the genetics of those seed stocks into everything that you pollinate using them. That means that following the pack gives you a better chance of being successful, and at the same time, allows you to upgrade your own seed stocks with the addition of a hot seed's characteristics.

The disadvantages of following the pack are that a limited number of seeds are being chased by hundreds of growers each year. Your chances of getting a hot seed to plant go down as the success of the seed goes up. Trading for hot seeds becomes tighter because those with the seeds want equally hot ones in exchange.

Buying hot seeds has become very prevalent in the last 3 years with many associations using hot seeds as auction bait to fund their operations. Single seeds have sold for more than $500, and reasonably good seed stocks easily receive $20-$25 per seed in auctions. This was unheard of just 5 years ago, and leads me to ponder what prices will be a couple years from now. In any event, if you follow the pack, it's going to get very expensive in upcoming years.

I have always stressed the importance of collecting seeds every year. A pumpkin grown this year has no track record for pumpkins produced by its seeds (it hasn't been planted yet), and this is precisely why it is easier to come by these seeds. If you exclusively follow the pack, you won't be trying to secure these seeds, giving everyone else the luxury of receiving them, just for the asking. Making it a routine to contact the growers you have come to know because of competitions or previous encounters, either by mail, email, or in person, allows you to collect a huge amount of seeds. These seeds are worthless at this point, but a year or two down the line, a few of them will stand out as high success seeds.

Each year, mail to as many growers as you know, asking to receive their seeds. Send to each of them, your own seeds produced each year, along with a self addressed and stamped bubble pack. This will make it as easy as possible for the grower to honor your request. Never begrudge another for not sharing their seeds – this will assuredly ruin your chances of ever trading or receiving seed from this grower – and besides, it's just common courtesy.

If you are going to use a follow the pack strategy to select seeds for each year's planting, make sure you do your homework every year, so you have the seed before it becomes hot.

94: So you want e a winner. Here, he top growers in in 1999 pose for ctures, from left: Rob Lanterman, d Calai with the amous 846, and ale Lanterman. Below: ons, decisions... seed do I plant?

The Dark Horse

I have always advocated planting proven seeds, but the strategy of seeking a dark horse, which seeks to find good performing, unproven seeds, has been embraced by some with much success. The tactics they use in discovering these unknown and unappreciated seeds rely, in many cases, on numbers gleaned from the lists of top pumpkins grown each year – the rest is a cerebral excursion that most of them are unwilling to describe.

Those that hint at tactics employed show a remarkable knowledge of the seeds available to choose from, and they spend a lot of time and thought in reviewing what has been grown every year. In addition, they network with many growers to get their takes on what looks good, but inevitably plant what they themselves choose.

In the end, they choose the most unlikely of seeds, never settling to just follow the pack.

A tactic used in recent years has been the evaluation of a pumpkin's estimated weight to its actual weight. Actual weight is the important weight (because it is the real one), but if a pumpkin's actual weight is 20% or more over its estimate, then this pumpkin does not conform to the averages based on physical volume. Estimated weights are averages of other pumpkins with the same physical volume, and these averages have been developed over a long period of time. Any pumpkin that deviates significantly from the averages, sends a red flag up for the dark horse strategist.

The mentality is pretty simple. If a pumpkin is supposed to weigh 600 pounds, but actually weighs 800 pounds, then something besides measured volume is contributing to the increase (because we have good, average estimates for volume). Thicker walls are most often inferred, especially blossom-end walls.

Some have hinted at a higher water content of the pumpkin's cells. Maybe, instead of cells carrying 80% of their weight in water, they carry 90%. What's heavier, a 5-gallon pail of grapes, or a 5-gallon pail of raisins?

Another tactic used is the evaluation of the rate of growth and the total period of growth. This information is harder to come by, but the ever curious dark horse strategist is always talking to other growers about their pumpkins. It has become a pretty standard practice to keep diaries of weight gains. From these diaries, it is easy to determine the rate of growth of a pumpkin at 14 days, or 30 days, and whether it stopped growing at 60 days. It was once considered a given that the *Atlantic Giant* pumpkin grew for only 60 days after pollination. That has essentially been disproven. Many growers now measure increased growth after 70, 80, and 90 days. It is slower growth, because growth naturally tapers, but the pumpkin does not stop increasing in weight. If it stops growing at 60 days, other factors besides the natural growth tendencies of the *Atlantic Giant* are at work.

Looking for a pumpkin that had daily weight gains in the 25-35 pound range for two or more weeks during the season sends shivers up the spine of the dark horse strategist. A pumpkin that grew for ninety days also beckons investigation, as does one that had extraordinary growth from pollination through 30 days of growth.

With the dark horse strategist, a number of factors influence decisions as to what seed is selected to plant – all of these factors combine to produce a cerebral representation of the most likely candidates. Some growers are particularly gifted in this respect, and they are very adventurous, risk takers whose success is shared by all other growers. A good seed stock would remain an unproven entity if everyone was unwilling to risk planting it.

The Charts

When you look at one of Marv Hick's compilations, you are bombarded with an awful lot of information. If you take Charlie Houghton's 1337.6, new world record as an example, you can determine what seed grew the pumpkin (845 Bobier), what plant he used as a male pollinator (712.2 Kuhn), the measurements in inches starting with the circumference, side-to-side, and then stem-to-blossom end (174-11-108), the total inches (392), the estimated weight as determined by a look-up-table for total inches (1201), the deviation of the actual weight from the estimated weight expressed as a percentage (+10.21%), the number of pumpkins that were grown on the plant (1), the number of segments, lobes, or stigmas in the flower (5), what vine it was grown on (PM - primary main), the distance out from the initial transplant (13'), the size of the plant in square footage (550), whether or not he shaded the fruit (Yes), when the seed was germinated (April 26) and transplanted to the garden (May 5), and, finally, when the female flower was pollinated (July 8). This line contains 17 pieces of data, and the 2002 Hick's compilation contained 228 pumpkins. This makes for almost 4000 pieces of information to review. So, where should you begin?

Looking at a hard copy of the entire list can be daunting. There is no way for you to rearrange the list without painstakingly going through the chart, noting significant data, and then writing it down or committing it to memory. Without a computer, the charts can become useless to anyone who does not commit many hours to its review. There is a necessity to eliminate information entirely to expedite the analysis, and if you are without a computer, or the ability to capture the data into a spreadsheet application like *Microsoft Excel,* you are faced with concentrating your review on a fraction of the

700+ Pumpkins 2002 — 1 of 6

	Weight	Grower	"	Est.	Δ	Weigh Site	Female Parent	Male Parent	C-SS-FB		# on plant	# of lobes	Vine	Out	Size	Shade	Germ	Set Out	Poll.
1	1337.6	Charlie Houghton	392	1201	10.21%	Topsfield, MA	845 Bobier '00 UOW	712.2 Khun '00	174-110/108		1	5	PM	13	550	Y	4/26	5/5	7/8
2	1215	Ben Hebb	399	1266	-4.20%	Windsor	875 Dill '99	sibbed	175-111.5-112.5		1	5	PM	10	800	Y	4/22	5/20	7/11
3	1186.4	Bruce Whittier	382	1112	6.27%	Topsfield, MA	582 Hester '01	723 Bobier '99 UOW	180.5-101-100.5		1	4	PM	12		Y	5/5	5/23	7/7
4	1178	Rock Rivard	376	1061	9.93%	Gentilly, Québec 9/28	723 Bobier '99 UOW	805 Pukos '00	174-104-98		1	5	PM	12	850	Y	4/27	5/5	7/13
5	1177.8	Jim Khun	385	1138	3.38%	Topsfield, MA	846 Calai '99	723 Bobier '99 UOW	175-107-103		1	5	PM	12	600	Y	4/25	5/5	7/6
6	1173	Kirk Mombert	377.3	1070	8.74%	Half Moon Bay	846 Calai '99	1064 Mombert 01*	166.25-112-99		1	5	PM	12	950	Y	4/28	5/1	7/4
7	1172	Bill Greer	386	1147	2.13%	Ottawa	846 Calai '99	1153 Eaton '00	173-110.5-102.5		1			10	600	Y	4/20	5/15	6/27
8	1156	David Larsen	359	926	19.90%	Canby, OR	898 Knauss '01	1062 Rivard '01	165-100-94		1	5	PM	14	667	Y	4/18	4/26	7/3
9	1112.5	Steve Handy	379.5	1095	1.57%	Canby, OR	695 Handy '01	955 Stelts '01	162.5-112-105		1	5	PM	9	1600	Y	4/23	4/30	6/30
10	1105	Greg Stucker	390	1183	-7.06%	Elk Grove, CA	846 Calai '99	801.5 Stelts '97	181-106-103		1	6	PM	10	620	Y	5/10	5/20	7/6
11	1101	Jake Van Kooten	372	1028	6.63%	PNWGPG	1016 Daletas '01	1262 Emmons '01	158-112-102		1	5	PM	12		Y			7/4
12	1097.8	Tony Ciliberto, Jr.	403.5	1313	-19.60%	Altoona	705 Stelts '99 UOW	845 Bobier '00 UOW	188-106.5-109		1	5	PM	14	600	Y	4/21	5/4	6/29
13	1097.5	Tom Beachy	372	1028	6.33%	Huber Farm Market 9/21	845 Bobier '00 UOW	723 Bobier '99 UOW	166-106-100		2	5	PM	16	1300			5/29	7/14
14	1096	Pete Glasier	366	980	10.58%	Half Moon Bay	845 Bobier '00 UOW	940 Mombert '98	175-90-101		1	4	PM	11	650	Y	5/13	5/18	7/4
15	1092	Dennis Dugle	372	1028	5.86%	Windsor	810 Dill '99	658 Emmons '98	165-108-99		1	5	PM	12	800	Y	4/28	5/20	7/7
16	1090	Mike Fisher	359	926	15.05%	Canby, OR	783 Daletas '00	open	166.5-96-97		2	4	PM	10	750	Y	4/18	4/26	7/3
17	1083.5	Jerold Johnson	376	1061	2.04%	Anamosa	735 Pukos '01	1007 Brown '00	159-113-104		1	4	PM	13	500	Y	5/7	5/20	7/13
18	1076.5	Quinn Werner	378	1078	-0.14%	OVGPG	845 Nesbitt '01	988 Khun '01	177.75-100.75-99.5		1	5	PM	10	575	Y	4/30	5/4	6/29
19	1074.0	Fred Calai	391	1192	-10.99%	OVGPG	801.5 Stelts '97	876.5 Lloyd '96	176-110/105		1	4	PM	10	800	Y	5/6	5/23	7/6
20	1066	Jack Vezzolo				Elk Grove, CA	845 Bobier '00 UOW	self											
21	1064	Jack LaRue	379.5	1095	-2.91%	Half Moon Bay	611.5 Hester '99	746 La Rue '01	182.5-97-100		1	5	PM	13	400	Y	4/25	5/1	7/14
22	1058	Charlie Houghton	359	926	12.48%	Hillsboro Fair- NH 9/5	712 Khun '00	845 Bobier '00 UOW	164-98-97		1	5	PM	14	600	Y	4/26	5/5	7/7
23	1058	Craig Sandvik	373	1036	2.08%	Shoreline, WA 10/12/02	652 Pukos '00	multiple	172-103-98		1	6	PM	12	500	Y	4/27	5/2	7/7
24	1056.5	Bob Ruff				Anamosa	748.8 Ruff '01	self											
25	1049.5	Fred Calai	372.5	1036	1.29%	OVGPG	720 Parks '00	879 Holland '97	166.5-104.5-101.5		1	4	PM	10	800	Y	5/6	5/23	7/4
26	1049	Clarence Koch	387	1156	-10.20%	Nekoosa (WI Record)	801.5 Stelts '97	712.2 Khun '00	185-103-99		2	5	PM	10	700	Y	4/28	5/16	6/28
27	1038	Geneva Emmons	361	941	9.34%	PNWGPG	846 Calai '99	723 Bobier '99 UOW	166-101-94		1	5	PM	10		Y	4/26	5/10	6/28
28	1037.5	Bill Bobier				Clarence, NY													
29	1035	Paul Handy	384	1130	-9.18%	Canby, OR	1026 Holland '00	955 Stelts '01	180-102-102		1	5	PM	10	750	Y	4/22	4/30	7/2
30	1027	Lisa Hester	374	1045	-1.75%	Half Moon Bay	1230 Daletas '01	1075 Daletas '01	176-104-94		1	4	PM	10					
31	1024	Joe Pukos	359	926	9.57%	Oswego	723 Bobier '99 UOW	self	160-99-100		1	5	PM	10	700	Y	5/6	5/11	7/7
32	1023	Arnold Vader	367	988	3.42%	Ottawa	787.5 Greer/Vader	1153 Eaton '00	172-102-93		1	5	PM	9	750	Y	5/4	5/15	7/5
33	1023	Brett Hester	370.5	1020	0.29%	Canby, OR	723 Bobier '99 UOW	sibbed	165-104-101.5		1	4	PM	14			4/22	5/1	7/4
34	1013.6	Dave Hampton	363	956	5.68%	Topsfield, MA	881 Hampton '01 UOW	805 Pukos '00 + 940 Mombert '98	161-101-101		1	4	PM	10	600	Y	5/1	5/10	7/1
35	1012.5	Andrew Papez	385	1138	-12.40%	Niagara Peninsula	846 Calai '99	712.2 Khun '00	167-118-100		1	5	PM	17		Y	5/3	5/15	7/4
36	1005	Kirk Mombert	374.8	1053	-4.78%	PNWGPG	723 Bobier '99 UOW	846 Calai '99	167-105.5-102.25		1	5	PM	10	950	Y	4/28	5/1	7/4
37	996.5	Paul Handy	367	988	0.85%	Canby 10/19	790 Daletas '00	730 Stellpflug '96	166-102-99		1	5	PM	7	660	Y	4/22	4/30	7/2
38	989.5	Brett Hester	358	918	7.23%	Canby 10/19	790 Daletas '00	705 Stelts '99 UOW	162-97-99		1	5	PM	14		Y	4/22	5/1	6/30
39	989.5	Dave Stelts	361	941	4.90%	OVGPG	801.5 Stelts '97	712.2 Khun '00	158-103-100		1	5	PM	11	700	Y	5/2	5/14	7/6
40	986	Larry Checkon	363	956	3.04%	Altoona	723 Bobier '99 UOW	815 Checkon '98	162-101-100		1	5	PM	10		Y	5/2	5/15	6/26
41	982.8	Geoff Pierce	355	896	8.83%	Topsfield, MA	723 Bobier '99 UOW	855 Khun '01	161-98-96		1	5	PM	15	650	Y	4/20	5/5	7/16

is chart ranks top pumpkins wn in 2002 by eight, starting th the largest.

pumpkins in the compilation. This is not entirely without merit, because the analysis of just the top ten weights can yield alot of information.

	Weight	Grower	Δ	Female Parent	Male Parent
1	1337.6	Charlie Houghton	10.21%	845 Bobier '00	712.2 Kuhn '00
2	1215	Ben Hebb	-4.20%	875 Dill '99	sibbed
3	1186.4	Bruce Whittier	6.27%	582 Hester '01	723 Bobier '99
4	1178	Rock Rivard	9.93%	723 Bobier '99	805 Pukos '00
5	1177.8	Jim Kuhn	3.38%	846 Calai '99	723 Bobier '99
6	1173	Kirk Mombert	8.78%	846 Calai '99	1064 Mombert 01
7	1172	Bill Greer	2.13%	846 Calai '99	1153 Eaton '00
8	1156	David Larsen	19.90%	898 Knauss '01	1062 Rivard '01
9	1112.5	Steve Handy	1.57%	695 Handy '01	955 Stelts '01
10	1105	Greg Stucker	-7.06%	846 Calai '99	801.5 Stelts '97

The beginner might look at the chart and say, "I have to plant the 1337.6 Houghton, because it is the largest pumpkin ever grown," and if he has any ability at deductive reasoning, he might say, "I'm going to plant the 845 Bobier, because it grew the world record 1337.6."

Also note that out of the top-ten pumpkins by weight, 4 of them were grown by the 846 Calai. To a grower following the pack, this would be all the information he would need to make his seed selection the 846, based on its multiple appearance. No other seed stock appears more than once on either side of the female/male pollinations except the 723 Bobier that appears twice, but only once as a female and once as a male. To a grower experienced in reviewing these compilations, or who networks with many other growers all over the country, this is not a surprise, but it is information none the less. If no Calai 846's showed in the top-ten, the experienced grower would be as surprised as the beginner at finding it 4 times. You can bet that the serious grower, and the serious beginner, are both going to try to obtain the 846 to plant.

Anyone analyzing just the top-ten would also see that 8 of the top-ten were over their estimated weights, and that David Larsen's 1156 was 19.9% over the estimates. Even a beginner

might conclude that this amount of deviation gives reason for further investigation of the seed that was used (the 898 Knauss).

So a beginner, or someone with experience but limited time to spend in review of the data, might come-up with the following list of seeds: 1337.6 Houghton, 845 Bobier, 846 Calais, and perhaps the 898 Knauss. Not a bad list for a beginner. I have given this example to show everyone how easy it is to find the best seeds to plant. If you are willing to look at just the top-ten pumpkins grown each year, you will probably be successful (however, obtaining the seed, and knowing what to do with it is another matter entirely). The important thing is that you would have a fair chance to compete with the best growers in the world if you planted these seeds.

If you went through the entire charts just to find occurrences of female parents, this review might take an hour to complete yielding the following results:

Female Parent	# of occurrences it appears
846 Calai '99	18
723 Bobier '99	18
845 Bobier '00	11

Again, a very good selection of seeds found by looking at just female parents.

If you've had any success at all with growing giant pumpkins, and you want to try to insure yourself that if you grow a big pumpkin, it weighs the estimated weight or above, you might decide to review only those pumpkins that weighed above their estimated weights. If you decided to go through the charts just to note the top ten positive (+) deviations from estimated weight, the ranking of the top-ten would be as follows.

Weight	Grower	Est.	Δ	Female Parent
1156	David Larsen	926	19.90%	898 Knauss '01
951.4	John Castellucci	775	18.54%	1260.4 Weir '01
719	Peter Carter	596	17.11%	805 Pukos '00
795	Jose Ceja	666	16.23%	723 Bobier '99 UOW
744	Jack LaRue	624	16.13%	968 Hester '00
771.5	Steve Krug	648	16.01%	746.8 Scherber '97
812.2	Robert Demers	684	15.78%	1020.2 Kuhn '01
1090	Mike Fisher	926	15.05%	783 Daletas '00
737.8	B & C Duffy	630	14.61%	828.8 Bresnick '00
772.5	Ron Wilson	660	14.56%	1028 Hester '01

If you chose just the top 4 female parents, your selections would include: the 898 Knauss, 1260.4 Weir, 805 Pukos, and the 723 Bobier – a very good list with potential for both a seasoned grower or someone with limited experience growing giant pumpkins.

Below is a page from Marv Hick's annual 700 pound-plus pumpkin compilation. I've organized it so that the difference (Δ) between the actual weight and the estimated weight is ranked . Many growers who are looking for an unproven seed (the dark horse) , will look for pumpkins that exceed their estimates significantly.

If you chose the 4 heaviest pumpkins, you might choose to plant one of these unproven seeds, 1156 Larsen, 1090 Fisher, 951.4 Castellucci, or the 812.2 Demers, or the the list of proven seeds (female parents) could be: 898 Knauss, 783 Daletas, 1260.4 Weir, and the 1020.2 Kuhn.

The important thing to remember is that Marv Hick's compilations can yield a significant amount of valuable information, with limited time spent in analysis. But, you do have to do some work (on your own).

Seed selection is also covered in great detail from a statistical analysis perspective in the chapter, *Genetics and Pollination Strategies*. Nic Welty uncovers the truth about proven and unproven seeds, and the necessity to plant both proven and unproven seeds every year.

ght: This chart ows pumpkins l by percentage deviation from imated weight.

	Weight	Grower	"	Est.	Δ	Weigh Site	Female Parent	Male Parent	C-SS-FB	# on plant	# of lobes	Vine	Out	Size	Shade	Germ	Set Out	Poll.
8	1156	David Larsen	359	926	19.90%	Canby, OR	898 Knauss '01	1062 Rivard '01	165-100-94	1	5	PM	14	667	Y	4/18	4/26	7/3
50	951.4	John Castellucci	338	775	18.54%	Topsfield, MA	1260.4 Weir '01	846 Calai '99	147-100-91	1	5	PM	14	600	Y	4/30	5/4	7/7
218	719	Peter Carter	309	596	17.11%	Rochester Fair NH 9/14	805 Pukos '00	712.2 Kuhn '00	138-88-83	1	5	PM	11	800	Y	4/24		7/9
143	795	Jose Ceja	321	666	16.23%	Safinas, CA	723 Bobier '99 UOW	801.5 Stelts '97	133-98-90	1	5							7/21
194	744	Jack LaRue	314	624	16.13%	Hunter's Shelton, WA	968 Hester '00	882 LaRue '00	145-87-82	1	6	SM	9	350	Y	4/20	5/5	7/13
167	771.5	Steve Krug	318	648	16.01%	Austin, MN 9/28	746.8 Scherber '97	712.2 Kuhn '00	150-80-88	1	5	PM	9	500	Y	5/4	5/12	6/8
128	812.2	Robert Demers	324	684	15.78%	Topsfield, MA	1020.2 Kuhn '01	self	141-90-93	1	5	PM	12	1000	Y	4/25	5/9	7/7
16	1090	Mike Fisher	359	926	15.05%	Canby, OR	783 Daletas '00	open	166.5-96-97	2	4	PM	10	750	Y	4/18	4/26	7/3
200	737.8	Bob & Christine Duffy	315	630	14.61%	Topsfield, MA	828.8 Bresnick '00	open	142-88-85	1	5	PM	10	1200	Y			7/5
166	772.5	Ron Wilson	320	660	14.56%	Canby, OR	1028 Hester '01	self	135-97-88	1	5	PM	13.5	460	N	5/1	5/16	7/12
102	851	Shellie Cramer	331	729	14.34%	Shoreline, WA 10/12	723 Bobier '99 UOW	656 Bhaskaran '00	143-96-92	1	5	PM	10	800	Y			7/13
46	959	Reggie Noonan	345	823	14.18%	Windsor	845 Bobier '00 UOW	700 Paynter '01 UOW	148-98-99	1	5	PM	17.5	1000	Y	4/28	5/15	7/15
98	854	Rock Rivard	332	735	13.93%	Ladysmith Quebec	805 Pukos '00	self	153-88-91	1	4	PM	14	900	Y	4/28	5/5	7/8
193	745	Steve Krug	317	642	13.83%	Anamosa	771 Krug '01	1097 Mombert '01	150-85-82	2	6	PM	13		N	5/4	5/14	
168	770	Bill Vanlderstine	321	646	13.51%	P.E.I Silver Bell 10/12	845 Bobier '00 UOW	945 Vanlderstine '01	139-89-93	1	5	PM	10	500	Y	4/28	5/27	7/16
212	728	Ron Wallace	315	630	13.46%	RIPGA 10/12	790 Daletas '00	705 Stelts '99 UOW	141-87-87	1	6	PM	10	450	Y	5/2	5/8	7/11
140	798.5	Chris Lyons	326	697	12.71%	Port Elgin	611.5 Hester 99*	960 Rose '01	154.5-81-90.5	1	4	PM	14		Y	5/4	5/26	7/19
69	910	Vince Zunino	341	795	12.64%	Elk Grove, CA	995.8 Carter '01	open	146-101-94	1	5	PM	18.5	800	Y	5/6	5/12	7/14
47	957	Kevin Companion	347	837	12.54%	Hillsboro Fair- NH 9/5	995.8 Carter '01	810 Dill '99	152-99-96	2	5	PM	15	1800	Y	5/1	5/6	6/28
22	1058	Charlie Houghton	359	926	12.48%	Hillsboro Fair- NH 9/5	712 Kuhn '00	845 Bobier '00 UOW	164-98-97	1	5	PM	14	600	Y	4/26	5/5	7/7
62	922	Joel Holland	343	809	12.26%	PNWGPG	846 Calai '99	940 Mombert '98	149-99-95	2	5	PM	11	1200	Y	4/28	5/2	6/19
88	878.5	Jim Beauchemin	338	775	11.78%		1020.2 Kuhn '01	846 Calai '99	148-101-89	1	4	PM	12	650	Y	4/26	5/9	7/3
85	883.5	Utoni Ruff	338.5	782	11.49%	Anamosa	960 Rose '01		156-5-93-89									
156	780	John Elliot	325	691	11.41%	Oswego	790 Daletas '00	self	146-86-93	1		PM	11	900	Y	4/30	5/10	7/9
52	935	Glenn Needham	346	830	11.23%	Ottawa	1230 Daletas '01	1056.5 Dueck '00 UOW	150-98-98	1	5	PM	16	800	Y	4/30	5/15	7/13
183	756	Jim Ford	322	672	11.11%	Rochester Fair NH 9/14	805 Pukos '00	self	140-93-89	1	4	PM	9	750	Y	5/1	5/15	7/8
150	788.6	Kevin Companion	327	703	10.85%	Topsfield, MA	810 Dill '99	995.8 Carter '01	149-93-85	2	5	PM	15	2000	Y	5/1	5/7	7/7
14	1096	Pete Glasier	366	980	10.58%	Half Moon Bay	845 Bobier '00 UOW	940 Mombert '98	175-90-101	1	4	PM	11	650	Y	5/13	5/18	7/4
106	842	Al Eaton	335	755	10.33%	Wellington, ONT 10/19	846 Calai '99	723 Bobier '99 UOW	160-86-89		4	PM	13	600	Y	5/6	5/18	7/11
1	1337.6	Charlie Houghton	392	1201	10.21%	Topsfield, MA	845 Bobier '00 UOW	712.2 Kuhn '00	174-110/108	1	5	PM	13	550	Y	4/26	5/5	7/8
72	907	Kirk Mombert	344.3	816	10.03%	Shoreline, WA 10/12	723 Bobier '99 UOW	860 Mombert '01	151-101.5-91.75	1	5	S	8	1000	Y	4/27	5/1	7/5
4	1178	Rock Rivard	376	1061	9.93%	Gentilly, Québec 9/28	805 Pukos '00	174-104-98	1	5	PM	12	850	Y	4/27	5/1	7/5
152	786.1	Eddie Shaw	328	709	9.81%	P.E.I Silver Bell 10/12	735 Dill '01	self	153-84-91	2	5	PM	13		Y	4/15	4/22	6/26
31	1024	Joe Pukos	359	926	9.57%	Oswego	723 Bobier '99 UOW	self	160-99-100	1	5	PM	10	700	Y	5/6	5/11	7/7
27	1038	Geneva Emmons	361	941	9.34%	PNWGPG	846 Calai '99	723 Bobier '99 UOW	166-101-94	1	5	PM	10		Y	4/26	5/10	6/28
217	721	Joel Holland	319	654	9.29%	Puyallup Fair, WA 9/6	935 Lloyd '97	846 Calai '99	141-88-90	2	4	PM	11	1600	Y	4/28	5/2	6/24

700+ Pumpkins 2002 **1** of 7

Seed Preparation

Seed preparation actually starts with seed storage, because without adequate safeguards, the healthiest of seeds are vulnerable to deterioration. Seeds which start-out incompletely developed, thin, or showing signs of disease, but nevertheless still capable of germinating, suffer the most from inadequate seed storage.

There has been much discussion on the proper way to store valuable seeds, and many opinions seem to be different but possess a common thread. The commonalities center on temperature and humidity, both of which must be controlled to insure the best environment for a seed awaiting planting.

Humidity must be maintained at levels that neither deplete the seed of moisture nor provide excess that may lead to decay. Keeping a stable level of humidity allows the seed to rest in its dormancy without disturbance. Oscillating levels of humidity often awaken the seed, depleting the finite energy stored for its start of new life. Humidity must be kept constant.

Temperature must be maintained at levels that are below 70 degrees, and are constant over time with little fluctuation. Temperatures over 90 degrees, for extended periods of time, can rob seeds of moisture and their stored energy. Freezing temperatures do not harm seed if they are accompanied by adequate and consistent humidity levels. In this respect, freezing seeds may be the best form of storage if they are properly packaged before freezing. Most freezers automatically defrost themselves. Defrosting is intricately tied to temperature. An automatically defrosting freezer controls the temperature so it does oscillate. This may seem bad, but the range of oscillation is so small that the mass of material in the freezer are untouched by the change. What is effected by the oscillating temperatures is the air within the freezer which acts far quicker than the bulky mass stored.

To far left: Drew and friends remo— seeds from a pur—

Left: Tom Beach reaches for that — and possibly, magical seed.

Defrosting depletes moisture from the air thus reducing the humidity level. If seeds are stored in airtight packaging, they remain immune from the damage of defrosting. Freezing should be considered a highly effective way of storing valuable seeds over long periods of time. Storing seeds outside of the freezer is a little trickier. When storing seeds in this way, attention must be given to the types of packaging in which seeds are stored. Airtight containers, placed away from direct sunlight, and heating and cooling devices are best.

Seed starting in various methods.

Finally, Time to Start

You are ready to start that precious seed that you traded for or parted with your cash for. Good seeds have become a valuable commodity, and the best seeds have become nearly impossible to obtain, unless you have developed a long standing relationship with the grower who possesses them, or you have very deep pockets.

In many cases, one seed from a proven seed stock may be all you have. You have only one chance at growing a plant from this seed stock. You better pay attention, because germinating *Atlantic Giant* seeds is not guaranteed. Just as in seed storage, temperature and humidity are the most important issues to address, but now in a way that is dramatically different from the way in which the seed was stored. Now, temperatures over 80 degrees and heightened humidity levels are welcomed.

Temperatures between 80-85 degrees are ideal. That's the easy part of germinating seeds. Getting you to understand the proper moisture level is far more difficult to explain. It is a given that you start seeds in soilless, sterilized media, and most of these commercial medias have an extremely high rate of water absorption and retention. Therein lies 99% of all the disappointments experienced in germinating AG seeds. Moisture levels must not be too high.

If you get the proper level of moisture to begin with, no additional water will be needed before the seed fully germinates and emerges from the media. If the media is too dry to begin with, sufficient amounts of water will not be absorbed through the seed coat to stimulate the beginnings of new life. If it is too wet, the seed may rot before it fully emerges from the media, and this is even more probable if temperature of the media is below 80 degrees. Wet and cold media account for almost all seed loss.

If you touch the media with your fingers and feel the faintest level of moisture in it, it is enough. When preparing the media beforehand, it should still be light and crumbly when handled, held together by a minimum of moisture. The peat pots that the seeds will go into should be soaked in water prior to filling them with media so they do not wick the moisture out of the media and expose it to air and evaporation. Adequately moistened media in presoaked peat pots should sustain the seed through germination and the full unfurl of its seed leaves. If temperatures are maintained between 80-85 degrees, most seeds will germinate in 3-5 days, with some taking as long as 7-10 days. The longer the seed is below media level, the higher the chances that it will rot before it fully emerges.

The key is to get the seed above ground as quickly as possible. That is why we elevate moisture level and temperature, but what else can we do to hasten germination?

Filing Seeds

Many growers file the edges of their seeds, exposing the seed leaves, and allowing water to penetrate the seed faster. Since seeds from properly grown AG's are generally very large and thick, this filing expedites absorption of water and allows the seed to germinate and move itself out of the soil faster. Remember, the longer the seed is in the soil, the higher the chance of problems. However, not all AG seeds should be filed. If a seed is very thin or underdeveloped, it may be wise not to file it. In the case of thin, underdeveloped seeds, we must assume that the seed will not have adequate strength to both germinate and defend itself against the onslaught of disease – which is always heightened when moisture levels are elevated. A thin seed coat may already provide for the absorption of sufficient moisture to stimulate germination. Elevating the amount of absorption may allow for disease to develop even before the seed is ready to spring to life. Preserving the seed's energy and allowing for germination to occur at seed readiness are two factors which are sustained under optimum temperature and moisture levels. Any artificial methods used to accelerate gemination (higher heat or faster absorption of water from filing) may do more damage than good with an underdeveloped seed.

Soaking Seeds

Many growers soak seeds, and many do not. Soaking seeds is also sometimes combined with the filing of their edges. Soaking is done especially to introduce water into the seed faster. This can be good or bad. Personally, I believe that if soil moisture is at an optimum level, and temperature is kept consistently between 80-85 degrees, then soaking or filing the edges of seeds is not necessary. Most of the time, anything we do to alter the seed's natural response, by elevating temperature and moisture, can be opportunities for disease to flourish.

Some growers also soak their seeds in water containing various ingredients. Some use a water soluble fertilizer like MiracleGro, and still others use seaweed and fish emulsion solutions. The jury is still out on a decision concerning the effects of any of these solutions.

Presumably, growers add these materials to their water for a reason. In the case of fertilizer, it may be to insure that adequate levels of plantfood are present when the seed begins to manufacture energy on its own. The seed leaves actually contain sufficient energy to push the seed out of the soil to begin the process of photosynthesis. Why not add plantfoods after the process begins.

Another reason may be to expose the seedling early to plant hormones, like cytochinins which are present in seaweed. Cytochinins have been shown to promote root growth. We will talk more about cytochinins and other plant hormones in the chapter, *Growth Regulators*.

At this stage of the plant's life – at or before germination, or at the seed leaf stage – delaying the introduction of plantfood or growth regulators will have no effects that cannot be replicated with later introductions of these materials.

eft: filing a seed.

: An average AG
ed at actual size.

Soil Preparation

Giant pumpkin growers have a love affair with organic material, and they apply manure, compost, and anything else available, in staggering amounts to soils already better than your average backyard gardener's.

Most growers aim for organic matter levels of 20% or more, and achieve it with year-after-year additions of organic materials. Below, Drew Papez spreads 6" of manure on his patch every year in the fall, and Quinn Werner from Saegertown, PA takes the addition of organic material to all new levels in a carefully executed delivery of hundreds of yards of manure to his patch.

John Castellucci of Smithfield, RI has raised the ground more than 2' in his patch by the addition of leaves, manure, and mushroom compost, and has won the Rhode Island State Giant Pumpkin Championship in six out of the ten years it has been held.

Ron and Dick Wallace of Coventry, RI added almost 200 yards of manure and mushroom compost to their patch over a 2-year period, and elevated their personal best from 400 to almost 900 pounds. That's Dick waving an American flag from behind a 10-yard dump of manure in the upper photo on page 185.

Spreading manur digging pits, improving the so — there is never enough organic material in the s for a giant pumpkin grower.

Transplanting

This is the most exciting time of the year for most of us who grow giant pumpkins. It has finally started to warm a bit during the afternoons, the sun is higher in the sky, and it's great to be outside gardening and working in the yard after a long, cold, winter.

This is the real beginning of the journey to the October competitions. Your mind is full of joyous anticipation and expectation, and all the longings of "Wait until next year," have vanished in the transplanting of a tiny seedling in warm and prepared ground, in early May.

The seed that you nurtured through germination just a week or two ago, now strains in its pot – its tiny white roots showing through the peat, and its first true leaf ready to grab all the sunshine of the lengthening days. It is a rare privilege that all growers of *Atlantic Giants* are blessed with – that of looking at a tiny seedling that fits in the palm of the hand, knowing that it could grow a fruit that several strong men together could not lift to their knees.

When is it Ready?

The seedling and the weather play important parts in the decision to set your transplant outside. Almost every year I challenge my decision for transplanting outside too early or too late.

One year I stress that plants really don't begin to grow until the soil warms up, and having them out early in cold soil and cold and damp weather can do them more harm than good. Then, I'll always say that everything evens out in late June and early July anyway. Plants set out two weeks apart may cover the same amount of ground with vines and leaves by late June, despite the fact that more chances were taken with the earlier seedling, and it required more work.

But another year, I'll say that I should have put the seedlings out earlier, because we had a very warm month of May, and now, if I had planted earlier, I'd be ready to pollinate my plants in late June rather than having to wait for opportunities in early to mid July. Because I hesitated, I lost two week's growth in the short season of my pumpkin's life.

It's really a very tough call – whether or not to plant early or late. It depends on circumstance, but it also depends intimately on your level of commitment. If you don't have the time, germinate and transplant your seedlings later. If you have the time and the commitment, here are a few ways to thwart the effects of mother nature, and take some of the effects of circumstance out of the picture.

All of the following can be used to create an atmosphere that is more conducive for optimum growth of a giant pumpkin plant. Black plastic placed on the ground around your seedling will heat the soil during the day and retard the loss of soil heat at night. Heating cables placed in the soil around the seedling can keep the soil temperature at 72 degrees at night. Mounding the planting area accentuates the effects of the sun warming the soil, and also helps drain away water that is more difficult to heat. Having a larger cloche or greenhouse over the plant insures a longer period of growth under controlled conditions. Most AGs will outgrow a 2' x 3' cloche in a couple of weeks, which dramatically shortens the time of ideal protection for the plant, putting the plant at the whims of the weather. Warming the interior of your cloche at night with a light bulb or portable heater will sustain whatever momentum your plant has acheived after a warm day in early May.

Cloches can be as simply built as a sawhorse wrapped with plastic, or as large and difficult to build as a 12' x 16' greenhouse requiring more attention to maintain. They are designed to reduce the harmful effects of wind on the seedling, and to give it additional warmth. The seedling will have to be protected for several weeks from wind, and as the plant outgrows the cloche, barrier fence should be erected.

Page 106: Young seedling showing first true leaf is ready to set out.

Right: Cloches can be made from a variety of materials and designs.

The Direction of Growth

The main vine's direction of growth will always be opposite the first true leaf. The first true leaf is the third leaf, if we include the two seed leaves that were already formed within the seed. As you observe the size of leaves as the plant develops, the first true leaf is rather small. At this stage, the seedling is working on mostly stored energy. The first true leaf begins the process in which the plant actually begins to manufacture its energy needs. It accelerates the growth of the plant, and provides for a second true leaf which is much larger and heavier. This extra weight causes the seedling to lean in a direction that is opposite the first true leaf.

Protecting the Transplant

The following represents a good list of the ways to insure that your transplant is properly protected.

Start the colonization of beneficial fungi and watch for early infestations of Cucumber Beetles (see the chapter on *Insect and Disease Control* for more discussion). Keep the plant cool on early, hot days by providing some misted water to prevent the scorching of leaves. Reduce the harmful effects of wind by installing temporary fences, pinning vines down, and burying side vines as soon as they begin to lengthen. And, protect transplants on cold nights by covering them.

Remember, protecting transplants will help to accelerate growth, and this early growth will provide for pollinations within a time zone that insures adequate time to fully mature your pumpkin.

All protection is for the maintenance of a continuous momentum of growth. Anything you can do to improve the microclimate of your transplanted seedling will pay you dividends later in the season. An extra day saved here could result in hundreds of pounds of additional weight at the end of the season. The time you lose now can never be fully recovered.

Direction of Vine Growth

Page 108 shows direction of vine growth from observance of leaves.

Left and right: More cloche designs and some methods for wind protection.

Feeding

The feeding schedule that I introduced in WCGP II in 1998 still has great information, and I advocate that anyone who is really interested in the philosophy of feeding *Atlantic Giant*s, refer to it on page 111 – but apply this strategy with temperance. Temperance is the practice of moderation. If I can fault giant pumpkins in any way (and I do not exclude myself here), we tend to apply too much plantfood to soils that are already "jacked". We apply manure and compost in staggering amounts, and then amend these ingredients with mineral and water soluble fertilizers. There comes a time when too much is too much. And, by observing the results of other growers over the past five years, I can say with a lot of confidence that we have overestimated the needs of the *Atlantic Giant* variety. Less plantfood may even be better, and particularly, less nitrogen may be better.

I have never seen an *Atlantic Giant* plant lacking for nitrogen when 5-10 yards of manure had been applied the preceding fall or in early spring. What I have seen is vines with accelerated growth, huge plants (sometimes covering 2500 square feet), blue and bloated leaves, and a propensity to abort many of the early fruit. Why? Way too much plantfood – way too much nitrogen. It's time for temperance; it's time for moderation.

It is important to feed *Atlantic Giants* aggressively, but many of us have our soils in such good condition, that we require only moderate use of fish, seaweed, and water solubles throughout the season. The importance of growing large plants has seen its day, and now the emphasis has shifted to raising smaller, more strategically pruned plants.

The Ohio boys summed it up nicely a few years ago, and now they are reaping the rewards from what they call developing the "food factory." That food factory has gone from recommendations that plants have 1000 leaves or more before setting fruit, and a minimum plant coverage of 1000 square feet, to pollinating early on plants covering only 300-500 square feet. And, that number is not set in stone. People are growing 1000 pounders using only 200 square feet of garden area. That's a long way from the gargantuan plants we all raised five years ago. I laugh at myself when I read my first book where I advocated spacing plants 36' apart. Now growers are spacing plants 20' or less, and deadheading side vines at 8'-10'.

These smaller plants do not need the abundance of plantfood we have been so used to applying. In fact, increased nitrogen, which activates vine and leaf growth, may even be a deterrent to keeping these "food factories" in a proper balance between feeding the plant and feeding the fruit.

The "food factory" is nothing more than the established plant behind the set fruit, and it is tremendously exciting to report that this plant area can be quite small. It could be as small as 20' x 10' (200 square feet), with more than enough ability to support the growth of a world record pumpkin. I will cover more about this idea of the food factory in the chapter, *Pruning Strategies.*

For now, follow the advice I gave five years ago. I include the chart that appeared in *How-to-Grow World Class Giant Pumpkins II* on the next page, but remember that moderation is the key ingredient in this program.

Organic or Chemical

This is a debate that we could have until the end of time, but the facts are that giant pumpkins respond more favorably to slower feeding than they do to quickly available sources of plantfood. We've all been disappointed by pumpkins that have split because growth was

Feeding Schedule
Plantfood Application

Week 1*	xx-**XX**-xx / Seaweed	Soil drench†
Week 2	xx-**XX**-xx / Seaweed	Soil drench
Week 3	xx-**XX**-xx / Seaweed	Soil drench
Week 4	xx-**XX**-xx / Seaweed	Soil drench
Week 5	**XX**-xx-xx and Fish / Seaweed	Drench-broadcast / foliar spray≈
Week 6	**XX**-xx-xx and Fish / Seaweed	Drench-broadcast / foliar spray
Week 7	**XX**-xx-xx and Fish / Seaweed	Drench-broadcast / foliar spray
Week 8	**XX**-xx-xx and Fish / Seaweed	Drench-broadcast / foliar spray
Week 9	**xx-xx-xx** and Fish / Seaweed	Drench-broadcast / foliar spray¥
Week 10	**xx-xx-xx** and Fish / Seaweed	Drench-broadcast / foliar spray
Week 11	**xx-xx-xx** and Fish / Seaweed	Drench-broadcast / foliar spray
Week 12	**xx-xx-xx** and Fish / Seaweed	Drench-broadcast / foliar spray
Week 13	**xx-xx-xx** and Fish / Seaweed	Drench-broadcast / foliar spray
Week 14	**xx-xx-xx** and Fish / Seaweed	Drench-broadcast / foliar spray
Week 15	**xx-xx-xx** and Fish / Seaweed	Drench-broadcast / foliar spray
Week 16	xx-xx-**XX** and Fish / Seaweed	Drench-broadcast / foliar spray∆
Week 17	xx-xx-**XX** and Fish / Seaweed	Drench-broadcast / foliar spray
Week 18	xx-xx-**XX** and Fish / Seaweed	Drench-broadcast / foliar spray
Week 19	xx-xx-**XX** and Fish / Seaweed	Drench-broadcast / foliar spray
Week 20-22	Seaweed only	Foliar Spray

* -Week 1 in New England would be approximately May 1-8 (about two weeks before the last frost).

† -Soil drench is done by completely dissolving plantfood in water and applying from the base of the plant and extending 3' out. As plant grows, a larger area will be fed and more plantfood will be used. High phosphorous (P) plantfoods (xx-**XX**-xx) like *EnP* (10-50-10) and *MiracleGro* (15-30-15) along with liquid seaweed should be used.

≈ -Drench-broadcast / foliar spray - This week marks a shift from high (P) plantfoods to high nitrogen (N) formulations (**XX**-xx-xx). Granular, high, (N) fertilizers can be applied to the ground at a rate of a half pound per 100 sq. ft. or water solubles used as a drench according to package instructions. Calcium Nitrate (16-0-0), and Urea are good choices. Granules should be applied just before anticipated rainfall or watered-in after broadcasting. Again, apply from the base of the plant and extend 3' out. Use liquid fish emulsion as a drench and begin using liquid seaweed as <u>both</u> a foliar spray and as a drench.

¥ -This week marks the transition from high N to balanced formulations (**xx-xx-xx**). We still continue to use fish emulsion as a drench and seaweed as <u>both</u> a foliar spray and as a drench. Balanced plantfoods could include granular 10-10-10, 19-19-19, 17-17-17 and others and water solubles like *Peters Plantfood* (20-20-20). Broadcast granules at the rate of one half pound per 100 sq. ft. and apply water solubles as a drench.

∆ -This week we begin the last push to harvest. Balanced formulations are now replaced with high potassium plantfoods (K) (xx-xx-**XX**). Muriate of Potash (0-0-60), Potassium Nitrate (14-0-46) and *Peters Plantfood* (15-11-29) are good choices. Broadcast granules at the rate of one half pound per 100 sq. ft. and apply water solubles as a drench. Use fish emulsion as a drench and seaweed as <u>both</u> a foliar spray and as a drench.

far faster than the fruit could adjust to. We all want fast growing fruit, but at some point this favorable attribute becomes a limiting factor in maximizing the potential of a particular fruit.

Atlantic Giants have an enormous appetite that, if not held in check, can lead to many problems. So, over the last five years, growers have begun to adjust feeding programs so that catastrophic failures do not happen as often. One of the ways they have adjusted is to reduce water soluble nitrogen products, and other sources of abundant nitrogen like uncomposted manures. Remember the epigraph that appears in the beginning of this book, *You're not growin' salad, you're growin' fruit."*

Nitrogen is the major plant nutrient responsible for vegetative growth (leaves and vines). Reducing nitrogen slows vegetative growth, allowing for a more consistent and controlled processing of the products of photosynthesis and the storage of plant carbohydrates in the fruit. Even pruning strategies have moved in this direction by reducing plant size so that more efficient and safer levels of fruit growth can be sustained.

There are times when chemical sources of plant food are advantageous. Early season cold soils do not allow for the adequate release of nutrients, so chemical, and/or water soluble sources are advocated then. Also, in-season foliar feeding has its benefits in assuring that all major plant nutrients are available, and this practice delivers the essentials while, at the same time, dispensing them in very small dosages. We feed water solubles in tablespoons per gallon via compression sprayers, and a gallon of solution can easily cover the leaf area of a single, well-pruned plant.

So, chemical sources of plant nutrients have their place in any giant pumpkin feeding program, but organic sources such as: composted manure, fish emulsion, kelp meal, and seaweed should form the major portion of plantfood.

The Major Essentials

Nitrogen, phosphorous, and potassium are the major, essential plant nutrients. Their part in plant growth and plant health have been discussed in detail in *WCGP I & II*. In general terms, nitrogen produces leaves and vines, phosphorous produces roots and flowers, and potassium produces fruit; but each performs other tasks that overlap one another in the supply of nutrients for plant functions.

Manure

Manure supplies all the major plant nutrients, and when applied at the rates giant pumpkin growers apply them, supply abundant sources of N, P, and K. But, not all manures are the same. Cow and horse manures contain less nitrogen than chicken and sheep manures, so it is essential to compensate for the use of poultry and sheep manure in a nitrogen limiting feeding program. Each contains by weight approximately the same amount of phosphorous and potassium, with horse manures having an edge in potassium amounts, and chicken manure having the edge in phosphorous.

Fish Emulsion

Fertilizers made from fish contain plant nutrients in an N-P-K proportion of approximately 2-4-.5. We apply fish emulsions in tablespoons per gallon, so they provide very small amounts of plant nutrients, and as such, enhance a program of slow growth. They also contain oils, that when sprayed on leaves tends to benefit the health of the leaf.

Kelp Meal and Seaweed Extracts

Products made from seaweed have even lower amounts of the major plant nutrients, and thus work well in a reduced feeding program. These products have become popular because the effects they have on plants are not related to their plantfood supplies, but rather to their supplies of certain hormones and growth regulators. This will be discussed in much greater detail in the chapter, *Growth Regulators.*

The Minors But Still Essential

More and more emphasis has been put on the amount and balance of several minor elements like Calcium, Magnesium, Iron, and Sulphur — all of which help or hinder the uptake of the major plant nutrients (N-P-K). I have devoted a whole chapter to Calcium which tries to explain its benefits and use in a strategy that attempts to balance the soil for optimal giant pumpkin growth. Although minor elements are required in infinitesimal amounts compared to the major plant nutrients, they have a limiting effect on growth if not available in even these small amounts.

Calcium aids in healthy cell structure and the building of plant proteins, but its key effect is the determining of soil pH and the availability of other plant nutrients. It works with and against other plant nutrients, like magnesium and potassium in a manner that determines what the plant's roots will absorb. Abundant calcium can thwart magnesium uptake, and vice versa, and both in abundance can thwart potassium absorption (the building blocks of carbohydrates stored in the fruit).

Magnesium is vital to chlorophyll formation and aids in the absorption of nitrogen, phosphorous, and sulfur. Excess magnesium can cause calcium deficiencies, even where abundant calcium is present. Only small amounts of magnesium are required for chlorophyll formation, and it is needed in greater amounts only during seed formation. Where magnesium is deficient, the addition of epsom salts (magnesium sulphate) late in the maturity of a fruit is advisable to insure good seed development.

Iron is essential in the formation of chlorophyll which is essential in the process of photosynthesis. Neutral to high pH soils tend to lock-up iron uptake, so many times yellowing leaves are diagnosed as nitrogen deficient even when nitrogen is abundantly available. The addition of small amounts of chelated iron (which does not have to go through additional breakdown in the soil to be available to the plant) often provides for the uptake of far more nitrogen.

Sulfur is a natural, non-metallic element that, under the right conditions, often combines with other elements in the soil to produce plantfood. Gypsum, or calcium sulphate, is just one of the ways sulfur combines with other elements to produce useable plant nutrients. Soils that are high in calcium can benefit from the addition of small amounts of sulfur to unlock calcium for plant uptake. Sulfur also reduces soil pH, and can be useful on soils where copious amounts of limestone have been applied. Potassium, ammonium, and zinc sulphates are other by-products of sulfur's combining nature.

Beware of N, Mg, and K

If it is not clear by now, I am advocating far less nitrogen in feeding programs, and far more calcium. In fact, I would advocate that you treat calcium as a major plant nutrient — elevating it from its status of a minor element.

With that said, beware of too much available magnesium and potassium in the soil as well. Both compete with calcium for plant uptake. A soil out of balance, but containing an abundance of calcium, magnesium, and potassium can be just as detrimental as soil with a deficiency of these elements. You'll see why in the next chapter on calcium.

Calcium

Calcium is essential for cell division and cell health, and is therefore very important in all phases of plant growth, but especially during fruit formation. Studies have shown that a single application of liquid, chelated calcium to fruit improves shelf life and mineral content, along with noticeably firming fruit flesh. This is a remarkable finding.

I've been thinking about this subject in a serious way for over two years now, and based on what I've learned from other growers, I can say with a great measure of confidence that calcium, and its relation to other minerals in the soil, and with certain growth regulators, cytokinins, auxins, and gibberellins, holds more potential for increased weights in *Atlantic Giant* pumpkins than any other cultural subject. More information on growth regulators is available in a chapter devoted entirely to them later in this book.

Calcium moves through the soil and through the plant very slowly, and the last place that water and minerals are delivered is the very end of the fruit – the blossom-end of the pumpkin. A fruit growing at an enormous rate may become deficient in plantfood essential to good health because of this slow movement of calcium in the plant's system. A deficiency in calcium can cause cell walls to rupture. This rupturing creates more stress on the surrounding cells until the fruit fails, much like what we see commonly in blossom-end rot of tomatoes. All the time, calcium is abundantly available in the soil and the vegetative portions of the plant show no symptoms of deficiency.

If a single application of calcium to melons and cucumbers can improve quality and lengthen life, it seems elementary to assume the same for giant pumpkins. Studies have shown that calcium can in fact be absorbed by the fruit. If calcium deficiencies are more likely to occur in fruit – the furthest plant part from the roots – and calcium can be absorbed by the fruit directly – it seems highly likely that applications of calcium to the fruit will thicken fruit walls, reduce the incidence of blossom end catastrophes, and noticeably improve the general health of a pumpkin.

While exploring this mineral, other subjects must be addressed as well. In fact, the subjects of soil pH and balancing soil nutrients take on even more importance, because having high amounts of calcium in the soil, or adding more in-season, does not automatically guarantee success.

Soil pH

The optimum soil pH range for growing giant pumpkins is between 6.5 to 6.8, however pH readings outside of this range have shown some measure of success – most notably, pH levels slightly above 7.0. Therein may be the clue to the importance of calcium.

Calcium is the most important mineral in determining soil pH. Additions of calcium in the form of agricultural limestone, over time, raises pH levels. Manipulating the soil pH remains the most valuable tool available to a grower. When we talk about the ideal pH range for a given crop, we do it with absolute assurance that within that range major and minor elements essential for crop health are not hindered from benefiting the crop. If the elements are present, and present in the right proportions to one another, the plant will absorb them.

The most important role that pH plays is the directing of mineral breakdown, and subsequently, the absorption of minerals by plant roots.

Soil Balance

Creating an ideal balance between calcium and other minerals in the soil remains the final goal after proper pH has been attained. There must be adequate supplies of all major and minor plant nutrients, but they also must be balanced with one another in order for optimal plant health to occur.

Calcium, magnesium, and potassium all compete in gaining entry through plant roots. I will not get into the electro-chemistry here (cation exchange capacity), but rest assured that individual levels of any one of these minerals can have major effects on the other's availability to the plant. Magnesium is an essential element responsible for chlorophyll formation, and therefore, the whole process of photosynthesis. Potassium is primarily responsible for the manufacture of carbohydrates – food-energy for the plant – of which the excess of this food is stored in the fruit. Potassium also plays a major role in protecting plants from disease. Both magnesium and potassium are essential to good plant health, as is calcium which, in addition to its role in determining

soil pH and the availability of several plant nutrients, also neutralizes the effects of toxic acids which form in plants as a by-product of normal plant metabolism and serves in building plant proteins.

Calcium, magnesium, and potassium must be balanced with each other in order that the effects of an imbalance – plant and fruit deficiencies – do not occur. First you must have the right pH, then adequate supplies of plantfood, and finally, a balance between these plantfoods.

Sources

Calcium sources will most likely come from agricultural limestone (if the pH needs upward adjustment), or gypsum (calcium sulphate, if no pH adjustment is needed). Using chelated calcium, dispensed through a compression sprayer or your watering system, is highly recommended in-season. In addition, calcium and nitrogen can be supplied simultaneously with calcium nitrate, but I recommend extreme moderation with the use of any product that will stimulate plant growth as much as 16-0-0.

...ndy measures ...ll thickness of ...view, WA resi- ...David Larsen's ...2002, 1156. ...ave's pumpkin ...eded estimates ...nds) by 22%. ...s were 8"-16" ...k, and surpris- ...thickest at the ...blossom end. ...e use calcium? ...s no, just good ...etics from the ...898 Knauss.

Magnesium is usually introduced to the soil in the form of dolomitic limestone or in-season with magnesium sulphate (Epsom Salts), which can be purchased at any pharmacy or supermarket.

Potassium can come from a variety of sources including manure, granite dust, greensand, potassium nitrate, muriate of potash, or sulphate of potash. Except for the organic sources, these products have a large percentage of potassium, and as a result should be used with great care. If your soil has adequate potassium, and it is in the right ratio to calcium and magnesium, more potassium should not be added.

Evaluating a Soil Test

We measure plantfood in soil in ppm's (parts per million), but we analyze the mineral balance as a percent of base saturation. Base saturation is the amount of available calcium, magnesium, and potassium expressed as a percentage of the total cation exchange capacity (CEC). CEC measures the capacity of soil to hold nutrients as opposed to leaching them. The higher the CEC, the higher the amount of Ca, Mg, and K. CEC is most notably effected by soil pH and the texture of the soil. Heavy soils have a greater CEC than lighter soils. CEC's can vary widely, so base saturation percentages, and their relationship to one another, are much more important than CEC amounts.

A good base saturation report for growing *Atlantic Giants* would see calcium at 75- 90% of the available base, with magnesium at 7-10%, and potassium at 3-5%. With these percentages as a guide, you can evaluate a soil test and make your own recommendations as to what should be added to, or refrained from, in bringing about a balance to the soil's base saturation.

For AG's, a good starting point for calcium would be 3000 ppm, with magnesium levels of 300 ppm and potassium levels at 150 ppm.

Feeding in the Right Balance

As a general rule for optimizing giant pumpkin plant and fruit health, there should be 10 times as much calcium as magnesium (except when seed formation is occurring at the end of the season), 15 times as much calcium as potassium, and a magnesium to potassium ratio of more than 2:1. Considerable leeway is afforded but large skewing from these ratios can lead to deficiencies in one or another of these elements, and a soil pH that is out of the proper range will retard the absorption of plantfoods regardless of their adequate supply or proper ratio to one another. Remember, adjust pH first, insure adequate plantfood next, then balance major and minor elements properly.

Application of Principles

Your calcium and soil balancing program should be taken care of before planting so you do not have to do much during the season. Because calcium is so slow to move through the soil, it is better to work it into the soil before planting (and apply it in the fall or very early spring). Using a liquid calcium chelate in-season will insure that calcium is available to all plant parts, and it can be run through an irrigation system using an injector. Spraying the leaves with calcium chelates will benefit the leaves, but studies have shown that calcium will not move from the leaf to the fruit. Spraying the fruit insures that calcium is available there, particularly the blossom end of the fruit which seems to always be thinner than the stem end and more susceptible to rots associated with calcium deficiencies. Some growers use calcium soaked blankets draped on their pumpkin during the day, but this method has still to be proved effective.

Additional K can be applied from late July through season's end with chelated calcium in a ratio of 15 parts Ca to 1 part K.

Alan Gibson and Tim Parks from the OVGPG analyze a recent soil sample result. They're right on top of things!

Insect & Disease Control

Wanting to spray less (because of the detrimental effects that it has on leaves), yet wanting to be totally free from Cucumber Beetles, Squash Bugs, Squash Vine Borers, and a myriad of diseases, both in the soil and in the air, I set a few of the more knowledgeable members of the RIPGA loose to explore the problem and return with answers. What they returned with gives hope to us all.

We wanted to spray less, so systemic chemicals appealed more to us than those that just coat the leaves and are washed away by rain and frequent watering. We also were cognizant of the new wave of synthetic pyrethroids that are combined with agents that help them to spread on the leaves and to withstand the weather and still maintain their effectiveness.

You may or may not recognize some of the names, and you may not be able to secure them, but here are insecticide and fungicide recommendations that will be very effective.

Insect Control

Much has been said about *Warrior T,* and justifiably so. With a 21 day residual period and systemic action, this 4th generation pyrethrin seems to obliterate anything that comes near it, and the amounts that an average giant pumpkin grower would use in a season could fit in a shot glass. The activity of this insecticide all but eliminates frequent spraying during the egg laying period of the Squash Vine Borer (SVB) when plants are lush and the crush of summer heat adds-up to produce significant damage when spraying. *Warrior T* may become the only insecticide you need apply through the whole season. Start spraying in mid May before Cucumber Beetles emerge, and continue every three weeks until late August.

The dosage amount is 6 drops (1/4 tsp.) per gallon, and since you do not have to spray underneath the leaves, a gallon of spray can go a long way. The downside of using an insecticide that is this effective is its non-selective nature. Bees and other beneficial insects will also be killed wherever *Warrior T* is exposed to them. A kinder approach to insecticide usage will only allow SVB and Squash Bugs to evade complete control.

An alternate program is outlined in *World Class Giant Pumpkins II,* in *Chapter 11, Insidious Insects and Demon Diseases,* under the subhead of *The No Spray Program.* In this program, *Imadacloprid (Merit),* a systemic insecticide sold at virtually every lawn and garden center as a granular grub control for lawns, does a good job in controlling SVB and other insect pests. Supplementing it with an occasional spray of *Carbaryl (Sevin)* when infestations of Cucumber Beetles become heavy will add effectiveness to this program.

Disease Control

Subdue, a granular, systemic fungicide is quite effective at reducing the onslaught of soil pathogens. It is very long lasting, and is applied to soil just before planting at a rate of 30 ounces per 1000 square feet. It kills pythium and phytophthora spores in the soil on contact, then is taken up into the plant to control most root and stem rots. Reapply at the same rate on August 1st to protect plants for the remainder of the season.

In soils constantly under the pressure of pathogenic diseases, more aggressive methods may be required. Starting in late June, spray every two weeks, alternating with *Daconil* and *Quadris.*

Daconil is still one of the best all-purpose fungicides, while *Quadris* is also quite broad in its effectiveness, but particularly effective on Powdery Mildew.

In late July, early August, apply *Kocide,* a copper based fungicide, on the off-week for either *Daconil* or *Quadris.* Continue spraying *Kocide* until late September. *Kocide* can burn leaves, so take every precaution in applying.

MycoShield is a tetramycin, bactericide which is very effective in preventing bacterial wilts not controlled by general fungicides. Spray once a month, beginning the end of May, and continue until the end of September, particularly in the wake of Cucumber Beetle or aphid attacks.

*Page 118 shows
Squash Bugs (also
known as Stink Bugs)
and nymphs, and a
Spotted Cucumber
Beetle.*

*Page 119 shows the
winged SVB (Squash
Vine Borer) adult.*

*Note: Warrior-T or
Lambda Cyhalothrin is
distributed under
a couple of other
names.
Landscape version
is called Scimitar.
The over the counter
one, which you can
find at your local
garden supply store, is
called Triazicide.
Triazicide is only
formulated at .5% of
active ingredient,
where as, Warrior T
and Scimitar are
formulated at
11.7% and 10.6%
respectively.*

Mycorrhizae

The future of disease control lies in the use of biological mycorrhizal fungi like those found in Natural Industries', *Actinovate* and *RootShield*. These beneficial fungi are applied as a drench in the spring as the transplants are set out, or right in the pot when seeds are started. These fungi colonize on the roots, reducing the attempts of non-beneficial fungi from entering the plant, in addition to performing other extremely valuable functions for their host plants including: shuttling plant nutrients from a far greater area than plant roots can access, regulating the uptake of nutrients in response to plant needs, and supporting the spread of other beneficial soil organisms. A second application, when the main vine is 10' long, concentrating on spraying the fungus on the soil, in and around the plant, is sufficient for the season. They are compatible with common, contact killing fungicides, but are limited by those fungicides that are systemic in action.

"Mycorrhiza is the natural linking of plant roots with beneficial soil fungi. Over millions of years, many plants have come to rely on mycorrhizae and no longer grow their own network of fine feeder roots. A plant missing its normal fungus partnership will have nutrient uptake problems. It will have to be treated as a 'heavy feeder'. Soil fumigation, fungicides, tillage, and overuse of synthetic fertilizers can destroy mycorrhizal fungi."

Bio/Organics, Inc.

The use of *Actinovate* and *RootShield* combines two different strains of beneficial fungi that allows for far broader control. This 1-2 punch may be all that is required in a patch where frequent rotation of crops is impossible.

For problematic conditions, fumigation of the soil may be advised, with inoculation of mychorrhizae fungi following sufficient passage of time.

Actinovate® Soluble Biological Inoculant

A high concentration of the Actinovate® microbe on a soluble carrier. Use as a drench down, transplant dip, seed soaking, or direct seed spray at planting.

Actinovate® Seed Inoculant

A high concentration of the Actinovate® microbe on a carrier that adheres well to seed.
Apply as a dry application, soaking or in a slurry.

Actino-Iron® Biological Soil Additive

A high concentration of the Actinovate® microbe on an iron and humic acid carrier.
Iron content is guaranteed at 15%.

Above: 3 products containing mychorrizal fungi from Natural Industries.

Below: A live Striped Cucumber Beetle feeding on a leaf.

*Background image shows thousands of dead Striped Cucumber Beetles after one application of insecticide.
However, it was too late for the seedling.*

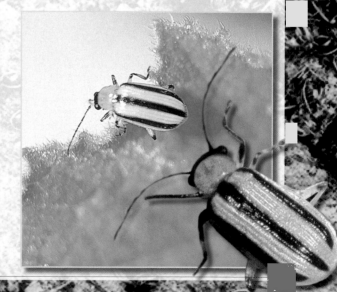

121

Kids, Good People, & Pumpkins

Right: The late, great, Barnesville Buckeye, Dick Beard celebrates.
Below: Sharon Breznick of Vermont entertains the contestants at the Topsfield Fair while sizing up Don Langevin's 2002, 953.

Right top:
Bobier's da
in a nice pl
his 1996, 7

Right: Todd
and Al Eat
pose in the
orange jack
the Interna
Growers' Se

122

Warming, Cooling, Warming

Make up your mind now. What is it – warm or cool? Believe it or not, attempts at controlling temperature are the most useful tools available to a giant pumpkin grower. Starting with the elevation of temperatures in seed starting, warmer temperatures extend over into the patch when early transplants are set into cool soil. Growers place black plastic to heat up the soil – starting weeks ahead of the transplant date. They construct cloches to elevate daytime temperatures, and use heating devices at night to maintain warmer conditions in the cloche. These warming devices are as simple as a light bulb, or soil heating cables placed around the plant. Some will actually go to the expense of heating the cloches with thermostatically controlled electric heaters. On the "flip side" of warming the cloche is the necessary ventilating of heat, and cooling of the interior of the cloche on a warm or sunny day. Leaving transplants in small cloches on warm days can end your season before it starts.

Mounding soil is another good method for warming soil. Some growers will actually transplant their seedling by placing it on the center of the raised mound, then pull the soil from around the seedling to bury it. This keeps the seedling roots in the warmest soil possible.

When your plants have outgrown their cloches and are beginning to run, unusually sunny and high temperature days can scorch new leaves. This is the time when cooling the plant can pay handsome dividends for you later. A misting system set to water plants for 3-5 minutes every 30 minutes (after temperatures reach 85°) can all but eliminate leaf scorch.

Above: Large wa[ter] filled black plas[tic] bags hold the st[ored] daytime heat to [ ] soil warming on [ ] cold nights.

Left: Tom Beach[ ] Indiana relaxes [ ] shade in a "bea[n] chair (pumpkin[ ]

124

During pollinating season, temperatures over 90° can abort almost every attempt you make at hand pollination. Cooling the micro-climate around the female flower can be accomplished by placing bottles of frozen water next to the flower.

Watering plants with warmed water has seen much attention the last 5 years. Growers will fill large black tanks with water, allow the sun to sufficiently warm, then gravity feed the water to irrigation units.

Shading fruit from punishing sunlight and heat is almost universally accepted by competitive growers, but conserving the heat absorbed by the fruit during the day has begun to attract interest as well. A simple blanket placed over the fruit when temperatures begin to decline in the late afternoon or evening can help conserve heat and enable the pumpkin to regain its growth momentum faster the next day. Most begin blanketing as soon as the fruit reaches basketball size.

And, let's not forget end-of-season warming where growers will erect large, lightweight plastic or Remay houses over their prized plant, allowing increased temperatures during the day and added protection from frost at night.

Right: Cooling a newly pollinated female flower/

...ading pumpkin harsh effects of ...nlight and heat.

...le: Black tanks ...ting cold water.

...n: Blanketing a ...before nightfall ...ld some of the daytime heat.

Growth Regulators

Plant hormones like cytokinins, auxins, and gibberellins have drawn more and more competitive giant pumpkin growers' attention over the years, and have shown great promise in optimizing growth of roots, plants, and fruit.

Each is present in seaweed products. And, in keeping with our recent fascination with calcium, observe in the next quotation from a scientific study, how the presence of cytochinins, auxins, and gibberellins provide further proof that the presence of both calcium and these plant hormones are essential for growth and development.

"The uptake of calcium is stimulated by numerous factors, for example by auxins, cytokinin, and gibberellins. The consequence of an increased calcium uptake by the cell [larger cells] may initiate a number of other processes. Growth processes and bud development, for example, are correlated with a rise of the intracellular calcium concentration. Bud development does not take place when calcium uptake is inhibited. A lack of cytokinins or auxins have the same effect." (OWEN, 1988).

Cytochinin and auxin, in combination with increased calcium may answer the question growers often ask, "Why do seaweed products work?" Both calcium and the compounds found in seaweed must be present for optimum growth. In fact, in their absence, growth stops.

Seaweed is a trace element treasure chest – containing not only the three major plant nutrients (N-P-K) and three major growth regulators (cytochinin, auxin, and gibberellin), but also a myriad of trace minerals including: magnesium, boron, manganese, zinc, calcium, aluminum, sodium, iron, sulfur, and humic acid. Since soils generally contain adequate trace elements, it is the growth hormones that get all our attention.

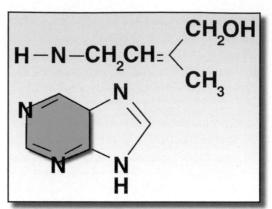

Chemical makeup of cytochinin.

Cytochinins

To some extent, cytochinin compounds are found in all plants, and are particularly concentrated in areas of the plant that are continuously growing, such as roots, young leaves, and developing fruit and seeds. Cytochinins promote cell division and cell elongation, both of which are the heart and soul of growth. They are believed to be taken in and synthesized by the roots, and then relocated to areas of the plant that are actively growing. This should encourage us to provide ample supplies to the roots, and less directly sprayed on leaves.

Seaweed has particularly high concentrations of this growth hormone either in extracts or in kelp meals. Kelp meal could be used to build soil supplies because of its bulk and weight, while seaweed extracts could be used in a spray program or through an injector via your watering system. Both have a place in the scheme of supplying ample cytochinins for active growth.

Cytochinins effect the plant in other ways, but our interest is perked because of its ability to promote cell division and enlarge cells in the fruit. Ample supplies of seaweed products should be applied to the soil to insure root synthesis and transport to the growing pumpkin. Cytochinins, along with increased calcium availability, should be every grower's goal.

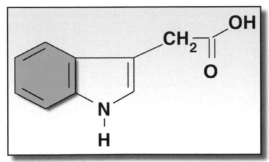

Chemical makeup of auxins.

Auxins

Auxins are also responsible for enabling cell elongation. They are able to do this by promoting the intake of water, and increasing the elasticity of the cell to cope with the increase of water taken in.

Because cells are made larger, auxins, therefore, regulate the amount, type, and direction of growth. They are most abundantly present in growth areas, like root and shoot tips (referred to as the meristems). Auxins affect many other plant processes besides cell elongation, including the formation of buds, roots, flowers, and fruit. Auxins are widely used commercially to produce more vigorous root formation, and to promote flowering and fruiting.

What is the biological significance of auxins? In low concentrations they aid cell elongation in leaves, roots, and fruit. However, if concentrations become too high, the effect reverses and elongation of cells is inhibited. So, like nitrogen and potassium, moderation is required with auxin laden seaweed products, and overall soil balance should still remain the central focus.

If you are familiar with the general weed killer, 2-4-D, and its detrimental effect on broadleaf plants, you'll understand the significance of over applying seaweed. 2-4-D is a highly concentrated, synthetic auxin. Yes, it is a growth hormone that in large dosages reverses the effect of elongating cells (normally caused by the presence of auxins), and subsequently, the death of the plant.

Gibberellins

"Gibberellins promote cell elongation and cell division. They also stimulate the germination of pollen and the growth of pollen tubes. They induce the development of fruits like apples, pumpkins, and egg-plants to twice the size of normal fruit." (P. HALMER; 1985)

The following is a list of functions for which gibberellins are held partially responsible: helps break seed dormancy, stimulates stem elongation by stimulating cell division and elongation; stimulates flowering in response to longer days; effects the determination of flower sex by inducing maleness in plants containing both male and female flowers, and can cause seedless fruit development.

Apical root cells, young fruits, as well as unripe or germinating seeds are all rich in gibberellins. The amount of gibberellin present, and the growth rate of apical cells, has been correlated. One of the reasons that pumpkin vegetative growth slows down when pumpkin flowers and fruit are actively growing is that an increase in gibberellins and a corresponding decrease in the effects of auxins in the growing tips of vines has occurred. Auxins and gibberellins work hand in hand in the process of shifting emphasis from vegetative to fruit growth.

There are many synthetically produced gibberellins with GA3 being the one most commonly referred to in research studies.

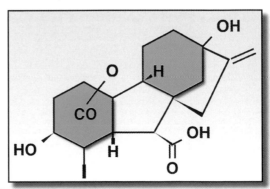

Chemical makeup of gibberellins.

Colchicine

Colchicine is a poison which when used properly can double the chromosomes (entire genetic material) of an organism. Colchicine is a microtubular poison that arrests the cell cycle by preventing the microtubuals from connecting at the spindle and separating the chromosomes. The result is that it kills many cells, but some will survive the treatment to escape the toxic effect of colchicine at the perfect timing to produce a growing bud with double chromosome number (4n). Normal cells are called diploid (2n), and then when the chromosomes are doubled, tetraploid (4n).

The advantages of doubling the chromosomes have been used in many other plant species. Such characteristics as increased fruit size, plant size, plant vigor, and disease resistance have been previously achieved in weaker species. Another reason for creating a plant with doubled chromosomes is the production of seedless fruit. All of these are wonderful benefits, but successful implementation of colchicine is not easy, as this scientific study excerpt points out:

"Seed yield of tetraploid lines in early generations is often only 50-100 seeds per fruit (vs. 200-800 for diploids). Another problem with raw tetraploids is poor seed germination, making it difficult to establish uniform field plantings. It may require as much as 10 years of self-pollination before sufficient seeds of tetraploid lines can be produced for commercial production of triploid hybrids."

McCuistion and Wehner

There is no specific recipe for using colchicine to create tetraploids, as it is species specific. From other research, I would recommend using concentrations of 2% or more. As soon as a seed has germinated, apply a drop of the colchicine right between the cotyledons where the first true leaf bud is developing. Applications should be made every 12 hours for three days, making a total of 6 applications. Some experimentation should be done in trials that vary concentration between .03%-3% before subjecting limited quantities of a prized seed stock. If concentrations are too high, it will simply kill the seedlings. The ideal concentration is only a little below a lethal dose.

*Left:
Chemical make[of colchicine.*

In order to determine if a treatment is successful, careful observation must be made. The best method is to count the chromosomes using a high power microscope. This is almost impossible for most giant pumpkin growers to do. An easier, and more accommodating, method is to check the guard cells on the underside of leaves using an inexpensive microscope. Compare the guard cell size and its number of chloroplasts to a leaf from a non-treated seedling. The guard cells should be noticeably larger, and should have roughly twice the number of chloroplasts. Other simple methods can also be used, but are not as accurate in determining the creation of a tetraploid. Such observations could be larger flowers, thicker vines and leaves, as well as, slower, stockier vine growth.

The creation of tetraploids and triploid hybrids using colchicine may be a method of increasing fruit size, but will take a great deal of work and years to accomplish successfully.

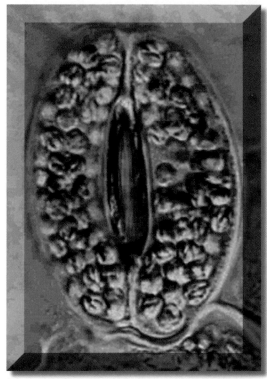

The rate of success in creating tetraploid plants with colchicine is only 1% (1 in 100), with most of the treated plants dying from the treatment or remaining diploid.

Leaf Section

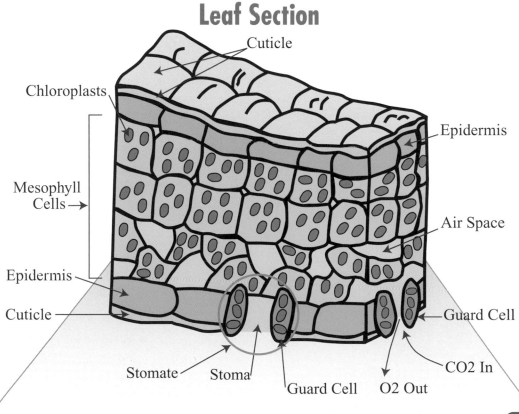

Cuticle

Chloroplasts

Epidermis

Mesophyll Cells →

Air Space

Epidermis

Cuticle

Guard Cell

Stomate   Stoma

Guard Cell   O2 Out

CO2 In

Genetics & Pollination Strategies

I am delighted to have collaborated with Nic Welty on the presentation of this chapter, *Genetics & Pollination Strategies*. With Nic and his associates, all specialists in their respective area of genetics, we hope to deliver to you a scientific explanation of AG genetics, and some strategies in using this information to develop your own world class giant pumpkin and a very "hot" seed stock.

I was first introduced to Nic at the International Giant Pumpkin Seminar held at Guelph University in Ottawa, Canada in March of 2001. There, he gave a workshop on basic genetics as they apply to *Atlantic Giants* that was both informative and exhilarating. I went home with great enthusiasm aimed at creating my own 567.5 Mombert, 935 Lloyd, or 723 Bobier (the hot seed stocks that year).

Although the subject matter can be quite complex and daunting at times, an underlying attempt was made at trying to keep the information basic. It was because of this basic delivery of the information by Nic at Guelph that I first became interested in the subject, and as a result, we chose the same methods in presenting the information to you here. It is our hope that we convey to all growers, even those not interested in scientific studies, the importance of these basic principles in choosing seed and pollinators. If you make only one good cross in your entire life because of this information, Nic and I will consider it well worth the time, effort, and space in this book.

Genetics Principles – A Primer for Pumpkin Breeders

The father of modern day genetics, Gregor Mendel, discovered in the 1800's most of the knowledge needed today for competitive giant pumpkin breeding. By conducting simple experiments with pea plants, he uncovered the basic principles of inheritance. This experimentation spawned the profound concept of independent inheritance, and the basic idea of genes functioning in pairs: dominant or recessive.

One of the most important aspects of understanding the genetics of pumpkins is understanding the process of pollination and seed production when genetic recombination and transfer occur.

To explain how genetic transfer and inheritance works, the process will be illustrated through a cycle of life. The cycle will be illustrated by beginning with the seed. Within the seed is a tiny embryo. This embryo originated from a single cell containing one copy of the complete genetic material for the plant. This genetic material is packaged in chromosomes, and these chromosomes exist in duplicate (called diploid, or abbreviated 2n). This duplication exists so that the halves can be systematically separated, and recombined, but both halves must be present in the pumpkin plant in order for normal development. The seed will grow and develop into a plant with the exact same set of genetic material in each cell. A cell is a small unit (a building block of life) joined together with all other cells in a plant, functioning with specificity to allow the plant to work properly as a whole. The plant will grow and develop – exactly replicating the genetic material in every cell throughout the plant.

The genetic material is exactly the same in almost all of the plant. except for the flowers where something special takes place. In flowers, the male and female gametes are produced. A gamete is the name used to refer to the specific units of egg and sperm that the female and male representatives of an organism produce in order to pass their genetic material on to future generations through reproduction. Within the immature seed, the gametes from the pollen and egg function in the mechanism of gene transfer. These gametes are produced such that each will contain exactly one half (haploid set of chromosomes abbreviated 1n) of the genetic material. Without going into too much detail on the specific mechanisms, it must be understood that every gamete produced will contain a different genetic makeup. Due to an independent assortment of the genes, when the chromosomes separate, every half is unique and complimentary to all other halves created. There are so many different combinations possible due to the immense number of genes, that it is statistically improbable for any two gametes to contain the exact same genetic material.

Each pollen grain contains half (1n) of the plants genetic material in a combination that is different from every other pollen grain. Within each female flower are many immature eggs waiting inside the immature seeds, also containing a unique half of the plant's genetic material.

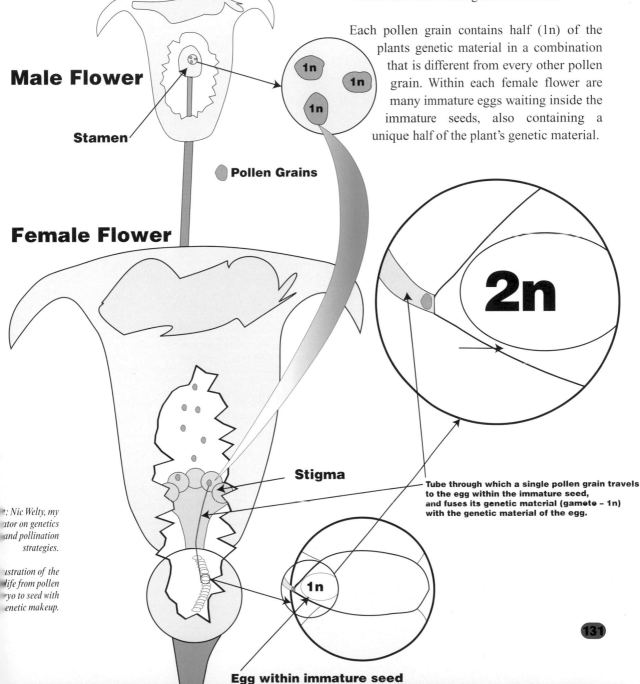

Male Flower

Stamen

Female Flower

1n 1n 1n

Pollen Grains

2n

Stigma

Tube through which a single pollen grain travels to the egg within the immature seed, and fuses its genetic material (gamete – 1n) with the genetic material of the egg.

1n

Egg within immature seed

*: Nic Welty, my
ator on genetics
and pollination
strategies.

ustration of the
life from pollen
yo to seed with
enetic makeup.

With this understanding of the pollen and immature seed, the pollination process can be described.

Take carefully protected male flowers, bearing the pollen grains harvested from one plant (or the same plant if you are self pollinating), to the carefully covered female flower. The pollen is transferred from male flower to the "lobes" of the female flower using the male flower like a paint brush. The pollen grains stick to the receptive surfaces of the female flower, and allow for a deliberate transport of the genetic material to the immature seed. This allows for a fusion of the pollen and the egg to produce a complete set of genetic material (2n). In this fashion, the father contributes the pollen, and the mother the immature egg within the immature seed, and both the mother and father contribute equal halves representing their respective genetic codes. This single cell, created as a result of the fusion of these gametes, continues to grow and divide, producing a complete embryo within the seed by the time the fruit is mature. This embryo represents a new combination of genes derived from its mother and father that will be represented throughout the plant that grows from this seed.

The implications of this process are vast and will affect all further genetic analysis. Here are some of the critical implications to the giant pumpkin breeder. Every seed is unique within a pumpkin, but represents a combination of the same two parental genetic make-ups (assuming the pollination is controlled). The mother and father give exactly equal contributions to the genetic makeup of the seed that is produced (there is a small exception, but those details are beyond the scope of this basic introduction). The father will only contribute an effect on the

offspring of the seeds of a fruit, and have no effect on the fruit itself that was pollinated.

It should come as no surprise that genes are most easily thought of as occurring in pairs. It takes both halves to form a functional gene. Genes will exist and may or may not be seen. Since there is no way that common giant pumpkin growers can see the genes themselves, we must rely upon what we can see, the characteristics and visual cues of the plants and fruit. These visual cues are termed the "phenotype" and are decidedly a result of the different genetic makeup that the plant being observed contains. The "genotype" is the term used to refer to the actual genetic makeup of the plant and is not easily observed or determined. The only tool available to a giant pumpkin breeder is examining the phenotype and making decisions based on such information.

What Gregor Mendel discovered studying pea plants was several specific examples of the function of genes in pairs. This is where the familiar terms of dominant and recessive

eft: a new female bud shows up at e end of the vine a tiny pumpkin base; the flower lops and finally to receive pollen m a male flower own to the right.

genes, working together to control the expression we see expressed by the plant, originated. Genes do work together in pairs as Mendel discovered, and in many cases they are related such that one gene is dominant, and can completely mask the expression of its counterpart the recessive gene. Unfortunately, no gene is known with absolute certainty in giant pumpkins. This eliminates the ability to analyze genes specifically in giant pumpkins. However, the principles that such inheritance implicate do provide a means of logic which can be very useful.

A simple example of a dihybrid cross will give a clear understanding of what is taking place. Remember, this is only a hypothetical situation, the actual nature of the traits in *Atlantic Giants* are unknown.

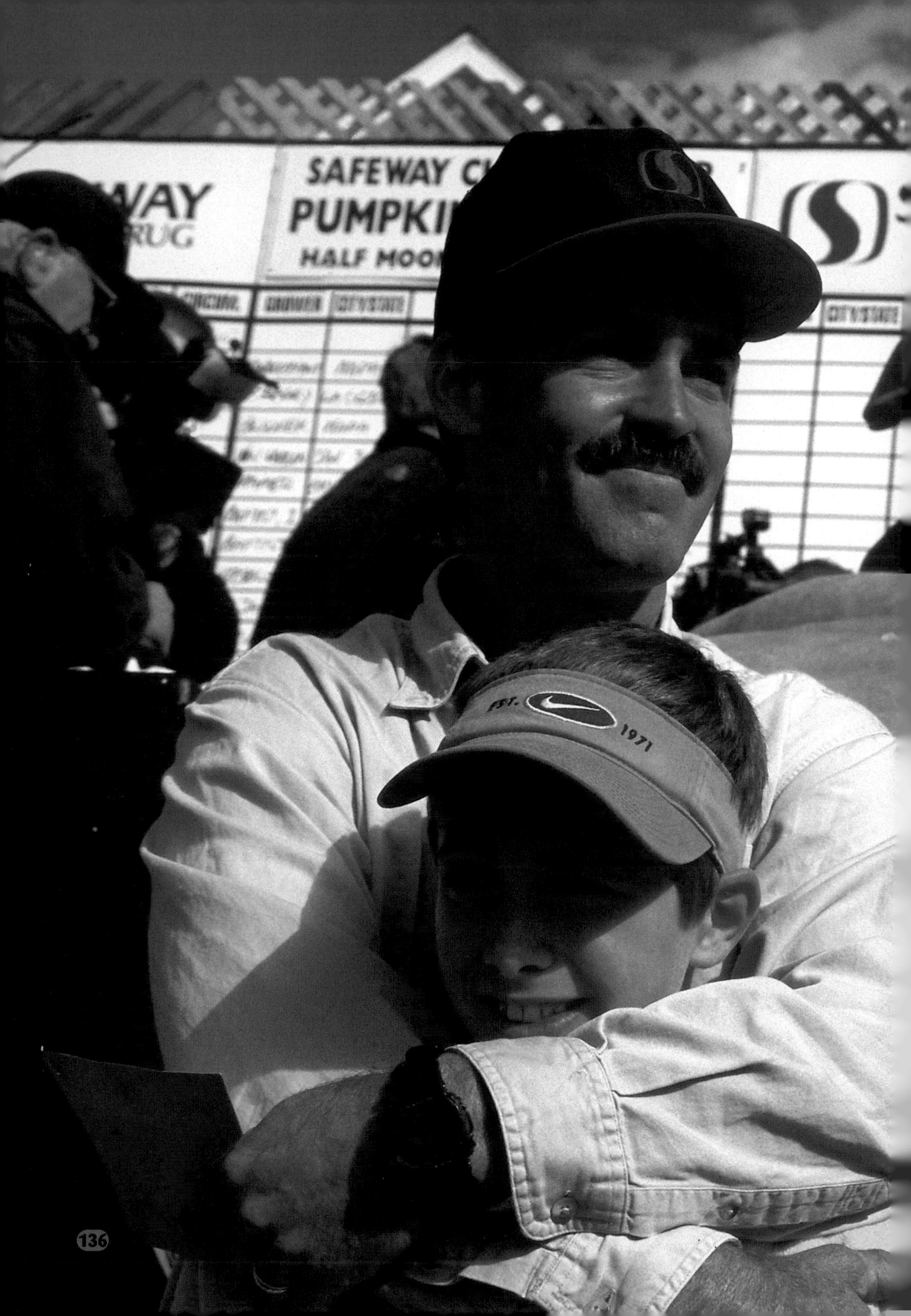
SAFEWAY C
PUMPKI
HALF MOO
EST. 1971

EWAY
& DRUG

Steve and Scott Daletas of Pleasant Hill, OR with their winning 2001, 1016 at the Half Moon Bay, CA weigh off.

A = tall (dominant); a = short (recessive);
D = split (dominant); d = no split (recessive).

Cross between Aa Dd
(tall split fruit heterozygous) and self

Demonstration of dihybrid cross:

⚲ gametes	A D	Ad	aD	ad
AD	AA DD	AA Dd	Aa DD	Aa Dd
Ad	AA Dd	AA dd	Aa Dd	Aa dd
aD	Aa DD	Aa Dd	aa DD	aa Dd
ad	Aa Dd	Aa dd	aa Dd	aa dd

Phenotypic result: tall split fruit = 9/16
(includes genotypes AADD, AADd, AaDD, AaDd)

tall solid fruit = 3/16
(includes genotypes AAdd and Aadd)

Short split fruit = 3/16
(includes genotypes aaDD and aaDd)

Short solid fruit = 1/16 (genotype aadd)

Thinking in terms of how a dihybrid cross works, and the implications this has on how an actual cross will work when all the genes of a pumpkin are involved, can help when considering how consistent the results will be from a given cross.

Statistics

Statistics is a powerful tool for analyzing nearly anything, so it is also very useful in studying the genetics of pumpkins. Terms such as mean, median, and mode should be fairly familiar to most individuals. Mean is the average, median is the middle value of a set of numbers ordered in sequence, and mode refers to the most often occurring value in a set of numbers. In the case of studying giant pumpkin genetics, we are looking at very large sets of numbers, and a wide spread of weights produced from a seed or seed lines. Finding the average weight of such sets of numbers is interesting, but much more insight can be gained by looking into further analysis. When analyzing a list of numbers, some idea of the distribution of the numbers must be understood. If you organize a group of numbers in order, the middle number is known as the median, and will be at the half way point in the series. Dividing the numbers into fourths, reveals two other interesting points: first and third quartiles. Starting from the left, we have the first quarter of the numbers, then the first quartile (a point), then another quarter, the median (a point), followed by the next quarter of numbers and then the point that is the third quartile, followed finally by the last quarter of numbers.

Distribution of Numbers

Another very useful means of analysis is the normal distribution. The bell shaped curve is a term many people are familiar with; it represents a normal distribution of numbers. That is a nice symmetrical ordering of numbers. If arranged in sequential order, the list of numbers will have most numbers nearer the mean, and increasingly fewer further from the mean in a symmetrical fashion. This symmetrical fashion is designed so that a value known as standard deviation can be used to give the percent of values in a specific range from the mean. When a set of numbers matches the normal distribution, a range of plus or minus one standard deviation around the mean will include 66% of all the numbers in the set. A range of plus or minus two standard deviations will include 95% of all the numbers in the set. From this, we can predict 2.5% odds of having a value that is more than two standard deviations from the mean.

Below is a histogram representing a normal distribution of numbers, frequency is on the vertical axis indicating how many numbers fall into the range represented by each bar in the table (in our situation the number of fruits within each range bounded by a bar on the graph). On the horizontal axis is the range of values of numbers (in our case this would be weight).

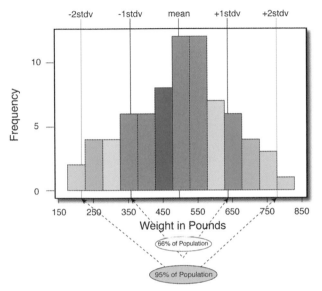

Normal, Random Distribution of Weights

mean = 484.9   standard deviation = 143.9

Now, it is very useful to note that the expected distribution of numbers for a population of any species is the normal distribution. From this distribution of numbers a measure of how far from the mean relative to that set of numbers can be calculated, and is called the standard deviation. On a normal distribution, standard deviation is defined to be a value that when added to the mean, two thirds of all values will lie within the range created, and that when you are two standard deviations from the mean, this parameter will enclose 95% of all values in the set of numbers. Generating the analysis of numbers relative to a normal distribution is best suited to statistical software, but is a powerful tool pumpkin growers should be using.

Population Genetics

Population genetics is a study of an entire population of organisms. In the case of giant pumpkins, this is using genetic principles to study the entire gene pool of competitive giant pumpkins. Here, what we are looking at is evolution of the giant pumpkin gene pool. Survival of the fittest is replaced in this situation by the selection by pumpkin growers for the most massive fruit.

World's Largest Fruit				
	1989-1995	Seed Year	1996-2001	Seed Year
	1090*	1995	1337	2000
	1061*	1995	1262	1998
	1010*	1994	1260*	2000
	1006	1994	1245	2000
	990*	1993	1236	1999
	975*	1994	1215	1999
	963*	1994	1190*	1998
	946.5*	1995	1186*	2001
	945.5*	1993	1178	1999
	939	1992	1177	1999
Mean	992.6		1228.2	
	123.7% increase			

indicates fruit grown from a new seed

This table indicates an overall picture of the evolution of the giant pumpkin population over the past decade. It shows an overall improvement of approximately 23% in the ten largest fruit grown. It must be understood that this figure is the result of a very complicated set of factors which also includes grower improvement, and a change in seeds being planted. This complication can be summed up in the following equation:

Variance = Genetics + Environment
23% = Improvement in Seed
+ Improvement in growing techniques

The difficulty in interpreting these figures is compounded by the fact that we can not distinguished how much of this variance is due to our improvements in growing technique or our improvement in the genetics. The general trend is obviously towards an increase in weights. This follows the general implications of the evolution of a species being selected for weight. Through the selection made, the population as a whole will increase in weight through the generations. From this aspect, strong indication is given for implementing seeds which have received the highest number of generations of selection. As noted earlier, the normal distribution is a good model of a population which has developed by random selection. Growers selectively picking the best seeds and making planned crosses, have an effect on the population generally referred to as artificial selection. It has been shown in several other plant species that selecting for a single quality defined as a number (such as yield or mass), the population will shift away from the normal distribution, and exhibit higher frequencies than expected at 1 and 2 standard deviations away from the mean towards the desired quality. What this means for a pumpkin grower is that through years of selective breeding, the population of seeds will improve. This improvement is exhibited when comparing to the set of numbers on a normal distribution – there will be more high weight fruits than expected by the 66% and 95% characteristic of the normal distribution. Through experimentation and calculations which are still incomplete, the following distributions were created modeling the population of giant pumpkins.

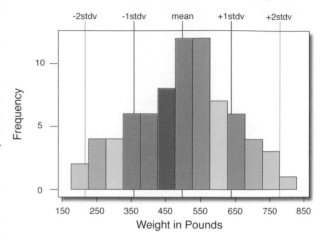

Normal, Random Distribution of Weights

Mean = 482.7 Standard Deviation = 143.9

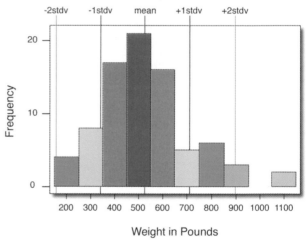

Histogram of older gene pool from 1989-1995

Mean = 525.4 Standard Deviation = 185

*Left: Nic
spies fror.
beneath s
pumpkin
during a
his patch
annual g
together
Ohio Val.
Giant Pu.
Growers.*

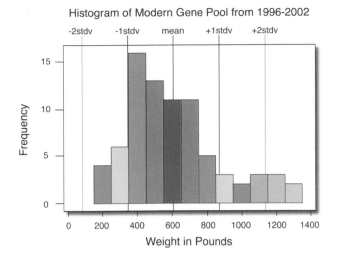

Histogram of Modern Gene Pool from 1996-2002

Mean = 609.7 Standard deviation = 262.9

One major indication of the reason for population genetics is that it appears that we are improving the population of giant pumpkins through our selection. With every year of planting and picking better seeds, our efforts have been, and will continue to be, rewarded by better seed every year.

Qualitative vs Quantitative breeding

What cross should we make to improve? The many investigations by Gregor Mendel indicated clear cases of dominance and recessive genes acting on specific known qualities. Breeding based upon these specific traits with known genes influencing the traits is called qualitative breeding. With giant pumpkins, we are not going to be directly using qualitative breeding because the genes are not known for any of the traits useful for producing the largest fruit. Breeding to select for a single characteristic defined by a number and controlled by a multitude of unknown genes influencing the trait is known as quantitative breeding. As giant pumpkin breeders, we must focus on quantitative breeding. Quantitative breeding is much more complex and relies heavily on statistics to attain the highest weight possible without knowing the mechanism of inheritance.

F2 Backcrosses

The method of using the F2 hybridization pattern of breeding shows success derived from the benefits of an F1 cross, and the F2 consistency outlined in the hypothetical situation. Now a general procedure for the F2 hybridization is as follows:

Begin with a productive seed that has done well for you or others in your region (has been very consistent in producing large offspring). When planting this seed, some flowers should be self-pollinated, and others on other plants, cross-pollinated. The cross-pollination should use males from a plant which is most genetically different from your original productive seed. Select this cross-pollinator based on something which you feel the original producer is lacking. This cross pollination produces an F1 hybrid and should be a productive seed. The F1 hybrid seed is then crossed with the self-pollinated original producer seeds, or the original producer itself. The result of this final cross can be considered an F2 hybrid. An F2 hybrid should be a consistent seed with most of the traits of the original producer and some new traits from the cross-pollinator. The F2 hybrid can then be treated like the original productive seed to repeat the process. In this fashion every year you will produce another good seed for planting the next season. (Welty, New England Giant Pumpkin Grower's newsletter June/July 2003)

The most successful F2 hybrid seeds will be produced by using the most pure parental line to make the backcross. An F2 seed itself is already a pure line to begin with since it is 75% the same material, but a self pollinated F2 that has undergone some selection for desirable characteristics under a large population will make an even better pollinator.

♂ Male

Large (% heavy) #2

Large F2 Fruit that consistently produces 1500 pounders

♀ Female

Large F1

Self

Largest F2 to date

New Line of % heavy long

Largest F2 to date

Self

Large desirable

Self

Good line

Large desirable

Large F1

Large F1

Large F1

Large F1

Self | Self
| 1061.5 Ciliberto

Large F1 | 1230 Daletas
| 1061.5 Ciliberto

Self | Self
| 1061.5 Ciliberto

Large F1 | 1230 Daletas
| 1061.5 Ciliberto

Self |

Self | Self
| Unrelated

Self | Self
| 1061.5 Ciliberto

Large F1 | 1230 Daletas
| 1061.5 Ciliberto

Hierarchy tree showing an example of an F2 hybridization pattern with the goal of producing world class seeds.

Left: The Dale
2001, 1016 is
cross as the 12
in the F2 tree c
(705 Stelts x 8

F1 Hybrid Seeds

The production of a seed which exhibits hybrid vigor is a very appealing prospect, but I must give a word of caution to those wishing to attempt such an endeavor. The success of an F1 hybrid is critically linked to how pure each parent is, and, equally critical, how complementary each parent is to the other. Creating a pure line is difficult, but cooperation among growers to select and purify a particular line of seeds, can produce good results. Determining the best lines to complement themselves is not easy, and there is no clear method of guessing which lines will produce the best hybrids when crossed, other than repeated trials and observation of many plants.

Selection of the Best Seed to Plant

Statistics plays a powerful role in determining which seeds to select for planting and which seeds to leave out of the collective gene pool. Here are a few useful patterns for determining the potential of a seed:

Average weight potential of mother and father weights ranked according to this equation:

[(weight of mother) + (weight of the father)]÷2 = estimated average weight potential

Because both the mother and father are equally critical to the success of the offspring, gathering information on the size of the fruit produced by the plant and the size of the fruit from the plant that donated the pollen, can yield a very useful means of analyzing seed potential. By taking the weight of the fruit from which a seed has been harvested (mother weight), and the highest weight of the pumpkin on the plant used to pollinate (father weight), an average of these two values can be generated for ranking seed potential. Take for example the 801.4 Ciliberto:

801.4 + 983 (father grown from the 946.5 Geerts) = 1784.4 (1784.4 ÷ 2 = 892.2).

This can be repeated for as many prospective seeds that are being considered for planting.

If there is a case where complete information is known about a patch, a value can be calculated to give reason for attempting some smaller weight seeds. Assuming that all the plants in a competitive patch receive equal and optimum care, a small scale population genetics approach can be implemented by setting environmental variance equal to 0 (in actuality this is a false assumption, but at present there is no way to ascertain the exact value, so this assumption will be used). Using the weights of the largest fruit produced for each plant, a series of numbers is created and analyzed as a normal set of data producing a mean of fruit weights and a distribution of weights from the mean in terms of standard deviation. The mean of mother and father in terms of standard deviations from the mean can then be calculated for each seed as in the previous example. This value can be calculated for a grower's own seed, and other seeds if complete information is known, to make an attempt at clarifying the true genetic potential of a seed. Here is some clarification by example:

Your patch produced 400, 550, 575, 605, 620, 650, and 715 pound fruit, and you are considering some seeds from Geneva Emmons' patch, where she grew an 850, 910, 990, 1010, 1025, 1030, and 1055 pound fruit.

Your mean is 587.9 pounds, with a standard deviation of 98.5 pounds. Geneva's mean is 981.5, with a standard deviation of 74.1 pounds.

The percent of variance from the mean in terms of standard deviation equals:

(fruit weight – mean) ÷ standard deviation x 100%

Your fruits' percent of variance from the mean are: -191%, -38%, -13%, +17%, +32%, +63%, and +129%. Geneva's fruit vary by: -177%, -96%, +12%, +39%, +59%, +66%, and +99%.

If you are considering your 715 seed (+129), and it was pollinated with the plant that produced your 620 pound fruit (+32), its mean ranking value would be: (129 + 32) ÷ 2 = 80.5% standard deviation above the mean.

Comparing that to Geneva's 1025 pound fruit, and assuming the 1025 (+66) was pollinated with the plant which produced the 850 pound fruit (-177), the 1025 ranking value would be: (66 – 177) = -111% standard deviation below the mean.

From this comparison, your 715 appears to contain a much higher level of genetic potential than a seed planted from a heavier pumpkin (1025). Many smaller weight seeds have hidden potential.

Ranking of seeds which have seen a considerable amount of planting is difficult because of the great variance in the environments where the seeds have been grown. General statistics, such as mean of fruit grown, or the number of fruit surpassing a particular weight (over 1000), can be useful, but other methods of analysis will also help in determining the best seeds to plant.

Regional Considerations

This should come as no surprise that some seeds and seed lines appear to perform well in some regions, but not as well in other regions. Some people have attempted to describe this as a function of the evolution of a particular seed line grown in a specific region. This is not a very accurate representation because it takes many more generations of growth and selection to produce such a result through evolution. A more likely reason is that there are some genes which may be influencing the success. Possibly some seed lines contain a gene which promotes

better performance at high temperatures, or the ability to grow quickly in a cold spring. The exact details of what these genes are and how specifically they are functioning remain unknown, but an observation can be reliably made that specific gene pools will complement different climates with differing levels of success. When considering seeds to plant, make a ranking of seeds which have performed well in your climate, and give them a serious consideration even if the weights are lower than other champion fruit in a different climate.

Consistency Factor

The quality of a proven seed is its capability to produce large fruit again and again. This is what makes the great seeds famous and more sought after. The world's best growers take these seeds and plant them repeatedly and are successful over and over. This is where the analysis of tested seeds, based upon their range of deviation from the average weight, becomes a very critical value. A seed with a 75% confidence rate of producing an 800 pound fruit will make it a very desirable seed. Consistency is critical because a competitive grower can then plant the seed with confidence, knowing how it will perform and respond to current growing technique to produce a world class fruit. For this reason, investigation into choosing good consistent seeds is one of the most important factors in seed selection. Determining the consistency of a seed, which has already seen significant planting, is difficult, but easier than making predictions on unplanted seeds. For the purpose of comparing expected consistency, I have developed a ranking system:

One:	F1 hybrid or F2 hybrid that is a success, or a true breeding self pollinated line (no giant pumpkin true breeder exists).
Two:	Planned F1s, some selfed F2s, and poor F2s.
Three:	Self pollinated F1s, or any unplanned crosses like open or multiple pollinators, and very poor choice F1 crosses.

This ranking is set so that one is the most consistent and three is the least consistent. This makes a great check for new seeds, but will have exceptions that are either more or less consistent than they appear from this ranking. Until there is a complete understanding of the inheritance of giant pumpkins, there will always be unexpected results that deviate from the predicted calculations.

Motive for a World Record

The decision making process must be altered if the goal of planting is aimed only at producing a world record fruit. Here, the target is to produce one single fruit which has the highest odds of achievement and the highest possible deviation from the mean. This is a very different factor than looking for something with high odds of producing a large fruit. Here, all that is considered are the seeds which produced the heaviest offspring. This can involve very complicated calculations in determining exactly which seed may provide the highest odds of producing a world record.

In selecting seeds based on greatest single weight of offspring, there is a pattern which is present that indicates startling difficulties.

In the years 1993, 1994, 1995, 1996, 1997, 1998, and 2000, the largest pumpkin in the world was grown from a new seed (a seed you would not have grown yourself because there was no record of large offspring).

New vs. Proven

The decision is always difficult when deciding what to plant. Many growers have seeds in their collection which are proven from past years to have grown very large fruit. Planting these proven seeds may appear to eliminate some of the guess work, and make the decision easier, but it may not be the best option. Planting a new seed is the best option for achieving the highest weight, but may not be as consistent or predictable. Planting a proven seed may allow for higher odds of a big fruit, but will not offer the highest odds of the biggest fruit. The simple reason for this is found in population genetics. A newer seed undergoing a greater amount of selection will have a higher probability of producing fruit at the largest size (greatest number of fruit produced which are two standard deviations from the mean). It may seem difficult to pick a new seed, but I recommend using the average weight potential estimate, and consistency ranking based upon the character of both parents of a new seed. Using this ranking will systematically help in determining which new seeds have the highest potential. For those with a few plants, it may be smart to plant one or two proven seeds to help increase the chances of having a respectable fruit, but also plant as many new prospect seeds to give higher odds of reaching that world record goal.

*ht: Dave Stelts
s-off his Ohio
number plate,
"POLN8R."*

AG Hybrid Vigor

"When it comes to seed selection for next spring, all growers want the "best" genetics. But what does that mean? And how do you go about deciding which seeds are the best? Often selections are made based on what a particular seed has produced in the past. Growers want "proven" seed – seeds that consistently produce big fruit. But, why do some seeds produce larger fruit than others? There has to be an explanation, and I propose one theory in the text that follows.

"Hybrid vigor occurs when two genetically different sources of DNA combine to form progeny that exhibit non-typical results. A horse and donkey cross produces a mule. It has the endurance of the horse, and strength of the donkey, but cannot reproduce. The same type of results are found in the plant world. Typical characteristics of hybrid vigor as it may apply to pumpkins include: consistent, marked increase in size of fruit and plant mass, increased growth rate, and lack of seeds, or sterile seeds.

"Looking back through the archives, there appear to be a few distinct groups of seeds that appear in most backgrounds. Some of these seed lines differ enough genetically that some degree of hybrid vigor may be expressed. As an example I will use the following seed line-seeds based on "Lloyd" genetics. I choose this line because the genetics behind the 935 Lloyd and 876.5 Lloyd are very pure, having a high degree of inbreeding within its lineage. When the 935 or 876.5 are crossed with another seed having no Lloyd genetics in its background, the resulting seeds typically produce above average vigorous pumpkins. The 723 & 845 Bobier, 846 Calai, and 712 Kuhn are good examples of what I have termed a "vigor cross". Many of the 1000+ lb pumpkins grown to date are the result of a vigor cross.

"Lets take the 845 Bobier as an example. This fruit was grown on the 935 Lloyd plant, and was pollinated by the 865 Mettler. The 865 Mettler is a cross between the 946 Geerts and 567 Mombert. The 935 is unique, in that both its parents came from the same self pollinated pumpkin. This cuts a possible 8 genetically different grandparents down to 2, producing very "pure" genetics. The genetic backgrounds of the 865 & 935 differ significantly, thus setting the stage for a hybrid vigor cross.

"In an attempt to validate the presence of hybrid vigor in AG's, a large amount of data was gathered and analyzed from the AGGC website. I calculated the average weight of fruit whose matriarchal grandma or grandpa was the 935 Lloyd or 876.5 Lloyd, and the opposite grandparent was neither of these fruits. This is the basic "vigor cross," in which one grandparent is the 935 or 876.5, and the other grandparent is any other seed that does not have Lloyd genetics in its background. After doing the math, I found 362 fruit resulting from a "vigor cross", with an average weight of 721.5 lbs. I then took the average weight of all non-vigor cross fruit registered at the AGGC between 1999 and the present. (I chose 1999 because that was the first year a "vigor cross" seed was planted.) This average was calculated at 634.9 lbs. Dividing this number by 721.5 gave a difference of 12.0%. The most basic interpretation of this data is simple, "vigor crosses" yield fruit that are an average of 12% heavier than other seeds.

"Initially, this sounds great. Who wouldn't plant a seed that offered an extra 12%? But unfortunately, we cannot conclusively interpret the data in this manner. There are a number of factors that can affect the interpretation of the data. The reason the "vigor cross" average is so high is that it contains fruit from seeds such as the 723, 845 and 846, which have performed very well recently. Have they performed well because it's in their genetics, or because they receive favor from the growers who plant them because of seed reputation? If an unknown seed grows a 1000 pound pumpkin, growers will jump on the bandwagon and grow the heck out of it the next year, often giving it favored attention in relation to other lesser-known seeds in their patches. This action may boost the average weight of fruit this seed produces regardless of its genetics. Typically, the more experienced heavy hitters will plant the seeds with the best reputation (which happens to be vigor crosses). These seeds will normally do better in an experienced grower's patch than in the patch of a less experienced grower, planting lesser-known quality seeds. Situations like these can skew the data, and making it difficult to solidify hybrid vigor. However, similar analysis for other proven seeds, such as the 801 Stelts and 567 Mombert were performed in an effort to disprove any possible grower influence on the outcome. In each case, none of the selected proven seeds came close to the average shown by the "vigor crosses". This suggests that increased weights may be due to something special in the seeds, and not just gardener favoritism.

Right: George and Deanna LLoyd with the legendary 1997, Lloyd 935.

"I believe that the genetics in the Lloyd fruit (935 and 876.5) differ enough from others to produce some degree of hybrid vigor. Keep this in mind though- hybrid vigor is not a day and night situation. There are varying degrees, and we as growers can manipulate the genetics of our seeds to maximize the degree of vigor introduced into a seed. The more "purified" a seed's background is, the better chance it has for exhibiting hybrid vigor.

"Of course I must say the evidence provided here is by no means conclusive. This is just another theory like many others out there.

However, I feel that this theory holds a significant amount of merit, which can be backed up scientifically. Here is a statement found in a chapter on squash breeding, from a book titled *Breeding Vegetable Crops*: '… investigators have found support for the idea that inbreeding in Cucurbita does not decrease vigor... absence of inbreeding depression does not signify that hybrid vigor in Cucurbita is lacking. A number of investigators have found significant evidence for hybrid vigor.' *Atlantic Giants* were not mentioned specifically in the book, the preceding text was in reference to all species of Cucurbita, which certainly includes the big pumpkins.

"Ever-improving grower knowledge and growing practices are likely the major cause of recent advances in giant fruit size. But, having an education in the field of biology exposed me to the importance of genetics in an organism. By adopting theories from both aspects of growing, i.e., environment and genetics, you will be well on your way to maximizing the potential of fruit in your garden."

by Joe Ailts

APOG

"The **A**wesome **P**ower **O**f **G**enetics must not be underestimated. There is no other plant on this planet which can produce fruit rivaling the size of an *Atlantic Giant*. With little attention, the fruit can grow to sizes up to 500 pounds, but with meticulous care are capable of reaching the current world record size of 1337.6 pounds. While the grower techniques used are the key to world class fruit, the ability to plant seed and expect such high weights is founded on genetics, and without the incredible genetic potential it would be impossible to achieve such tremendous weights. The genetic potential is present within the giant pumpkin and squash strains associated with *Atlantic Giant* to continue reaching the most impressive fruit weights of any species on our planet."

Pruning Strategies

Nothing has changed more dramatically over the last 10 years than the idea that you must have a large plant to grow a world class giant pumpkin. In my first book, I referred to growers who stressed leaf counts of a 1000 or more in determining the ideal sized plants, and wrote of spacing between plants of 35 feet or more.

In my second book, I introduced the term "primary vine," and a multiple fruit strategy on individual plants. In other publications, I even coined some names for these pruning strategies, like the "wishbone" (a two-fruit strategy), and the "cross" (a four-fruit strategy). How things have changed!

If you have been seriously following the trends in growing giant pumpkins over the last four years, you have heard the, then occasional and now more prevalent, stories of 1000 pound pumpkins being grown on plants that covered less than 400 square feet of ground. The success of these smaller plants has ushered in a whole new cast of characters in the sport who excluded themselves 4-5 years ago because of a lack of garden area, but now grow with a vengeance on a fraction of the space previously recommended. These growers awakened us all to the possibilities that, perhaps, large plants were not necessary, and even more startlingly, perhaps they were a detriment.

Many of the more progressive, veteran growers, who previously grew plants ranging in size from 1000-2500 square feet, now started to experiment with the idea of aggressively pruning to reduce plant size. Certainly, their success did not decline because of the smaller plants, and the bonus was that now they had the opportunity to grow even more plants in the same area that they had previously planted. Where once they grew one plant, now they grew two or three, increasing the probability of planting a "magical" seed.

It is not difficult to see where I am going with the introduction to this chapter. If you are still growing huge plants in hope of growing multiple world class giant pumpkins on a single plant, or you cannot bear the thought of growing more plants than you presently do each year because of the work entailed in taking proper care of them, consider the following carefully.

Left: Joe Pukos patch shows: christmas trees, heated and gravity fed water, and drip irrigation.

Visiting Christmas Past

Although the Christmas Tree method of pruning plants is not new, it has never been explained in any of my books up to now, and the variation described here is modified slightly to show the present day use of this method. Simply, if you took an aerial photograph of your plant at the end of the season, it would be shaped like a Christmas tree with the largest side branches of the tree branching from the oldest part of the plant. The first side vines off the main root would be the longest, and the side vines furthest from the main root would be the shortest, and all side vines would be perpendicular to the main vine.

I first heard the expression, "Christmas Tree" from Norm Craven of Stouffville, Ontario, Canada, back in 1993, who mentioned it to me in passing after he grew an 836 pound pumpkin of considerable renown back then – although I cannot attribute the creation of this expression to him with any certainty. It sounded pretty basic, but it still employed the idea of producing as big a plant as possible. Although third stage growth was immediately removed, second stage growth was allowed to grow indefinitely, making side vines as long as 30' or more, and pushing plant size well over 2000 square feet.

The Christmas Tree

Main Vine

Primary Vine

= Secondary Vines

t: The christmas ...uning method is ...ectly executed by ...Gibson of Ohio. ...p: One of Craig ...ir's early season ...ants pruned as a christmas tree.

The new Christmas Tree method took the same pruning strategy, but reduced the length of the secondary vines. Many chose to deadhead all secondaries when they reached 10'-12'. Some, like Geneva Emmons (grower of the 2001 World Record - 1262 pound pumpkin) also removed every other secondary (side) vine. As this method has slowly evolved from Norm Craven to present, almost every improvement in it has come from reducing the amount and area of the plant. This method has evolved from a large plant strategy to a small plant strategy!

Observations of the *Atlantic Giant* pumpkin growing tendencies has revealed that when the pumpkin is growing the fastest, the main vine ahead of the fruit grows the slowest, or altogether stops. There has always been a debate over whether a pumpkin receives the most contribution from the plant behind it or ahead of it. If you polled those growers that use the Christmas Tree method, they would most likely tell you that the fruit gets all of its growth from behind it, and none from the slowly growing portion of the plant ahead of it. Some even believe that deadheading the main vine is necessary to achieve the maximum potential of the pumpkin, and they choose an arbitrary number of feet past the pumpkin for stopping all vegetative growth in the plant.

The growers from the Ohio Valley Giant Pumpkin Growers Association coined the expression, "food factory," for the area of vegetative growth behind the pumpkin. They believe that it is essential to build this factory early, and push it into fruit production as soon as possible.

What is certain with the new Christmas Tree pruning method is, you decide how big you want your plants to be, when to stop all vegetative growth, and when the time is right to switch gears to all fruit growth. This method really puts the grower in charge, as opposed to the natural aggressive tendencies of the *Atlantic Giant* plant.

Growers experiencing the most success have limited the width of their plants to 20' -24' (making side vines on either side of the main only 10'-12' long). Some are pushing the envelope even further, reducing the plant's size to what seems ridiculously small. The final answer to the question of, "What is the best plant size," has not yet been given. I can say with a measure of confidence that it is definitely under 1000 square feet, and probably lies somewhere between 300-500 square feet – holy crap!

Two pruning methods have been embraced by the majority of experienced growers — the christmas tree and the wishbone. None of those growing giants successfully and consistently can say that they just let their plants go unattended and unpruned. All growers use one of these methods or a modified version of them.

Before we begin any discussion of pruning methods however, let us first try to understand the vocabulary of the giant pumpkin grower. The definitions of main and secondary vines used to be fairly straight forward until I introduced the terminology "primary vine." This became a source of confusion for some growers, but when the definition of this term is grasped, a better understanding of pruning methods can be obtained. The necessity to add this term became evident when growers began to grow multiple world class giant pumpkins on a single plant. As growing methods have evolved over the last eight years, many came to believe that it is foolhardy to grow just one pumpkin on a plant, while others vehemently held that if you want a world record you have to take a chance, and the chance you take is growing one fruit on the main vine. I consider a single vine as a single and distinct plant. This view has translated into a whole new way of looking at fruit sets. A single strong vine can have a single fruit regardless of the number of other vines and other fruit contained on the plant. The number of pumpkins grown to maturity on a single plant can be increased to two, or even three, if there are the same number of strong vines coming directly off of the main vine within 18"-24" of the main root, and these are called the primary vines. These are the strongest vines on the whole plant. With the main, these 3-4 vines are designated the primaries, and each could support a pumpkin.

The Christmas Tree in Detail

Growing one, long main vine was the forerunner of a method that has become known as the Christmas Tree. Only the main vine is left unpruned. Secondaries off the main are allowed to grow at right angles to the main and are dead headed when they reach the edge of your patch or a prearranged distance. In this method, there are no "back door" vines, so the plant is started at the furthest end of your garden, and growth is trained in a straight line across the widest area of your patch, or two plants are started in the middle of your patch and each is trained in opposite directions to one another. Several fruit are set along the main vine with all but the best performer culled by August 1st. One vine, one fruit, and absolutely no growth off the secondary vines (third stage growth).

Every Other Vine

This is a modified version of the Christmas Tree where every other secondary vine is pruned immediately after appearing at the leaf axil. This action spaces vines and leaves out, thus helping with ventilation and disease control. I've used this method and have observed that leaves become larger, allowing for a good leaf canopy over the soil, and easier access to the main vine between secondaries. In our attempts to reduce plant size and vegetative growth, this method holds much promise.

*es 152 and 153,
Tom Beachy and
patch at various
during the season.*

*ght. A schematic
e actual patch of
Drew Papez of
ntario, Canada.
Two plants share
out 750 sq. ft. of
garden space.*

The Flag

The Flag is a modification of the Every-Other-Vine method. In removing every other side vine, we are in fact reducing vegetative growth by half. The Flag method takes this fact one step further. All secondaries are pinched from the plant on one side or another of the main vine, creating half a plant, or half a christmas tree.

Below: Two plants are "double planted," then trained in opposite directions to one another. Many growers are now planting two plants where they once planted only one — doubling their chances of growing a "magical seed," and reducing vegetative growth in favor of faster growing pumpkins and a more manageable patch.

The Wishbone

The Wishbone is a modification of the Christmas Tree method. Under this method, you can double the number of fruits you grow, and still get the benefits of increased vigor that comes from streamlining a plant by pruning. It's simple. The main and only one other primary are allowed to grow. The main and first strong primary are trained about 60 degrees apart. This "V" resembles a wishbone, hence the name. All other pruning is the same as described with the christmas tree method.

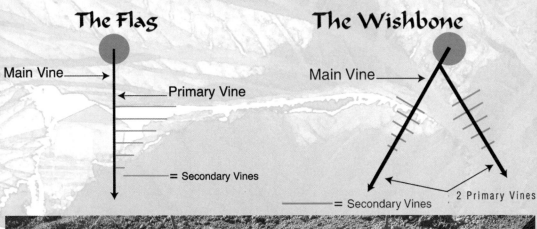

The 400 Square Foot Patch

Plant size is gradually moving towards smaller square footage, and I Believe that the perfectly sized plant – one that takes advantage of the "food factory" – may be as small as 400 square feet. This area allows for 10' side vines and the opportunity to pollinate several pumpkins on the main vine before the time remaining in the season limits their growth potential. A 20' main vine gives you the chance to set 3 or 4 pumpkins before the plant shifts gears into fruit growth – when vine growth beyond the set pumpkins is dramatically curtailed.

And, the principle of deadheading all side vines, and in many cases, deadheading the main vine after the fruit is set and aggressively growing, works well with a plan to limit plant size to just 400 square feet. Most world class giant pumpkins are set at a distance of 8'-15' out, so a garden that reserves space for a 20' main vine is not limiting the growth potential of an AG plant or its fruit. In most cases, a fruit set within this average range of 8'-15' out will have slowed vine growth that will be easily contained within 20'. Some growers even advocate deadheading the main vine 8'-10' after the pumpkin. I have observed many instances of pumpkins growing at world class pace, where the main vine never reaches an additional 8'-10' beyond the pumpkin. The fruit's aggressive weight gains all but stop main vine growth, and the plant is nicely contained within a 400 square foot area.

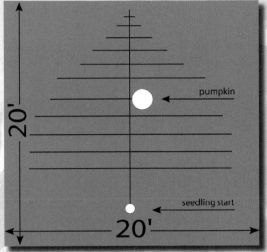

Trouble Shooting

Most of the fruit problems that you will encounter will be concentrated around the stem, blossom end, or a "Dill ring" if present.

Stem stress resulting from the rapid growth of the fruit or poor positioning on the vine can be contained by cutting tap roots at each leaf axil on either side of the pumpkin. How many you cut will be determined by how much the vine must be elevated to relieve stem stress. In some instances, the vine will have to be supported or lightly pulled away from the shoulders of the fruit, or slightly moved even after reaching 400 pounds or more. Rotating a bulging shoulder away from the vine can be done safely with one person rotating the pumpkin and another supporting the vine and stem.

Some growers successfully reduce stem stress by ramping the fruit, keeping the blossom end of the pumpkin higher than the stem end. This can be done with soil when the fruit is very young, or with a wooden ramp placed under

the fruit before it reaches 200 pounds. By pitching the fruit back towards the stem and vine, much of the stress associated with a rising vine is eliminated.

Having a stem that stays too low can also present problems. Some fruit will have a tendency to do this resulting in the blossom end moving to an upward facing position. They are commonly called "birdbaths" because of the water that collects in the concaved fruit. There is not much you can do to avoid this from happening, but you should still take precautions in relieving stem stress. Carefully

Top: Stem has p
from the vine be
anchor roots we
pruned.

Left: Ramping
back towards th
can also reduce

Far left and abo
some methods
elevating the vi
reduce stem str

excavating soil from under the stem and vine can help to relieve the increasing weight of the pumpkin from totally pinning the vine.

With better control of stem stress, and the planting of seed stocks with less likelihood of stem splits, many stem stress related problems have been avoided in recent years. The same cannot be said for "Dill Rings." Most of the catastrophic failures of giant pumpkins today come from cracks that develop at the intersection of a rib and a slightly indented ring that runs at right angles to the rib. The deeper the rib or ring, the stronger the likelihood of a split that exposes the cavity of the fruit to air. The use of calcium, either sprayed on the fruit every 4-5 days, or soaked in a towel that is draped over the rib-ring area shows some promise in avoiding some Dill ring failures. More than likely, Dill rings will become less encountered only after growers insist on not planting seed stocks that have an inclination to produce them.

Ribbon Vines

Ribbon vines, or flat vines, have become very prevalent the last 5 years, and may be the consequence of inbreeding aggressive plant behaviors. In a normally growing vine, there will be a set of plant parts at each leaf axil consisting of: one leaf, one male flower, one tendril, and sometimes one female flower. This is not so with ribbon vines. They may have 2, 3, or more sets of plant parts which all but totally disrupts pruning strategies and fruit positioning. I have had many over the years, and have had only minimal success at eliminating them. Some growers will try to battle a 2 or 3 ribbon vine by carefully cutting away all but one of the vines at the end of the main. Others will cut the ribbon vine off at a side vine that does not show ribbon tendencies. In many cases though, this side vine will eventually develop into a ribbon vine. If the plant is from an outstanding seed stock, the extra work is worth the effort to a point. If fruit are not set on normal vines before July 25th, you might do what most growers do at the first discovery of a ribbon vine – pull the plant out!

Right:
An extreme
example of a
ribbon vine.

Patching

You'll spend some time mending and patching your pumpkin as it grows. Stem splits, blossom end splits, damage from animals, or just your own carelessness will all require some attention.

I use a fungicide like *Captan* or *Benlate* mixed with a few drops of water to make a paste that is the consistency of thick paint. Using a soft artist brush, paint over the areas that are cracked and weeping, or anywhere where damage has occurred. Let dry and keep dry for several days until the wound is fully healed. Some growers have even used the pumpkin's own secretions to fill cracks, and claim that it miraculously heals. Try it yourself and see if it works. Poke a few pin pricks in the stem end of an expendable pumpkin. It should begin weeping within minutes. Collect the material and fill the cracks in your prized specimens, covering any large crack with a layer of insulating foam.

Late Season Precautions

Protecting your pumpkin during the month of September can reduce your chances of experiencing some kind of failure as a result of splits, cracks or rotting. Most experienced growers assume the worst will happen and take measures to reduce their chance of incidence.

Disinfect your pumpkin's skin routinely (once a week) with a solution of bleach and water (1 part bleach to 10 parts water). Spray with a plastic hand sprayer and lightly wipe the skin with a soft towel. Inspect the pumpkin for splits and cracks in the skin and stem. Paint either Captan or Benomyl into the cracks with a 1" soft bristled paint brush. The fungicide should be mixed with just enough water to produce a thick paste.

Left: Ray Bare applies a fungi paste on a blos end split.

On forecasted cold nights, cover your pumpkin with a thick blanket, and then cover this with a waterproof tarp. Your shade structure should be removed to get the maximum benefit from the sun during the day. The key is to keep your pumpkin dry at all times, and to try to hold some of the daytime heat and moderate the temperature changes that swing drastically from day to night in the fall.

There are also some last minute procedures you can perform to really make your giant pumpkin look its very best on weigh off day. I have used all of these and have never experienced any detrimental effects to the pumpkin. Most of these procedures revolve around cleaning, disinfecting and increasing the luster of the pumpkin's skin.

Cleaning

With a mild dish detergent, mix a pail of soapy water. Also make sure that you have a small, soft bristled brush, a tooth brush, a sponge, and some old towels for drying and buffing. Thoroughly wash your pumpkin with the soapy water, using the brush to dislodge dirt or fungicide you have used to coat the skin and stem. It is important that all this fungicide be removed because it is a mandatory requirement at most weigh offs, and it's just common sense when dealing with public exhibitions where people, and especially kids, will be present. Use the tooth brush to get into small and difficult crevices in the ribs and around the stem.

Disinfecting

Rinse the soapy water off with clean water that is laced with bleach. One capful to a gallon of water is sufficient. This will disinfect the surface of the pumpkin, killing most of the pathogens or disease spores that may be present. If you use *ZeroTolerance* in your spray program, this can be substituted for the bleach.

*A fan is used to
y a crack in the
blossom end.*

*Don Langevin
disinfects his
kin with a light
y cleanup with
ZeroTolerance.*

159

Estimating Weight - Estimating Growth

Estimating the Weight of Giant Pumpkins

The last update of the weight estimating tables was done in January 2001, and was based on 1194 measurements made from 1989 - 2000. Data was compared for approximately 800 fruit grown in 2001 and 2002 with all data since 1989. Len Stellpflug, the creator of the original equations for these tables says, "On my graphs, it is obvious that pumpkins grown in recent years have been heavier for the same measurements, therefore the tables that appear here are primarily based on the 800 fruit grown in 2001 and 2002." Most of the data was provided from AGGC files submitted by Mike Nepereny. The tables provide estimates for fruit measuring as little as 31" circumference, and 91" over-the-top (which is approximately 21 pounds).

David Martin from Little Britain, Ontario, Canada used multiple regression analysis to obtain equations that best fit this data.

The *Circumference Method* uses only the circumference measurement. This method does not provide good estimates for unusually high, flat, long, or short fruit. Only about 50% of the estimates will be within +/-10%. This method is useful for estimating day-to-day increases, but I use the over-the-top method weekly to provide a better estimate. The circumference measurement should be the largest circumference possible; taken approximately parallel to the ground. See the illustration on the next page. The length of that measurement can be compared with Table 2 (C) on page 167 to determine weight in pounds.

The *Over-the-Top Method* provides the best estimates of weight, and about 80% of these estimates will be within +/- 10%. This method requires adding 3 measurements: the circumference (measured precisely as directed in the circumference method), side to side, and stem to blossom end; then finding the total inches on Table 1 (OTT) on page 166 to obtain the estimated weight. The over-the-top measurements, from ground-to-ground in both directions, should be over the highest point of the fruit. The tape must be allowed to hang straight down from the widest part of the pumpkin – see the illustration below. Allowing the tape to follow the contour of the fruit to the ground lengthens the measurement, and will overestimate weight.

Example

Circumference = 169"
Table 2 (C) estimate = 1069 pounds
Side-to-side = 106"
End-to-end (stem to blossom end) = 107"
Total = 382" (169 + 106 + 107)
Table 1 (OTT) estimate = 1139 pounds
The actual weight was 1092 pounds, or -4% under the OTT estimates, (1139-1092)÷1092. Growers would refer to this as being 4% light.

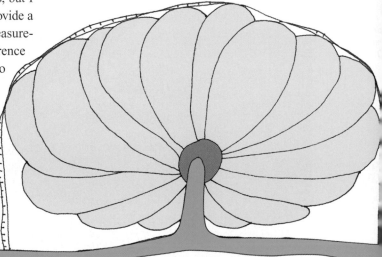

How close will either of these methods estimate actual weight? See the chart that follows.

Accuracy Range		
	Table 1 **OTT**	**Table 2** **C**
within 5%	49%	27%
within 10%	80%	51%
over 10%	20%	49%

In the OTT method, you will be within 5% of the actual weight 49% (almost half) of the time; while with the C method, you will only be within 5% of the actual weight 27% (about a quarter) of the time.

David Martin's equations can be obtained by email request at stellnix@aol.com.

*page: shows the
way to make an
the-top, side-to-
e measurement.*

*evin Smith with
2001 squash in
Elk Grove, CA.
stimating tables
rk with squash.*

*shows the tech-
e for measuring
umference and
e-top, stem-to-
ossom end; also
Welty and Len
the genetics of
ins that do not
m to the tables
OVGPG picnic.*

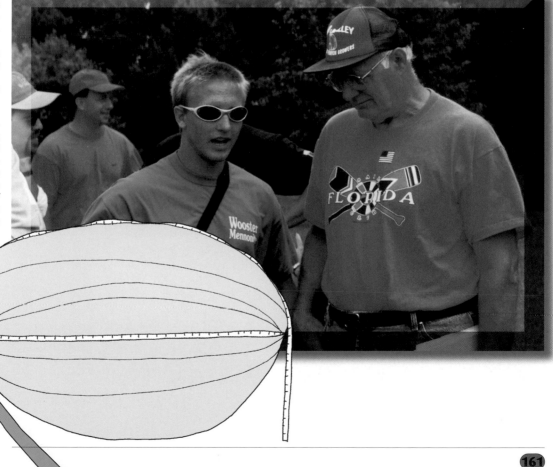

Estimating the Growth of Giant Pumpkins

This subject is not something I've written about before, and much of it is my own personal observations with no scientific methodology used. It is differentiated from weight estimating in that it tries to predict the weight of a pumpkin at the end of the season based on the rate of daily growth at a particular time during the season. It also helps to organize data collection in a more standard way so that your pumpkin's growth can be compared with that of other pumpkins you have grown, and also with pumpkins other growers have grown. This method is based on days from pollination, so all pumpkins are compared on an equal basis. Measurements are taken at 14 days and 30 days, and then at every 5-day interval. By doing this with every pumpkin, every year, you will develop data that will alert you to which pumpkins are growing the best, and make culling decisions easier. It will also allow you to compare the

growth of your pumpkin with other world class giant pumpkins in which data is available. In *World Class Giant Pumpkins II,* I referred to this as the *Tale of the Tape.*

How I get from a weight estimate now to estimating weight at the end of the season relies heavily on the following assumptions. Pumpkins do not grow at the same rate throughout the season. They start slowly, steadily accelerating, and then they peak and finally taper-off. This assumption is contrary to what I have written in the past in which I explained that the cycle of fruit growth lasts only about 60 days. For many pumpkins this is true, but for many others, this growth period can extend another 10-30 days – all dependent on the rate of current growth. The basic assumption made here is that a pumpkin does not begin at a certain rate and then suddenly stop growing. Its growth rate tapers-off rather than just stopping altogether. If it does stop altogether, it is symptomatic of a failure of the

Left: The India Giant Pumpki Growers take measurements confirm estime weight and to a for improving equations and estimate tables

fruit associated with environmental factors such as weather or disease. If a pumpkin suddenly stops growing, it is not because its time has come. It is because a problem exists that you must eventually determine if you are to improve your chances of growing a fruit that grows for the entire season. The *Atlantic Giant* pumpkin does not stop growing unless there is a problem, or it has fully matured. Those are the assumptions, now let's look at estimating weight at the end of the season based on the current rate of growth.

The 953

In this example, I will use my 2002, 953 to demonstrate this method. The following is a chart representing the estimated weights at five-day intervals after the initial estimate at 14 days from pollination. The measurement in inches at 14, 30, 40, and 50 days is a good comparison check for how fast a pumpkin is growing in relation to other pumpkins in your patch, pumpkins you have grown in previous years, or a significant pumpkin for which data is available.

Date of pollination (P): July 9, 2002

Days from P	Est. Wgt.	Δ	Avg. Daily
14	20		
30	326	306	19.1
35	466	140	28
40	607	141	28.2
45	709	102	20.4
50	802	93	18.6
55	866	64	12.8
60	907	41	8.2
65	937	30	6
70	956	19	3.8
75	972	16	3.2
80	988	16	3.2

From this table, you can see that the maximum, average, rate of growth per day, over an interval of 5 days, was 28.2 lbs.. Almost every serious grower I know insists that a pumpkin must

achieve daily gains of over 25 lbs. to have the potential to reach 1000 pounds. Many growers have reported daily gains of 30, 35, or 40 lbs. or more per day, albeit for short periods of 3 or more days. Growers agree that weight gains of over 25 lbs. must be sustained for 20 days or more to have a chance at breaking 1000 pounds. Having weight gains of 25 lbs. per day over just a 15 day period yields a net gain in weight of 375 lbs. (only a little over 1/3rd of the growth needed to reach 1000 lbs.). Something else must also occur to have a pumpkin top 1000 lbs., and that is a long cycle of growth.

Average daily weight gains rise, then fall, but a true world class giant pumpkin will rise to over 25 lbs. per day, and then fall at a much slower rate. It is not the nature of an AG to fall rapidly in daily gains. If it does, it is more an indicator of problems existing that interrupt the momentum of growth. Disease, weather, or feeding and watering practices can all lead to catastrophic failure of a fruit. An AG will decline slowly in average daily gains if it is healthy, and will continue to grow as long as health and the length of the season permit.

Tom Beachy of [Ind]iana holds up a [sign] showing OTT [mea]surements and [esti]mated weight of [100]6 pounds at 57 [days fr]om pollination [Sept]ember 9, 2002.

Left: Don Langev.
2002, 953.

Page 165 top: The
"Doing the Dew."

Page 165 bottom:
Alex Sandercock
grower-Dad, Ned,
document size on
July 21, 2002 of
eventual 797.

A good measurement at 14 days will not predict a pumpkin's rate of growth, but it does help to determine which pumpkin you keep on a plant that has multiple fruit sets. The 30-day measurement is far more reliable in predicting end of season weight (provided you keep the pumpkin in good health, and avoid the myriad of variables that can effect health, and subsequently growth). If you multiply the average daily weight gain from 14 to 30 days by 50, you will be close to your end of season weight (in this example: 50 x 19.1 = 955).

Peaking

Somewhere between 30 and 50 days, a healthy AG will reach its maximum rate of growth for the season. This is where daily gains must exceed 25 lbs. – and the longer it is sustained, the better. Exceeding 25 lbs. does not guarantee that a pumpkin will make it to 1000 lbs., as is demonstrated in this example in which 28 lbs. per day over 10 days did not lead to 1000 lbs.. A period of peak growth must exceed 2 weeks (15-20 days) for anyone to become excited about a pumpkin's potential. At 40 days, if the rate of growth exceeds 25 lbs., multiply the rate of growth by 33 to get an estimate of end of season weight.

The Taper

Somewhere between 40 and 60 days, a healthy AG will begin to decline in average daily gains, setting the stage for a long gradual decline. After the peak growth rate has ended, approximately 1/3rd of the average daily gain will be lost over every 5 day interval (or, about 50% over every 10 days). If you determine at a 5-day measurement that your pumpkin has declined in average daily gains, multiply the average daily gain by .50 to determine an estimate of daily gain over the next 10 days, and add ten-times that amount to your estimated weight to predict the weight at the next 10-day measurement. To estimate 10 days further, add 50% of the added weight to predict the next 20-day measurement. The formula looks like this:

Estimated weight + [(10 x daily gain) x .50] = next 10 day estimate.

20 days out would look like this:

Estimated weight + [.50 (10 x daily gain)] + .50[.50 (10 x daily gain)]

or Estimated weight + 7.5 x daily gain

If a pumpkin is estimated at 800 lbs. at 50 days, and is averaging 20 lbs. per day over the last 5 days (and that is a decline from its peak growth), then its estimated weight at 70 days would be: 800 + [.50 (10 x 20 lbs.)] + .50[.50 (10 x 20 lbs.)] = 950

800 + [100] + [50] = 950

The following table is presented for use in predicting end of season weights for healthy AG's.

From P	Est. Wgt.		Avg. Daily	Prediction
14				
30			AD x 50	
40			AD x 33	
50	EW	+	AD x 7.5	
60	EW	+	AD x 7.5	

How would the 953 fare under these rules?

From P	Est. Wgt.	Δ	Avg. Daily	Prediction
14	20			
30	326	306	19.1 x 50	955.0
35	466	140	28	
40	607	141	28.2 x 33	930.6
45	709	102	20.4	
50	802	+	18.6 x 7.5	941.5
55	866	64	12.8	
60	907	+	8.2 x 7.5	968.5

How would your pumpkin fare?

Table 1: Over-the-Top Inches vs. Estimated Weight

"	lbs.	"	lbs.	"	lbs.	"	lbs.	"	lbs.	"	lbs.	"	lbs.	"	lbs.	"	lbs.	"	lbs.	"	lbs.
91	21.3	121	44	151	80	181	131	211	201	241	293	271	412	301	561	331	743	361	962	391	1221
92	21.9	122	45	152	81	182	133	212	203	242	297	272	417	302	566	332	750	362	970	392	1230
93	22.5	123	46	153	83	183	135	213	206	243	300	273	421	303	572	333	756	363	978	393	1240
94	23.2	124	47	154	84	184	137	214	209	244	304	274	426	304	578	334	763	364	986	394	1249
95	23.8	125	48	155	86	185	139	215	212	245	308	275	430	305	583	335	770	365	994	395	1259
96	24.5	126	49	156	87	186	141	216	214	246	311	276	435	306	589	336	777	366	1002	396	1268
97	25.1	127	50	157	89	187	143	217	217	247	315	277	440	307	595	337	784	367	1010	397	1278
98	25.8	128	51	158	90	188	145	218	220	248	319	278	444	308	600	338	791	368	1019	398	1288
99	26.5	129	53	159	92	189	147	219	223	249	322	279	449	309	606	339	798	369	1027	399	1297
100	27.2	130	54	160	93	190	149	220	226	250	326	280	454	310	612	340	805	370	1035	400	1307
101	27.9	131	55	161	95	191	152	221	229	251	330	281	458	311	618	341	812	371	1044	401	1317
102	28.6	132	56	162	96	192	154	222	232	252	334	282	463	312	624	342	819	372	1052	402	1327
103	29.3	133	57	163	98	193	156	223	235	253	338	283	468	313	630	343	826	373	1060	403	1337
104	30.1	134	58	164	100	194	158	224	238	254	341	284	473	314	636	344	833	374	1069	404	1347
105	30.8	135	59	165	101	195	161	225	241	255	345	285	478	315	642	345	840	375	1078	405	1357
106	31.6	136	60	166	103	196	163	226	244	256	349	286	483	316	648	346	848	376	1086	406	1367
107	32.4	137	62	167	105	197	165	227	247	257	353	287	488	317	654	347	855	377	1095	407	1377
108	33.1	138	63	168	106	198	168	228	250	258	357	288	493	318	660	348	862	378	1104	408	1387
109	33.9	139	64	169	108	199	170	229	253	259	361	289	498	319	666	349	870	379	1112	409	1397
110	34.7	140	65	170	110	200	172	230	256	260	365	290	503	320	672	350	877	380	1121	410	1408
111	35.6	141	66	171	112	201	175	231	260	261	369	291	508	321	678	351	885	381	1130	411	1418
112	36.4	142	68	172	113	202	177	232	263	262	374	292	513	322	685	352	892	382	1139	412	1428
113	37.2	143	69	173	115	203	180	233	266	263	378	293	518	323	691	353	900	383	1148	413	1439
114	38.1	144	70	174	117	204	182	234	269	264	382	294	523	324	697	354	907	384	1157	414	1449
115	39.0	145	72	175	119	205	185	235	273	265	386	295	529	325	704	355	915	385	1166	415	1460
116	39.9	146	73	176	121	206	187	236	276	266	390	296	534	326	710	356	923	386	1175	416	1470
117	40.8	147	74	177	123	207	190	237	280	267	395	297	539	327	717	357	930	387	1184	417	1481
118	41.7	148	76	178	125	208	193	238	283	268	399	298	545	328	723	358	938	388	1193	418	1492
119	42.6	149	77	179	127	209	195	239	286	269	403	299	550	329	730	359	946	389	1202	419	1502
120	43.5	150	78	180	129	210	198	240	290	270	408	300	556	330	736	360	954	390	1212	420	1513

Table 2: Circumference vs. Estimated Weight

"	lbs.	"	lbs.	"	lbs.	"	lbs.	"	lbs.	"	lbs.	"	lbs.	"	lbs.
31	12.5	51	48.0	71	112	91	210	111	345	131	537	151	770	171	1111
32	13.7	52	50.5	72	116	92	215	112	353	132	548	152	784	172	1133
33	14.9	53	53.0	73	120	93	221	113	360	133	558	153	798	173	1155
34	16.2	54	55.7	74	125	94	227	114	368	134	569	154	812	174	1177
35	17.6	55	58.4	75	129	95	233	115	377	135	580	155	827	175	1201
36	19.0	56	61.2	76	133	96	240	116	385	136	591	156	841	176	1224
37	20.4	57	64.0	77	138	97	246	117	393	137	602	157	857	177	1249
38	22.0	58	67.0	78	142	98	252	118	402	138	613	158	872	178	1274
39	23.6	59	70.0	79	147	99	259	119	410	139	624	159	888	179	1299
40	25.2	60	73.1	80	152	100	265	120	420	140	635	160	904	180	1325
41	27.0	61	76.2	81	156	101	272	121	431	141	646	161	921	181	1352
42	28.8	62	79.5	82	161	102	279	122	442	142	658	162	938	182	1380
43	30.6	63	82.8	83	166	103	286	123	452	143	669	163	955	183	1408
44	32.5	64	86.2	84	171	104	293	124	463	144	681	164	973	184	1436
45	34.5	65	89.7	85	177	105	300	125	474	145	693	165	992	185	1466
46	36.6	66	93.2	86	182	106	307	126	484	146	706	166	1010	186	1496
47	38.7	67	96.8	87	187	107	314	127	495	147	718	167	1029	187	1527
48	41.0	68	100.6	88	193	108	322	128	506	148	731	168	1049	188	1558
49	43.2	69	104.4	89	198	109	329	129	516	149	744	169	1069	189	1590
50	45.6	70	108.2	90	204	110	337	130	527	150	757	170	1090	190	1623

Right: Kim Thomas and Chuck Ibey demonstrate the proper way to measure a giant pumpkin.

08/05/99
507 LBS

*Andrew Papez, son of Drew Papez,
documents estimated weight for Dad
on August 5, 1999 at 507 pounds.*

Loading & Safety

All pumpkins are not loaded the same, but some basic steps are common to all. First of all, a carrying device must be placed under the pumpkin. This is accomplished by rolling the fruit, side-to-side to a position of balance, while someone places the carrier under the pumpkin. Then, the fruit is lowered back to the ground, and is rolled side-to-side in the opposite direction. The carrier is then pulled through to the other side, and the pumpkin is adjusted so that it sits in the center of the carrier.

A carrier with hand-holes like the one to the right is preferred, to prevent slippage while lifting, and to avoid injuring hands. The carrier should be large enough to accommodate the pumpkin with at least 18" of free space all the way around. This insures that lifters will not have to bend over to the ground to get a hand hold. Where possible, lift to your truck with a machine or winch. Any pumpkin over 500 pounds is a difficult move without mechanical assistance, but any pumpkin, regardless of weight can be moved by hand if you follow this simple rule. Have at least one person for each estimated 100 pounds of weight, and additional lifters, if possible, to facilitate the lift. If you have a pumpkin that is estimated at 1000 pounds, you will need 10 lifters to get it from the ground onto a pallet for lifting to the truck. Fewer than 10 people risks injury to the lifters or damage to the pumpkin.

Once the pumpkin is in your truck, much care should be given to its placement. Many pumpkins over 800 pounds will have side-to-side or stem-to-blossom widths of more than 4'. This means that your pumpkin may have to be turned to one side or another just to fit it in the bed of your truck. Also, some trucks have wheel wells that reduce the width even more, and sometimes an additional pallet or two under the pumpkin is necessary to raise it above the wheel wells.

Adjust your pumpkin so there is as little movement as possible. If you can rock your pumpkin in any direction, additional padding should be wedged under the fruit to retard movement. A bale of straw placed between the front of the bed and the pumpkin, and the tailgate and the pumpkin is strongly advised.

All of us at one time or another have had to readjust the position of a pumpkin so it would not be injured by a wheel well, tailgate, or the front of the bed. Turning corners at high speeds or sudden stops can negate all the precautions we take in protecting our giants from injury.

Take this story as a warning against the perils of traveling with your prized specimen in tow.

Dave Rushia was returning to work from his lunch hour at the Norton Post Office. It is just a 4 mile journey, but no one, including myself, could ever have foreseen what was about to happen. Dave will be the first to admit that he was not particularly attentive this day. After all, he had travelled this same route, back and forth, for over thirty years. A sharp curve in the road concealed a line of traffic poised at a dead stop. When he finally saw it, it was too late. He applied the brakes and rear-ended the last car in the line of traffic.

The front bumper was completely turned under, but that was the least of what turned out to be enormous damage. His 342-pound pumpkin was hurled at 40 mph into the rear of his cab. You wouldn't think much about this until you saw what it did. It split the truck bed, severing the rolled top of the bed about 3". The

front of the bed was bellied forward 6" (similar to the image in the lower portion of page 170). The sliding windows on the rear of the cab could not be moved, the cab was literally pushed in 3-4". It looked as if a 4' wrecking ball had crushed the cab.

Remember, this was not a world class giant pumpkin. If a pumpkin weighing 700-800 pounds had been catapulted into the rear of the cab, injury to the driver would have been sustained. May this be a warning to all growers, if you still insist on carting your best pumpkin around for show — beware of the loose canon rolling in the bed of your pickup.

...ft and right shows ...he many ways that ...iant pumpkins are ...fted so they can be ...en to weigh offs — ...ually, by winch, or by machinery.

World Wide Web

Nothing propels you up the learning curve faster than a community of like-minded individuals sharing what they know. And in this day and age, the internet provides almost every individual the opportunity to communicate with like-minded people. I have always maintained that the introduction of the *Atlantic Giant* pumpkin variety was the modern beginning of this sport. My books helped accelerate learning and introduce the subject of giant pumpkins to a wider, like-minded audience, but then, the internet took all of that and put rocket boosters on it.

In 1993 when I wrote my first book on giant pumpkins, the worldwide web (www) was something only academic scientists and computer junkies knew anything about. Ten years later, and www has become one of the most important parts of almost every home in America, challenging television for the discretionary leisure time of the family.

Remember that nonsense about the paperless society? The personal computer is the biggest boom for the paper companies since the invention of the printing press. Fifteen years ago, who could have imagined that in a single year, with a computer hooked up to the www, we'd all consume more paper than we'd used in all our previous years on earth. And, what about that nonsense of becoming illiterate because of all that entertainment available on the www, and the need never to write another letter to a friend or business associate? I know that my kids became better writers and spellers because of incessant email and messaging with their friends, and also became adept at carving out 60 words per minute on their keyboards (something I always considered to be a fundamental communication asset which eluded my every attempt at mastering). And, has anyone bought a set of *Encyclopedia Britannicas* lately, that wasn't artfully wrapped in a CD envelope? No paper went into the production of those books, but thousands of pages made their way to little laser printers that ate letter sized sheets reams at a time.

The worldwide web made information, we didn't even dream existed, available to anyone capable of launching their internet browser software. It was easy to find, easy to copy, and easy to print. So, the young and the restless (otherwise known as the serious giant pumpkin growers), embarked on an information gathering marathon that not only put them in the midst of their own kind, but stimulated the participants to such an extent as to push them years ahead of those not willing to risk their complacency in the unfamiliar territory of a PC.

Out of all of this comes the obvious, yet still somewhat startling observation, that if a large number of people seek the same information, then others, for reasons that cover the gamut from economics to sociology, will provide that information. As a result of the demand for information on giant pumpkins, the internet has spawned a river full of websites, all poised to hatch out at a moment's notice on the computer that finds their location. Amongst the many, a few of them must be called significant places of travel. Going even further in endorsing them, some hold the very keys to your success at growing giant pumpkins. Beyond the seed variety and my books lies the knowledge that will put you a cut above the rest – and that knowledge is on the web somewhere. Here are my best-place-picks, and mandatory travel itinerary on the worldwide web. There are many more great websites including:
www.backyardgardener.com/wcgp/index.html
http://web.raex.com/~ldnwelty/,
www.pumpkinnook.com/giants.htm,
http://V.webring.com/hub?ring=giantpumpring, but starting with those featured on these pages will help you find the rest.

AGGC – www.atlanticgiantgenetics.com
by Mike Nepereny

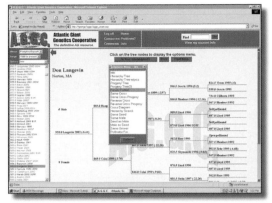

"The original idea for the AGGC was simple: create an application that would allow the user to input pumpkin information and render hierarchy trees on demand. Information on each pumpkin would be stored in separate database records, and the trees would be generated dynamically. Simple enough.

In the software business, we use the term, "scope creep," to describe a project whose definition and functionality just seems to grow exponentially with each passing day of development. Projects that succumb to scope creep generally evolve into something that only vaguely resembles the original concept. Along the way, they're subjected to numerous upgrades, updates, and enhancements all in the name of creating a better product.

"Such was the case with my little pumpkin application. Before long, it had facilities for tracking pumpkin, grower, and weigh-off site information. It rendered hierarchy trees, progeny trees, and cross pollination diagrams. It reported weigh-off results and averages, 'rated' pumpkins by performance, supported photos, and even had its own query builder. I dubbed the product *CucurByte* and a new era was born.

"I began to distribute the program to other people. At one point, several of us were taking turns entering data. When each was finished, we would email the database on to the next person. It was definitely not the most stream-lined of processes, but it worked and the database began to grow.

"*Cucurbyte/web* was my first attempt at creating an online web site dedicated to *Atlantic Giant* genetics. It consisted of static web pages depicting hierarchy trees, progeny trees, photos, and more. Many of the images on the web site were basically screen prints from the *CucurByte* program. The site quickly gained a loyal following and a whole new generation of folks interested in giant pumpkin genetics was born. The web site took an incredible amount of work to maintain however, and it was clear that a better solution was needed. As the database grew, there seemed be no way I could keep the web site updated. Also, I needed more widespread access to the information coming out of the weigh-off sites.

"The *Atlantic Giant* Genetics Cooperative became the solution both organizationally and technically. I set about creating a web site whose content would be driven dynamically by the contents of the CucurByte database. It would, in effect, become a web-based, read only version of the original CucurByte program. I envisioned an organization, working in cooperation with existing pumpkin groups and weigh-off sites, obtaining and sharing pumpkin and grower information. I gathered a geographically diverse group of growers and asked for their help and support in gathering weigh-off statistics. In the end, Quebec grower, Rock Rivard would be the most helpful and enthusiastic and was designated database coordinator. I appointed myself as director and developer of the web site and the organization. On January 1st, 2000, the AGGC web site went online and the *Atlantic Giant* Genetics Cooperative was born. On November 1, 2001, the site became a members-only resource with membership given to those helping support the site both in fees and content.

"Today, the website boasts information on over 3600 pumpkins and squash, 800 growers, and 100 weigh-off sites. It has become the definitive source for information on the *Atlantic Giant* pumpkin and the people who grow them.

"The *Atlantic Giant Genetics Cooperative* serves the needs of a select group of growers, people who demand the most detailed and accurate information available. Some have even credited the AGGC with the dramatic increase in pumpkin weights over the last couple years."

I can attest to Mike's final statement. There is just no way that a new grower can have the kind of success we have seen in very recent years without access to information found in the AGGC. In years past, this kind of information found its way by word of mouth to only a select few growers and their very close friends. Now, all this information is only a "click" away at www.atlanticgiantgenetics.com.

www.backyardgardener.com/pumkin.html

Duncan McAlpin's website, *The Pumpkin Patch* is always up to date and loaded with valuable information and data. This is one of the first places to look for worldwide weigh off results and lists of the top pumpkins and growers.

BigPumpkins.com

This website is the most user friendly and sociable, offering almost everything that a sophisticated site, devoted to a much broader topic, offers: chat rooms, webcams, archives, grower diaries, and on and on. This site is an absolute must-see on your internet browsing.

GiantPumpkin.com

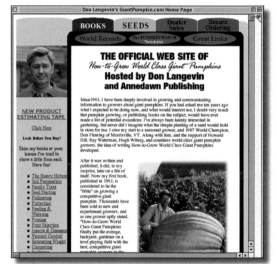

GiantPumpkin.com is the author's website, and is designed and maintained by Don Langevin. Its major goal is to introduce people to the world of giant pumpkin growing, to give some basic information on growing, and to offer books and competition-strain giant pumpkin seeds for sale. Those wishing to seriously pursue their dreams of growing a local, regional, or world record will find much here that is extremely helpful.

Giant Pumpkin Message Board

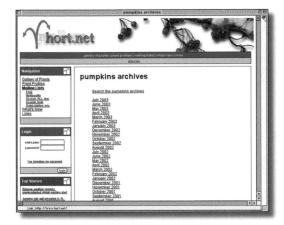

HowardDill.com and PandPSeed.com

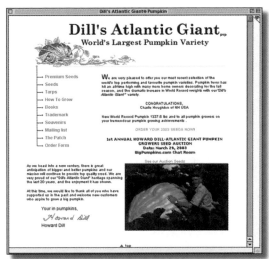

This message board is devoted to discussion on the growing of giant pumpkins. It has many very, high caliber growers who generously respond with comments to questions asked by other members. It is also the "grapevine" for what's happening currently, and it can keep you up to date on where and who is growing the big ones each year.

To become a member of this list, send an email to majordomo@hort.net with the message text SUBSCRIBE PUMPKINS in the body of your email. You will then automatically receive an email response with an authorization code and instructions on how to complete your enrollment. Newcomers are advised to spend some time listening before asking questions. Most of the rudimentary questions have already been discussed in great detail on other threads devoted to them. Before asking a question, please visit a searchable archive available at: http://www.hort.net/lists/pumpkins/. An archive like this can be a tremendous learning tool for anyone seriously interested in giant pumpkins.

Many of the people on this list have grown 1000 pound pumpkins, and those who have, credit the list for support. Getting to know the people on this list is one of the quickest ways to find answers to questions, information about seeds grown by list members, or news of any sort relating to giant pumpkins.

Both websites, above and below, deserve special mention for they are offered by the founding fathers of modern time giant pumpkin growing.

Howard Dill (howardddill.com) and Ray Waterman (pandpseed.com) have contributed vastly to giant pumpkin growing and the sport. Without Howard and the seed, and Ray and the organizational and marketing savvy, giant pumpkin growing, as we know it today, would be arguably non-existent. I owe much of my success to these two men, for they created a demand for information that I was fortunate enough in time and circumstance to satisfy. I thank both of these men for their contributions.

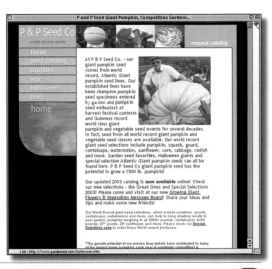

Above: A group of attendees at the International Giant Pumpkin Seminar in Niagara Falls rummages through quality seed at the annual seed sale.
Below (back row from left): New Hampshire growers, Matt Mongeon, Charlie Houghton, Jim Kuhn, and Robert Demers at the conference.
Front row: Danny Dill, Don Langevin, and Howard Dill rekindle friendship in pre-seminar hospitality room.

Right: George Hoomis (NEPGA Director) and Ron Wallace of Coventry, RI enjoy the festivities.

Groups & Associations

You can go it alone in this sport, but if you do, you miss most of the joy, and limit your opportunity to grow in knowledge and success at growing giant pumpkins. Within the groups, organizations, and associations lie new friends and new relationships. New information also comes to you faster than the every-five-year book I publish, by way of newsletters and correspondence that keeps you abreast of what's going on. There are scores of these groups all over the world, some consisting of only a few members, and others boasting memberships over 500. Most of them are regional in orientation, and most of the large regional associations have members from all over the world.

Your regional association is the epicenter for weigh off information. Most of the weigh offs staged in the United States and Canada are part of the annual activities planned and implemented by these associations for their members. Almost all of these associations stage competitions as open events, including members and non-members alike. Anyone not willing to support an association that freely provides the opportunity for an official weighing of his giant pumpkin, hinders only himself in the pursuit of friendship and personal achievement. For the average cost of $10 - $20 per year, these associations provide essential information and a network of people that you can rely on.

Left and right: A panoramic view o, 2002, Topsfield F All New England Giant Pumpkin Championship w saw a new world in Charlie Hough 1337.6 which ap in the lower left c

Far left: The Circleville, OH Pumpkin Festiv Left: A pre-weig off photo-op fo members of the PNWGPG. Below: The RIF annual seed starting party on April 27, 20

178

Right: A group of growers from the RIPGA pose with Howard Dill at the International Giant Pumpkin Growers' Seminar in Niagara Falls, Ontario, Canada on the occasion of his acceptance of a Lifetime Achievement Award in 2002. From left to right: John Castellucci, Fred Macari, Glenn Cheem, Dave Hampton, Dick Wallace, Howard Dill, Ron Wallace, Eddie Giarrusso, Don Langevin, Joe Jutras, and Stephen Sperry. Missing from photo is Alan Reynolds.

Left, from top:
The South Dak
Giant Pumpkin
Growers Weigh
a lifting team ar
Port Elgen Pump
and weigh off, a
some of the me
of the Southern
Growers Associ

Right, from top
1999, Napa Va
patch tour, and
Bitterroot Gian
Pumpkin Weig
in Hamilton, M

Left: Growers s
through a roast
at the OVGPG
summer picnic

Without groups and associations, weigh off organization would not exist, and your opportunity to gain recognition for your gardening efforts would be limited to the geographical scope of your neighborhood, and you would entirely limit your opportunity to make new, very good friends. There is a list of over 100 weigh offs on pages 182 and 183 that will provide you with contacts for groups and associations in your area.

t: Dave and Tom Beachy indicate eir finish in the diana State Fair Weigh Off.

left: Dave Stelts cts a patch tour at the OVGPG ner get together.

Top right: Joel land poses with rs in Japan on a e won as a prize through giant n competitions.

Indiana State Fair Giant Pumpkin Contest Weigh-Off

1st	John Barenie– Griffith, IN 635
2nd	Brad Walters– Greenwood, IN 612
3rd	Mark Pistono– Wisconsin Rapids, WI
4th	Winston L. Wyckoff– Burbank, OH
5th	William Hughes– Versailles, IN
6th	David L. Beachy– Woodburn, IN
	John Maston– Columbus, OH
8th	Bruce Gatewood– Noblesville, IN
9th	Gus Smithhisler– Columbus, OH
10th	Jim Gatewood– Rochester, IN
11th	Mark Seest– Mulberry, IN
12th	Bill Gatewood– Noblesville, IN
13th	Jim Gatewood– Rochester, IN
14th	Thomas Beachy– Woodburn, IN
15th	Bill Skidmore Huntington, IN
16th	Pat Hansen– Greenfield, IN
17th	
18th	
19th	
20th	
21st	
22nd	
23rd	
24th	

Weigh Offs and Associations

State	City		Contact	Comments	
AZ	Phoenix	USA	Sam Kelsall		
CA	Auburn	USA			
CA	Dixon	USA			
CA	Elk Grove	USA	Zack Jones	Elk Grove Community Harvest & Pumpkin Weigh Off	
CA	Fairfield	USA	Mike Green		
CA	Half Moon Bay	USA	Jack Olsen	Half Moon Bay Art and Pumpkin Festival	
CA	Salinas	USA	Tom Borchard	California State Giant Pumpkin Weigh Off	www.giant-pumpkins.com
CA	Santa Cruz	USA		Santa Cruz County Fair	
CA	Santa Rosa	USA	Sonoma County Harvest Fair		
CO	Colorado Springs	USA		Bear Springs Park	
CT	Durham	USA			
CT	New Milford	USA	Brian Kitney		
FL	Sanford	USA	Pete Hirst	Florida State Agricultural Inspection Station	
GA	Gainesville	USA		Hall County Farmers Market	
GA	Oakwood	USA		Southern Pumpkin Growers Association	
IA	Anamosa	USA	Greg & Nancy Norlin	Mid-West Pumpkin Growers Association Weigh Off	
IA	Sanbom	USA	Fred Boer		
ID	Rexburg	USA			
IL	Des Plaines	USA	Chris Pesche	Illinois Weigh-off	
IL	Lockport	USA	Paul Siegel		
IL	Morton	USA	Mike Badgerow	GPC Pumpkin Capital Weigh Off	
IL	Prairie View	USA	Didier Farms	Barbara Didier site contact	
IN	Indianapolis	USA	Brad Walters	The Great Indiana Giant Pumpkin Weigh Off	
IN	Indianapolis	USA	Indiana State Fair Weigh-off		Joe Huber
IN	Noblesville	USA	Jim Gatewood	IPGA Weigh Off	
IN	Starlight	USA	Joe Hubert, Jr.		
IN	Starlight	USA	Joe Huber's Family Farm Weigh-off		Joe Huber
IN	Versailles	USA	Clyde White	Versailles Pumpkin Show	www.ripleycountytourism.com
MA	Marshfield	USA	Ray McKay	Marshfield Fair	http://home.ici.net/~marsfair/marshfa5.html
MA	Topsfield	USA	Hugh Wiberg	All New England Giant Pumpkin Championship	
MA	West Springfield	USA		Big E Eastern States Exposition	
MI	Detroit	USA			www.michiganstatefair.net/
MI	Dundee	USA	John Harnica	The Great Harnica Farm Giant Pumpkin Weigh Off	
MI	Grove City	USA			
MI	LaSalle	USA	Michael Huggins		
MI	Monroe	USA			
MI	Saline	USA		Saline Fair	
MI	St. Johns	USA	Andy Todosciuk	The Great Michigan Giant Pumpkin Weigh Off	
MN	Austin	USA	David Andree	SE Minnesota Weigh Off	
MN	Byron	USA	Tom Tweite	Minnesota Weigh Off	jdandree@hotmail.com
MO	Republic	USA	Jack Meunch	Great Missouri Weigh Off	
MT	Hamilton ·	USA	Bitterroot Giant Pumpkin Weigh Off		Weigh Off Coordinator - Kim Thomas
MT	Hamilton	USA	Ravalli County Fair	Fairgrounds Mgr. - Gary Wiley	
NC	Mooresville	USA	Ron Johnson	NC Giant Pumpkin and Vegetable Weigh Off	
NC	Raleigh	USA		Weeks Seeds Contest	
NH	Deerfield	USA		Deerfield Fair	
NH	Goffstown	USA			
NH	Hillsboro	USA		Hillsboro County Fair	
NH	Milford	USA		Milford Pumpkin Festival	
NH	Rochester	USA		Rochester Fair	
NV	Fallon	USA	Richard W. Lattin		www.lattinfarms.com/home.html
NY	Amagansett	USA	Andy Sabin	The Great Long Island Giant Pumpkin Weigh Off	
NY	Collins	USA	Ray Waterman	World Pumpkin Confederation Weigh Off	www.pandpseed.com
NY	Elmira	USA	Bradley Farms	Northern Tier Giant Pumpkin Growers Club	
NY	Oswego	USA	Joe Crisafulli	Port City Pumpkin Weigh Off	
NY	Riverhead	USA		Riverhead Agricultural Fair	
OH	Barnesville	USA			
OH	Canfield	USA		Ohio Valley Giant Pumpkin Growers Association	
OH	Circleville	USA		Circleville Pumpkin Show	
OH	Frankfort	USA	Tony Vanderpool, Southern Ohio Giant Pumpkin Growers		www.geocities.com/sogpg
OR	Canby	USA	Hoffman Dairy Garden	Canby Giant Pumpkin Weigh Off	
OR	Canby	USA	Hoffman Dairy Garden	The Terminator	

State	City		Contact	Comments	
OR	Eugene	USA		Lone Pine Farms	
OR	Junction City	USA		Lone Pine Weigh Off	
OR	Mulino	USA	Pacific Giant Vegetable Growers (PGVG)		www.pgvg.org
OR	Portland	USA	Joel Holland	Pacific Northwest Pumpkin Growers Weigh Off	
OR	Salem	USA			
OR	Sauvies Island	USA			
PA	Altoona	USA	Marvin Meisner, M.D.	Pennsylvania Pumpkin Bowl	
PA	Altoona	USA	PGPGA	Marv Hicks	www.PGPGA.com
PA	Bloomsburg	USA			
PA	Milan	USA		Northern Tier Giant Pumpkin Contest	
RI	Warren	USA	Don Langevin	RI State Giant Pumpkin Championship	
SD	Sioux Falls	USA	Bill Hartman	Great South Dakota Weigh Off	
TN	Allardt	USA	C. Jeffers	Allardt Pumpkin Festival http://members.aol.com/TNpumpkin/fest.html	
TX	Floyada	USA	Assiter Punkin Ranch	www.floydadachamber.com/punkin.htm	
UT	Leki	USA	Laurie Stokes Bott		
UT	Salt Lake City	USA	Larry Sagers	The Great Salt Lake Giant Pumpkin Weigh Off	
UT	Thanksgiving Point	USA			
VA	Richmond	USA		Virginia State Fair	
WA	Auburn	USA	Mari Lou Holland	SuperMall	
WA	Centralia	USA		Centralia Fall Festival	
WA	Dew Moines	USA			
WA	Puyallup	USA	info@thefair.com	Puyallup Fair	www.thefair.com/
WA	Shoreline	USA		Central Market Weigh Off	
WI	Greater Keyeser	USA	Mark McGinley		
WI	Nekoosa	USA	John Weidman	Nekoosa Giant Pumpkin Festival	
WI	Oconomowac	USA	Jack Marks	Great Western Lakes Weigh Off	
WY	Riverton	USA			
	Seegräben	SWT	European weigh-off and Swiss Championship		
	Ludwigsburg	GER	Jucker Farmart	www.juckerfarmart.ch	
HA	Broughton	ENG	Greyhound Pumpkin Club Weigh Off		
AB	Bellis	CAN	Barry Wood		
AB	Smokey Lake	CAN	Barry Wood		www.smokylake.com/unmountain/pumpkin/weigh off.htm
BC	Armstrong	CAN	Patti Noonan	The Great British Columbia Giant Pumpkin Weigh Off	
BC	Nanaimo	CAN		Vancouver Island Weigh Off	
MB	Roland	CAN	Jake Neufeld	Roland Pumpkin Fair	
NS	Millville	CAN			
NS	Windsor	CAN	Howard and Danny Dill	Atlantic Pumpkin Growers	
ON	Arkona	CAN	Pete Geerts		
ON	Battersea	CAN			
ON	Emo	CAN	Ken McKinnon	Rainy River Valley Agricultural Society www.twspemo.on.ca/rainy.htm	
ON	Fonthill	CAN	Jerry Howell	The Great Niagara Falls Giant Pumpkin Weigh Off	
ON	Fonthill	CAN	Howell Family Pumpkin Farm		Jerry Howell
ON	London	CAN		Western Fair - held in September	
ON	Ottawa	CAN	Glenn Cheam	The By Ward Market Giant Pumpkin Weigh Off	
ON	Picton	CAN	Jim Ives	Prince Edward County Pumpkinfest mjives@post.kosone.com	
ON	Port Elgin	CAN	portelgin@sunsets.com	Port Elgin Pumpkinfest www.sunsets.com/portelgin/pumpkinfest/	
ON	Rockton	CAN			
ON	Sarnia	CAN		Sarnia Sunripe Rotary Weigh Off	
ON	Simcoe	CAN			
ON	Spencerville	CAN			
ON	Stittsville	CAN	Bruce Kaye	OSLGA Weigh Off	
ON	Toronto	CAN	rwfair@netcom.ca	Royal Agricultural Winter Fair	
ON	Troy	CAN	Fred Cooper		
ON	West Carleton	CAN	carpfair@istar.ca	Carp Fair	
PE	Springvale	CAN	Dr. Jim Murphy		
QB	Ladysmith	CAN		Fall festival named Ocktoberfest.	
QB	Gentilly	CAN	Rock Rivard	http://potirothon.mrcbecancour.qc.ca/index.htm	
QB	Lennoxville	CAN			
QB	St. Croix	CAN	Claude Colbert		
QB	St-Étienne-des Grès	CAN	Rock Rivard	Le Wezinage	

Alan Reynolds of Durham, CT pilots a 798.4 pound squash boat in Lake Quonnipaug in Guilford, CT. in 1999.
— Photo by Kathy Hanley of The Hartford Courant.

Sailing Giants

Yes, they sail, race, and do battle on water with giant pumpkins, and you should see the look on people's faces (both participants and spectators).

The first pumpkin boat made its maiden voyage in 1996, skippered by Wayne Hackney of New Milford, CT. Wayne successfully crossed a two-mile lake with his 746 pound "Mighty Mabel."

This set the stage for an annual exhibition, and sparked the interest of numerous grower groups all over North America. Central Park in New York City has staged a race every year since, however, race entries must be equipped with electric outboard motors (you can't have all the pollution created by those leaky 2 cycle engines competing with millions of cars. – can you?).

There are pumpkin regattas held in at least a dozen cities in the US and Canada, including the event shown on these pages in Goffstown, NH. Here, Jim Beauchemin (dressed in his lobster fishing apparel) eludes the large, man-made pumpkin, the "Pumpkin Eater." Several men are inside the "Eater," suggesting the thought that the Trojan Horse had nothing on these guys.

Proceeds from this day of fun and games goes entirely to the *Goffstown Main Street Program*.

All of the yachts are engineered using a patent pending contraption invented by Alan Reynolds of Durham, CT. Alan is shown on pages 184 and 185 sailing solo in his 798.4 pound squash boat in 1999. He successfully reconnoitered Lake Quonnipaug in Guilford, CT. The image was captured for posterity by photographer, Kathy Hanley of *The Hartford Courant*.

Alan was kind enough to make his boat plans public, and they are shown on page 189.

Alan reminds everyone that safety is first. "Life preservers, wet suits, bilge pumps, oars, additional fuel, food, walkie-talkie (or cell phone), first aid supplies, compass, maps, a detailed itinerary submitted to the US Coast Guard, and a co-navigator (if room) should all be taken care of before launch. And, in case of severe weather, or high seas, always remain with your boat. A pumpkin will never sink."

As Alan told me, "My toilet seat design revolutionized the pumpkin sailing industry, enabling half-wits of all ages to compete. In 2004, I plan to introduce new designs which will include a water-saver flusher, life boat attachments, water-tight port holes, anchor assembly, mast and sail, and optional global tracking (GTS)." I can't wait!

Making a Pumpkin Boat

Start by turning the pumpkin over so that the flat bottom is up. Place the plywood mounting assembly on the pumpkin and position it so it is equally spaced side to side, and the motor mount portion is not obstructed by the fruit. Trace the outline of the plywood cut-out onto the pumpkin with a black marker. Also mark the bolt holes. Take the mounting assembly off the pumpkin for now. Depending on how wide your pumpkin is, you may have to cut the hole smaller than the traced outline. There should be enough flat surface on the pumpkin, outside the traced outline, for the bolts and the assembly to be mounted properly. After cutting a hole large enough for you to get through, and small enough to accommodate the assembly, place the assembly back on the pumpkin, lining up

the bolt holes. Drill holes and bolt the plywood to the pumpkin. Washers in contact with the pumpkin should be as large as possible, and made of wood or a soft material if available.

Use spray foam to caulk between the pumpkin and the underside of the mounting assembly.

Motor Mount

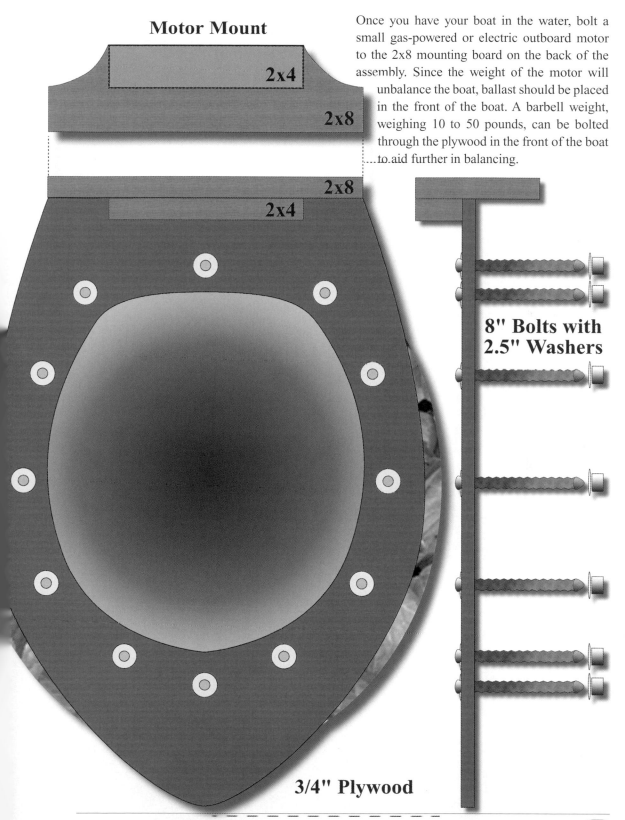

2x4

2x8

Once you have your boat in the water, bolt a small gas-powered or electric outboard motor to the 2x8 mounting board on the back of the assembly. Since the weight of the motor will unbalance the boat, ballast should be placed in the front of the boat. A barbell weight, weighing 10 to 50 pounds, can be bolted through the plywood in the front of the boat to aid further in balancing.

2x8

2x4

8" Bolts with 2.5" Washers

3/4" Plywood

More Kids & Pumpkins

Right: Al Eaton's 6-week-old, 12 pound granddaughter on his 12-week-old, 2002, 1236 pound pumpkin
Below: Some curious sculpture designs are the norm when using Atlantic Giants as media.

How-to-Grow World Class Giant Pumpkins
by Don Langevin
128 pages, 200 color photos
$14.95 (plus shipping and handling).
Order online at www.giantpumpkin.com
Or, call 800-985-7878
Considered to be the "bible" on growing giant pumpkins, this book put the average backyard gardener on a level playing field with the best giant pumpkin growers in the world. Published in 1993 and still considered the definitive text on the subject. Covers everything from A to Z. The perfect companion book to *How-to-Grow World Class Giant Pumpkins, II.*

How-to-Grow World Class Giant Pumpkins, II
by Don Langevin
160 pages, 250 color photos
$17.95 (plus shipping and handling).
Order online at www.giantpumpkin.com
Or, call 800-985-7878
Totally updated with all new photos and illustrations. Published in 1998, containing new information, data and cultural practices, yet covers everything you need to know to grow a world record pumpkin. Great for both the experienced or new grower — a "must read" for any serious giant pumpkin grower.

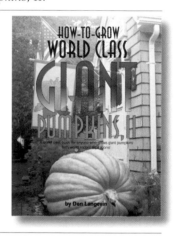

How-to-Grow World Class Giant Pumpkins, III
by Don Langevin
192 pages, 500 color photos
$29.95 (plus shipping and handling).
Order online at www.giantpumpkin.com
Or, call 800-985-7878
The evolution in growing giant pumpkins continues with this 2003 publication. After ten years, and three books on this subject, many of the closest held secrets are now public information.
This book is not for the faint of heart; it takes giant pumpkin growing to a new level – applying all that has been learned from the very best giant pumpkin growers in the world.

World Class Competition-Strain Giant Pumpkin Seeds
These seeds come from cross pollinations of heavy, top producing seed stocks. Each packet is marked with the pumpkin's weight, female and male parents, and significant offspring produced by parents.

5 seeds per packet for $5 (plus shipping and handling).

Giant Pumpkin
Weight Estimating Tape Measure

16' (192" long)

Measures pumpkins from 42-1422 lbs.

No need to buy two, 10' tapes to measure pumpkins over 420 pounds.

Made from, soft, flexible, and durable fiberglass; printed with weather resistant inks.

Measures inches and estimated weight of your pumpkin. Estimates printed right on the tape at each half-inch interval.

One-step estimating (no tables to refer to).

$10 or 3 for $20, or buy any book-combo and receive one free!

Measure Up To 1422 lbs.

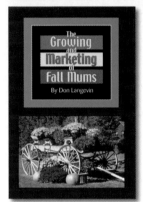

The Growing and Marketing of Fall Mums

by Don Langevin

228 pages, many photos and illustrations

$19.95 (plus shipping and handling).

Covers everything you need to know about growing prize winning fall mums for sale. Covers all aspects of growing and marketing your product — from securing cuttings and making your soil mix to pinching, feeding, and profitably selling everything you grow. The only book of its kind. Thousands sold to new and experienced commercial growers. Start your backyard flower business today!

Buy all three books (#6)
Get a free tape measure
A $72.85 value
You pay $49.95
plus s&h
Save $22.90

Item	Qty	Description	Price	Totals
#1		World Class Giant Pumpkins I	14.95	
#2		World Class Giant Pumpkins II	17.95	
#3		World Class Giant Pumpkins III	29.95	
#4		2-Book Combo (WCGP I and II)	29.95	
#5		2-Book Combo (WCGP II and III)	39.95	
#6		3-Book Combo (WCGP I, II & III)	49.95	
#7		Estimating Tape *Free Tape with Item #4, #5, or #6*	10.00	
#8		Competition-Strain Pumpkin Seeds (5 seeds/pk)	5.00	
		Sub Total		
		Shipping & Handling		5.00
		Total		

To order books, seeds, or tape measures directly from Don Langevin, write to: Annedawn Publishing, Box 247, Norton, MA 02766, order online at: www.giantpumpkin.com or call me toll free at **800-985-7878**

American Express, Mastercard, Visa, and Discover cards accepted.

Garden Center and Farm Store Manager, Fund Raising Chairman, or Weigh Off Coordinator:

We have 4 displays that will make you the one-stop shop for the best seeds and the best information on growing giant pumpkins.

We offer discounts from 50% - 60% off, and we ship right to your door with UPS.

To learn more about the contents of the displays, pricing, and ordering info, call 800-985-7878, or email us at annedawn@aol.com for a flyer, price list, and order form for download. You can also order online at *www.giantpumpkin.com*.

We sell the best books ever published on how-to- grow giant pumpkins. More than 35,000 sold, and every competitive giant pumpkin grower considers them "bible." Our displays contain the legendary, *Dill's Atlantic Giant* pumpkin variety, which holds every world record since 1979. The world record produced from this seed is 1,337.6 pounds, and many beleive that 1500 pounds will soon be broken! Will it be you?

Actinovate® Agricultural Inoculants

Actinovate® is a powerful inoculant for use in a wide variety of agricultural seed and soil applications. Actinovate® products contain high concentrations of a naturally occurring beneficial soil microorganism (Streptomyces lydicus strain WYEC 108) that, when applied, benefits plants in many ways.

When introduced into the soil (or applied to seed), the Actinovate® organism colonizes and grows around the root system of the plant. While settling in the root system, the microbe forms a synergetic relationship with the plant, feeding off of the plants waste materials while secreting beneficial and protective by-products. This combination of the colonization and the protective secretions forms a defensive barrier around the root system of the plant. Finally, the by-products of the Actinovate® microorganism also aid in plant health, complexing minerals found in the soil and, thus, allowing easier uptake. This symbiotic relationship between plant and microbe is the optimum balance for a natural, healthy soil environment. Actinovate® makes it happens.

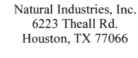

The Actinovate® microbe was not cross-bred or genetically modified. It was isolated by scientists from the root system of a linseed plant. Actinovate® products contain an extremely high concentration of this unique Streptomyces strain. This allows the plant to receive the maximum benefits of the microbe.

Actinovate® Benefits
1) Grows on the root system, shielding it from environmental hazards
2) Breaks down minerals and micronutrients making them more readily available to the plant
3) Creates larger, more robust root systems
4) Promotes plant vigor and strength
5) Increases plant size and mass
6) Reduces or eliminates the need for chemical fungicides

Name

Address

City

State

Zip Code

Mail this postcard for more information.
or visit our website at www.naturalindustrie.com

Postage Required

Natural Industries, Inc.
6223 Theall Rd.
Houston, TX 77066